Digital Disability

CRITICAL MEDIA STUDIES
INSTITUTIONS, POLITICS, AND CULTURE

Series Editor
Andrew Calabrese, University of Colorado

Advisory Board
Patricia Aufderheide, American University
Jean-Claude Burgelman, Free University of Brussels
Simone Chambers, University of Colorado
Nicholas Garnham, University of Westminster
Hanno Hardt, University of Iowa
Gay Hawkins, The University of New South Wales
Maria Heller, Eötvös Loránd University
Robert Horwitz, University of California at San Diego
Douglas Kellner, University of California at Los Angeles
Gary Marx, Massachusetts Institute of Technology
Toby Miller, New York University
Vincent Mosco, Carleton University
Janice Peck, University of Colorado
Manjunath Pendakur, Southern Illinois University
Arvind Rajagopal, New York University
Kevin Robins, Goldsmiths College
Saskia Sassen, University of Chicago
Colin Sparks, University of Westminster
Slavko Splichal, University of Ljubljana
Thomas Streeter, University of Vermont
Liesbet van Zoonen, University of Amsterdam
Janet Wasko, University of Oregon

Recent Titles in the Series
Floating Lives: The Media and Asian Diasporas,
    edited by Stuart Cunningham and John Sinclair
Continental Order? Integrating North America for Cybercapitalism,
    edited by Vincent Mosco and Dan Schiller
Social Theories of the Press: Constituents of Communication Research,
    1840s to 1920s, second edition,
    Hanno Hardt
Privacy and the Information Age,
    Serge Gutwirth
Global Media Governance: A Beginner's Guide,
    Seán Ó Siochrú and Bruce Girard

The Global and the National: Media and Communications in Post-Communist Russia,
  Terhi Rantanen
Newsworkers Unite: Labor, Convergence, and North American Newspapers,
  Catherine McKercher
Digital Disability: The Social Construction of Disability in New Media,
  Gerard Goggin and Christopher Newell

Forthcoming in the Series

Critical Communication Theory: Power, Media, Gender, and Technology,
  Sue Curry Jansen
Principles of Publicity and Press Freedom,
  Slavko Splichal
Internet Governance in Transition: Who Is the Master of This Domain?
  Daniel J. Paré
Recovering a Public Vision for Public Television,
  Glenda R. Balas
Herbert Schiller,
  Richard Maxwell
The Party System and Public Service Broadcasting in Italy,
  Cinzia Padovani
Contesting Media Power: Alternative Media in a Networked World,
  edited by Nick Couldry and James Curran
Harold Innis,
  Paul Heyer
The Blame Game: Why Television Is Not Our Fault,
  Eileen R. Meehan
Elusive Autonomy: Brazilian Communications Policy in an Age of Globalization and Technical Change,
  Sergio Euclides de Souza
Film Industries and Cultures in Transition,
  Dina Iordanova

Digital Disability

The Social Construction of Disability in New Media

Gerard Goggin and Christopher Newell

ROWMAN & LITTLEFIELD PUBLISHERS, INC.
Lanham • Boulder • New York • Oxford

ROWMAN & LITTLEFIELD PUBLISHERS, INC.

Published in the United States of America
by Rowman & Littlefield Publishers, Inc.
A Member of the Rowman & Littlefield Publishing Group
4720 Boston Way, Lanham, Maryland 20706
www.rowmanlittlefield.com

PO Box 317, Oxford, OX2 9RU, United Kingdom

British Library Cataloguing in Publication Information Available

Library of Congress Cataloging-in-Publication Data

Goggin, Gerard, 1964–
    Digital disability : the social construction of disability in new
media / Gerard Goggin and Christopher Newell.
        p. cm.—(Critical media studies)
Includes bibliographical references and index.
    ISBN 0-7425-1843-4 (cloth : alk. paper)—ISBN 0-7425-1844-2 (paper :
alk. paper)
 1. Computers and people with disabilities. 2. Digital media—Social
aspects. 3. Sociology of disability. I. Newell, Christopher, 1964– II.
Title. III. Series.
    HV1569.5 .G64 2002
    303.48'3—dc21

                                                            2002009977

Printed in the United States of America

♾™ The paper used in this publication meets the minimum requirements of American
National Standard for Information Sciences—Permanence of Paper for Printed Library
Materials, ANSI/NISO Z39.48-1992.

For
Denys and Margaret Goggin,
and Jill Newell,

with thanks for your love, encouragement and nurture,
and for all you are and all that you do.

Gerard and Christopher

Contents

Acknowledgments   xi

Preface   xiii

Part I: Technologies of Disability

1   Encountering Technology, Media, and Culture   3

2   Disability in Its Social Context   19

Part II: Networks of Disability

3   Holding the Line: Telecommunications and Disability   39

4   Disability on the Digital Margins: Convergence and the
    Construction of Disability   63

Part III: New Mediations of Disability

5   Getting the Picture on Disability: Digital Broadcasting Futures   89

6   Blind Spots on the Internet   109

7   Cultures of Digital Disability   129

Part IV: The Politics of Disabling Digitization

8   Rewiring Disability   147

Bibliography   155

Index   175

About the Authors   183

Acknowledgments

Endorsing the disability rights motto "nothing about us without us," we wish to thank the international disability rights movement who cooperated and supported, and who have provided the inspiration for a piece of research that seeks to bring together in dialogue the academy and a diverse social movement.

Similarly we are indebted to our colleagues in the Australian consumer movement, activists with whom we have shared many meetings and forums on telecommunications and new media, especially Trish Benson, Phil Harper, Elizabeth Morley, and Ian Wilson. Robin Wilkinson, AM, deserves our special thanks for constantly reminding us of why our research is important, and for the gifts of her encouragement and love.

We have been fortunate to have received generous support from many academic colleagues including Trevor Barr, Mike Bourk, Mike Clear, David Holmes, Helen Meekosha, Andrew Jakubowicz, Lelia Green, Jock Given, Justine Lloyd, Baden Offord, Tom O'Regan, Trevor Parmenter, Shelley Tremain, McKenzie Wark, and Helen Wilson.

In the telecommunications industry, Robert Morsillo, Margaret Portelli, Ted Benjamin, and Graeme Ward stand out as particularly important, in being willing to enter into frank dialogue. We have learned much and, even when we could not always agree, gained crucial insights into the commercial world of telecommunications.

A number of people generously gave of their time and resources in the pursuit of international research for this book. In particular we thank: Carol-lee Acquiline, Elizabeth Ager, Gunela Astbrink, Judy Brewer, Mairian Corker, Jan Delvert, David Edwards, Gerry Field, John Gill, Larry Goldberg, Ingar Beckman Hirschfeldt, Rachel Hurst, Gunnar Hellström, Andrew J. Imparato, Margita Lundman, Annette Lovell, Thomas Johansson, Erkki Kemppainen, Jan-Ingvar Linström, Margita Lundman, Scott Marshall, Aulikki Rautavaara, Patrick Roe, Jeffrey T. Rosen, Hans Smedberg, Karen Peltz Strauss, Clas Thorén, Bob Twitchin, Mary Watkins, and Elisabeth Wessel.

Gerard wishes to thank Southern Cross University for a recruitment award, which enabled him to conduct background research in the United States, the United Kingdom, Sweden, and Finland in January/February 2001, and to friends in the School of Humanities, Media, and Cultural Studies for their encouragement. Andrea Mitchell and Graeme Turner in the Centre for Critical and Cultural Studies, University of Queensland, provided much appreciated support and a congenial environment for the completion of this book. Matthew Kay cheerfully stepped in with timely research assistance.

Gerard gives his heartfelt thanks to Leigh Carriage, and his family, for their love, encouragement, and conversation over the years in which this book took shape. He is deeply grateful to Jacqueline Clark for her love and support while this book was finished.

Christopher expresses his appreciation to his family for their forbearance with his many absences and preoccupation. Special thanks to his wife, Jill, who sustains and loves him in the everyday.

Finally we are grateful to Brenda Hadenfeldt, Andrew Calabrese, and Rowman & Littlefield for publishing this book when so often the word "disability" leads to glazed eyes and rejection slips from publishing houses.

Preface

> If the category disability is to be produced in ways different from the individualized pathological way it is currently produced, then what should be researched is not the disabled people of the positivist and interpretive research paradigms but the disablism ingrained in the individualistic consciousness and institutionalized practices of what is, ultimately, a disablist society.[1]

Disability—it is an issue, a label, a statistic, an experience, and a complex space. However one views it, many people feel uncomfortable with disability. It remains enshrouded in misconceptions, myths, stereotypes, exclusion, and discrimination. Yet approximately 20 percent of all people live with disability. A World Bank report estimated the number of people with disabilities in the world in the year 2000 to be between 235 million and 549 million.[2] The amount of economic, social, and cultural activity associated with some hundreds of millions of people with disabilities is a very large sum. In narrow commercial terms, such a large class of people makes a very large market—a population roughly twice the size of the United States of America, for instance. Given the scope and scale of disability, why then do people with disabilities still continue to be an afterthought when it comes to most aspects of everyday life? How does the peculiar state of affairs with disability continue to exist, even in an area that is thought by many to hold out the promise of redressing the disadvantages of disability—namely, new digital communications technologies?

New digital communications technologies, or new media, include the Internet and broadband networks (fast, high-capacity data services), advanced telecommunications networks (offering services such as caller ID, digital mobile phones, third-generation mobile telecommunications, video telephones), and digital broadcasting (with digital television). There is a bewildering proliferation of communications and media technologies that are promised to revolutionize our lives. These technologies are called "digital," because they receive and transmit information in digital form. Digital forms of technologies are gradually replacing their older, analog counterparts—in many countries digital mobile phones are already supplanting analog ones; digital television is nudging out its predecessors; and the digitization of telecommunications exchanges, lines, and networks is nearly complete. Digital technologies allow the power of computers and software to be harnessed. They also allow what is called "convergence"—information stored and transmitted digitally can be shared across previously separate devices: computers and phone lines come together; video, audio, and text mix to become multimedia; Internet TV is becoming a reality; mobile phones send text messages; and third-generation mobiles will allow video communication. New industries have already formed around business plans for new digital technologies: one high point of this new electronic ("e-") economy was, of course, the dot.com fever of 1999, with its inevitable and predictable sequel, the dot.com crash (also known as the "tech wreck"). Another high point came with the popularity of telecommunications privatizations and initial public offerings in the late 1990s. This digital economy may not be so "new," but its sheer size is extraordinary. Estimates vary wildly, but the net worth of the various telecommunications, communications, and media companies around the world runs easily into hundreds of billions of dollars.

It is at the intersection of these two big pictures of disability, on the one hand, and digital communications and media technologies, on the other, that this book unfolds. Staring at the blank screen on a laptop in a hotel room, we wondered how to start a book about disability and new media, especially one that goes beyond taken-for-granted notions of what seems to be so obvious—"disability" and "new media," two spaces with their own logics, often felt to be "self-contained" and quite separate. Yet as we looked at the spartan hotel room, welcomed the cool of the air-conditioning in the midst of a hot Brisbane summer, and reveled in our conversations, we realized how the everyday has much to teach us about disability and technology, especially new digital communications and media technologies. We looked again at how the taken-for-granted technologies of the everyday reflect our taken-for-granted values, artifactually represented in how we design airplanes and sterile motel rooms, and also new communications and media technologies. Our hotel room was brimming over with values, with norms of design, and even with built-in disability—if we would but recognize it.

Christopher, who lives with disability and has long been active in the Australian disability rights movement and disability studies, had just arrived from Hobart. He was recovering from traveling on aircraft where he was the objectified "wheelchair in row 4E" rather than "Dr. Newell," the esteemed customer. It had been another circumstance in which he was defined as having "special needs." And where his different view amounted for nothing. This experience has fed Christopher's many years of advocacy and research regarding disability issues. The routine rejection of the knowledge of people needlessly handicapped by society has sparked this book.

Gerard, the other person staring at the rapidly filling laptop screen, brings to our encounter a deep and long-standing passion about disability and new media. Having first worked with people with disabilities and their representative organizations in the telecommunications area in Australia in the early 1990s, since that time he has collaborated with Christopher to research, write, and intervene on disability issues, bringing his engagement with media and cultural studies to bear on their dialogue.

We first commenced working together on disability and telecommunications issues in the early 1990s. Christopher was a consumer representative with the Disabled Peoples' International (Australia), now defunct, and Gerard was policy advisor for Consumers' Telecommunications Network, the national coalition of consumer and community organizations advocating for residential consumers of telecommunications in Australia. For some years we worked collaboratively with other activists on the macro and micro issues affecting the everyday lives of people with disabilities in telecommunications. It became evident that the thorough changes in communications and media were having enormous effects on the lives of people with disabilities. Yet, much to our frequent dismay, such transformations were given little attention by governments, regulators, and corporations that dominated the shaping of new technologies. People with disabilities were left off networks (old and new), were a problem and liability to be managed rather than accorded priorities as customers, were excluded or marginalized as citizens in the eyes of governments, were constantly reminded how "special" their needs were, while the needs of the majority were unremarked.

In order to achieve lasting and serious recognition of the continuing inequality people with disabilities face, in the face of the great promise of digital technologies, we have sought since the mid-1990s to publish our work. As we reviewed the literature we were struck by the dearth of books regarding disability and technology in general, particularly since other social categories are increasingly explored. For instance, there are substantial studies considering technology and a variety of social groups: women, developing countries, indigenous people, impoverished people, to name but a few. While our work for years has focused on the telecommunications policy arena, the policy environments in which we have been most active, convergence made possible with digitization makes an integrated approach important. Hence we wish in this book to sketch a broad argument about the social construction of disability in respect to a range of digital technologies. We suggest that for far too long disability has been an invisible and indeed rejected knowledge with regard to every aspect of society, but especially to technological systems such as the new media. We seek to cast a critical gaze upon the very technologies that are supposed to provide the solution to disability—and show how new media technologies actually build in disability. In so doing we bring together a variety of disciplines. Inevitably we cover a great deal of ground, and are conscious that we are not able to provide detailed treatments of each of the technologies we discuss—cochlear implants, telecommunications, digital broadcasting, and the Internet. Our focus is not so much to provide definitive treatment of these topics, but to identify and utilize particular critical tools in interrogating and bringing together those complex technoscience worlds of disability and technology. Likewise, while we have sought to provide examples from a range of countries, clearly we are unable to do justice to all national cultures, policy environments, disability movements, institutions, and political arrangements. Instead, the analysis we offer can be a starting point for further critical work. Just as technology and disability are changing spaces we would suggest that future work must inevitably honor such spaces as inherently temporal. Indeed, another book we identified in our research is that great unwritten tome on disability and technology across the ages.

In this project, we write from within the disability rights movements that arose in most Western countries in the 1970s and 1980s, and draw upon their intellectual and political energies.[3] For too long, members of our society have talked *about* people with disabilities, rather than talking *with* us. Here we wish to begin a different dialogue and enter into conversation with dominant accounts of digital technology, design, commerce, and policymaking. One of our purposes is to show the importance of people with disabilities taking a powerful role in shaping digital technologies.

Accordingly, we bring together the transdisciplinary tools of disability studies and media and cultural studies, as well as the insights of science and technology studies. We combine this with a strong flavoring of the practical experience of disability. We seek to do no less than to turn the world upside down in showing how disability is created and reproduced in digital communications and media technologies. In so doing we question the "commonsense" notion of people with disabilities inherently benefiting from new technologies.

*   *   *   *

In chapter one, we explore technoscientific worlds, namely the social, political, and cultural dimensions of science and technology. Technology is seen to have inherent values built into it, and those values actively operate to disable some people—those we call people with disabilities. There has been much hype regarding the benefits of technology, with dominant accounts seeing it as inherently good and yet paradoxically good for people with disabilities. We look at critical accounts of technology, which highlight its social shaping—something especially useful when seeking to explain disability and technology. We also consider the key concepts of "culture" and "media," both particularly important when considering new media and communications technologies.

We introduce the topic of disability in chapter two, elaborating our interdisciplinary approach whereby disability is seen as a sociopolitical space with defining discourses and related epistemology. The dominant knowledge in society, and indeed in much literature to do with technology and culture, is that disability is an inherent attribute of deviant bodies as opposed to the social construct this book suggests. The use of discourse analysis shows how culture operates in defining and regulating disability via the discourses of disability influenced by various partisan players. There are important connections with the insights offered in chapter one, in terms of technology, media, and cultural studies. To provide a sense of how such a framework might operate, we look at the cochlear implant, the discussion of which extends our understanding of "culture" and "disability." The Deaf community is shown to be a culture in terms of sociolinguistics, as well as having a markedly different understanding of the world in contrast with the dominant "hearing culture." Technologies are seen to reflect these values. Hence that which is "normal" according to a cultural worldview is reflected in taken-for-granted technological systems. Deaf people in various countries see themselves as disabled by a hearing culture that uses an oral approach, rather than inherently having a deficit. An excellent example of the clash of cultures is found in the cochlear implant, which is shown to be inherently ethical from the perspective of the hearing world, but unethical and destructive of culture from the perspective of the Deaf community. The politics of such technology are found in examining the construction and perpetuation of such technology, and supporting discourse and policy that perpetuate the hearing status quo. Finally we consider the emerging diversity literature, which offers important intellectual focus but does not yet sufficiently engage with disability.

Following these two introductory chapters, we take up the example of telecommunications, a technology central to new media and communications technologies. In telecommunications, we see at play dominant notions of technology and disability that hold that technology, especially high-tech technology, is inherently good for people with disabilities. Yet telecommunications too often exclude people with disabilities in their very design, and thus also creates disability. The role of the state is important here, perpetuating disablist norms and narrow notions of economics. Regulation and legislation play particular roles in creating the category "disabled" and in tacit ways fostering narrow norms. As well as traditional voice telephony and teletypewriters (TTY) (also known as telecommunications devices for the Deaf or TDD), we also discuss the example of digital mobile telephony and design of terminal equipment.

We broaden our discussion of telecommunications in chapter four, "Disability on the Digital Margins: Convergence and the Construction of Disability." Here we analyze the discourses on new media in the 1990s, arguing that the dominant views of concepts such as the "information superhighway" (and its cognates such as the "information society") leave fundamental issues of access and equity for many people with disabilities by the roadside. It is argued that the life experiences, needs, and aspirations of socially marginalized people were not at the forefront in the conceptualization of information superhighways in the mid-1990s—especially in the case of people with disabilities. Thus there is a need to reconceptualize the discourse on information superhighways so that the consumers are involved in defining and controlling new media. In particular, there must be a clear process for the dynamic redefinition of universal service in telecommunications that takes into account the changing sociopolitical spaces of consumers and technology. This means that people with disabilities, as well as all other citizens and consumers, must be able to participate in policy making, research, and knowledge construction on new media. Many social groups—often referred to as "minority groups" yet taken together they comprise the majority of citizens—are excluded from government and corporate policy making. Further, their knowledges and cultural practices are systematically marginalized, constituting historically "rejected knowledge." In government and corporate discussions on new media, telecommunications policymakers can be seen to persist in assigning people with disabilities to the marginal zone of "special needs." In this light, it is suggested that it is fundamentally important for people with disabilities, as well as other citizens, to have the economic, institutional, and conceptual space and independence to conduct their own sustained reflection and research on converging communications technologies.

Our discussion of discourses on the "information superhighway" sets the scene in chapter five for looking at a key but underexamined area of new media technology: digital broadcasting. Digital television already shows signs of being well on the way to matching the Internet as the new medium of choice of many people. Many more people at present have radio or television sets in their homes, rather than personal computers. So how will people with disabilities fare in the introduction of digital television? We look at the representation of people with disabilities on television in the 2000 Olympic and Paralympic Games, then turn to consider how disability is getting constructed in digital television policy.

From digital television we turn, in chapter six, to the construction of disability on one of the most rapidly growing mass medium of recorded history: the Internet. In romanticized histories of the Internet, the typical narrative tells of the often anarchic, countercultural, communal, and public-spirited space. Disability has played a pivotal role in Internet myth, but Internet theory has yet to properly engage with the realities of the lives of people with disabilities. While disability is evoked yet eclipsed in Internet myth and theory, it is often mentioned with regard to accessibility of the Internet—particularly the World-Wide Web. We note how accessibility for people with disabilities was only achieved with difficulty as computers and computer network developed. The 1989 invention of the World-Wide Web made the Internet much easier to use for many, but for many people with disabilities "surfing the Web" offers barriers and challenges, as well as pleasures and opportunities. We examine the development of standards on accessibility of the World-Wide Web, and how such standards have been put into practice. We analyze how disability is constructed in these standards and debates about applying them, with particular attention given to blind people and those with vision impairment—a group of citizens who have often been held out as those with most to gain from the Internet and computing, but whose needs, desires, and aspirations are still rarely taken into account in the cultural and social shaping of these technologies.

Having considered the construction of disability in computing and the Internet, we focus, in chapter seven, on the possibilities for cultural production and generation of alternative representations of disability by people with disabilities themselves in new media. Our starting point is the proposition that there are cultural spaces being transformed and created through digitization that have important implications for how disability is understood. We critically examine the claim that new media heralds a shift from consumer to producer, from "couch potato" to "couch commando." The sorts of embodiment and subjectivity implied by such claims needed to be examined, as the way these are constructed discursively often naively purports to include but then actually exclude people with disabilities. We look at the phenomenon of "chat groups" featuring people with disabilities and disabilities issues. These chat groups on the Internet constitute new cultural spaces for people with disabilities and give us insights into what the politics of such digitization might be. What are the conditions of possibility for emerging new media spaces for people with disabilities to provide more than disabling practices in the margins of digitization?

In the culminating section of the book, we consider the questions our study raises for more humane and enabling discursive practices in new media practice and cultural production. Instead of adopting the overly optimistic view that new media will confer opportunities on people with disabilities to create cultural artifacts, it is suggested that policymakers need to rethink their analytical frameworks for understanding disability and new media. The starting place for such realignment, we contend, is a realization of the emerging nature of cultures of people with disabilities in and through digitization. From this knowledge—provided directly from people with disabilities as experts about their lives and opportunities—a different understanding of people with disabilities and the new media can be fashioned. This requires us to recognize and affirm in practice different ways of knowing the world and to map the diversity of abilities people have in our societies. It is only when we understand disability in its emerging digital incarnations and recognize the importance of a critical understanding that incorporates difference into policy and cultural formations, and the construction of technological systems, that we will have a society that embraces all and lives out diversity. In the end this is a question not just of having regard for people identified as having disability but all who are on the margins.

NOTES

1. Mike Oliver, *Understanding Disability: From Theory to Practice* (London: Macmillan Press, 1996), 143.

2. R. L. Metts, *Disability Issues, Trends and Recommendations for the World Bank* (Washington, D.C.: World Bank, 2000).

3. Margaret Cooper, "The Australian Disability Movement Lives," *Disability & Society* 14 (1999): 217–26; D. Driedger, *The Last Civil Rights Movement: Disabled Peoples' International* (London: Hurst & Co; New York: St. Martin's, 1989); Sharon N. Barnartt and Richard K. Scotch, *Disability Protests: Contentious Politics, 1970–1999* (Washington, D.C.: Gallaudet Press, 2001); Doris Zames Fleischer and Frieda Zames, *The Disability Rights Movement: From Charity to Confrontation* (Philadelphia: Temple University Press, 2001); Paul K. Longmore and Lauri Umansky, eds., *The New Disability History: American Perspectives* (New York: New York University Press, 2001); Tom Shakespeare and Nick Watson, "Making the Difference: Disability, Politics, and Recognition," in *Handbook of Disability Studies* (Thousand Oaks, Calif.: Sage, 2001), ed. Gary L. Albrecht, Katherine D. Seelman, and Michael Bury, 546–64.

Part One

TECHNOLOGIES OF DISABILITY

Chapter One

Encountering Technology, Media, and Culture

[T]echnology must inescapably reflect the contours of that particular social order which has produced and sustained it. And like any human enterprise, it does not simply proceed automatically, but contains a subjective element which drives it, and assumes the particular forms given it by the most powerful and forceful people in society, in struggle with others. The development of technology, and thus the social development it implies, is as much determined by the breadth of vision that informs it, and the particular notions of social order to which it is bound, as by the mechanical relations between things in the physical laws of nature.

—David F. Noble, 1977[1]

[T]echnology is always a form of *social* knowledge, practices and products. It is the result of conflicts and compromises, the outcomes of which depend primarily on the distribution of power and resources between different groups in society.

—Judy Wacjman, 1991[2]

Technology is a preoccupation of contemporary life. It provides ways of doing things, makes work, creates material goods and services, supports ways of life, and even, in the case of genetic engineering, reshapes bodies and promises to create life itself. Technology is present in everyday life, in ways that we often do not notice once we become accustomed to and reliant upon it. It also carries many other meanings, having a special place in debates about how societies are governed, what their futures are, how their economic and cultural arrangements work.

These features of technologies are evident in the case of new media and communications technologies: visions of utopian and future society such as Alvin Toffler's 1974 *Future Shock*,[3] Nicholas Negroponte's 1995 *Being Digital*,[4] and

3

Bill Gates's 1995 *The Road Ahead*[5] assume a key role for networked digital technologies. And while early digital prophets were crying in the wilderness, in the 1990s such pipe dreams were routinely incorporated into government policy, corporate business plans, not-for-profit organization strategic planning, and household budgets. Science fiction utopia and dystopia in books, such as William Gibson's *Neuromancer*[6] (which contributed the word "cyberspace" to the English language), or movies, such as the 1999 film *The Matrix,* saw so-called high technology become part of the myths and folklore of everyday life and language. This book seeks to interrogate new media and communications technologies, and to question the way that disability is shaped or "made" in them. Before introducing our understanding of disability, however, in this chapter we wish to establish a critical perspective on such technologies and their media cultures.

In the first section, we provide a brief overview of new media. Following this, we turn in the second section to a discussion of the "technoscience worlds" of disability. In the third and final section, we investigate media and culture, suggesting the importance of both these dimensions of new digital technologies for appreciating digital disability.

WHEN MEDIA AND COMMUNICATIONS TECHNOLOGIES ARE NEW

Communication is central to human society.[7] It has long been supported by, and indeed is often inseparable from, technology. Historians of communication have pointed to humans using technologies such as fire, pictures, and other material practices as ways of conveying language, concepts, emotions, and ideas. The advent of writing was made possible by technologies, such as the chisel, stylus, quill or pen, and the tablet, papyrus, and paper.[8] The invention of the printing press heralded a new epoch in human communication, with the appearance of new media, the printed book, pamphlet, newspaper, and magazine. In the nineteenth and twentieth centuries, new media and communications technologies abounded: photography, film, radio, television. From a historical perspective, the use of the adjective "new" to describe media and communications technologies needs to be used judiciously. At the present time, "new" does extra work, in conjuring up the allure of such technologies as attractive, exotic, and urgently needed. Many media and communications technologies, such as the ones discussed in this book, are routinely described as "new." They include the telephone and telecommunications, computers and the Internet, digital television, digital radio, electronic books, portable digital assistants. Such new media technologies share at least three features: they are digital, converging, and networked.

Firstly, these new media are digital, or at least in the process of moving from older technological modes to digital ones. By digital, we refer to communications technologies that take the forms of encoding information in "ones" and "zeros." Older, analog technologies used other ways of recording, storing, and transmitting information. For instance, radio programs were recorded on tape recorders, then transmitted over airwaves, to be received by radios tuned to the correct frequency. Digital radio makes it possible for sound to be recorded digitally, edited more precisely than analog, digitally encoded for transmission over airwaves, and then received by digital radio devices. Such digital information can be stored with relative efficiency, especially using digital compression techniques. It is easily manipulated using computers and software. In theory, such information can be reproduced faithfully without any loss of quality.

Secondly, these technologies are in a process of converging. If media and communications technologies are in digital form, it is possible for information stored in one mode, channel, or device to be incorporated into another. So, for instance, our computers are "multimedia": they combine text, image, sound, and video. We no longer require a radio receiver to listen to radio programs, as well as a newspaper or magazine to consult a program guide. Listening to radio on the Internet or through a digital radio transmitter may allow us to receive information in both aural and written forms. We no longer need to read a book as one activity, and write a letter as a completely distinct one. Using a computer or web or digital television, we can read a text in electronic form and send an e-mail, with the text of interest attached.

Digital and converging new media and communications technologies are also often networked, a third noteworthy attribute. The telephone and the computer have converged, courtesy of the modem, allowing telecommunications networks to carry electronic mail and other data communications. Because of their shared digital elements, other technologies can also use telecommunications to access and interface with other devices: in a "smart" house, the refrigerator may have its in-built computer chip, memory, and software and be connected to a computer or telecommunications network, allowing remote diagnosis or recipes to be displayed on a built-in console for the chef-at-home's cooking ease.

Of course, there are many more complexities to new media and communications technologies, indispensable to a fuller understanding of the topic, some of which will be alluded to in later case studies.[9] For the present, however, we wish to stand back from the details of new media, to consider how to delve deeply into the nature of technology. We start our discussion with the idea of "technoscience" worlds and how this casts light on technology and disability.

THE TECHNOSCIENCE WORLDS OF DISABILITY[10]

The idea of the "technoscience world" makes explicit the constituent relations of science, technology, and society. Turnbull points out "a doubly-confounding paradox" with regard to our relationship with the world, a paradox that looms all the larger when looking at the relations between technology and people with disabilities.

> Not only are our scientific and technological enquiries manifestly both very productive and very destructive, but we will inevitably come to depend on them to resolve the very contradictions they have created. What compounds this even further is that we know little about the nature of enquiry: we hardly know what science and technology are, let alone what "makes them tick" or how to control them. We know little about them because, as Langdon Winner points out, the intimate connections between knowledge and power have led to the promulgation of myths about the nature of science and technology.[11]

Turnbull observes that his purpose "is to try to unravel some of the myths about science and technology."[12] Certainly, much science and technology literature in the 1980s and 1990s, for example, sought to correct "myths" that suggest that science is inherently objective, distinct from technology and society and its structures and power relations.

With regard to the wheelchair, the archetypal symbol of disability, notions of objective truth may differ depending on whether one is a consumer, a non-disabled professional, or a woman, to give a few examples. Likewise, for people with the values of the hearing world, including most professionals in the relevant fields, the cochlear implant is an inherently neutral technology, capable of beneficial application to problems of deafness. For members of the Deaf culture around the world, it can be an inherently destructive and unethical artifact, as we consider in chapter two.

Turnbull identifies the inherent contradiction in relying upon science and technology to resolve social questions they themselves have created. In this sense, the wheelchair and the cochlear implant demonstrate how disability may be created by such systems, which are then appealed to, relied upon, and promoted as ways of ameliorating the situation for which they are in part responsible. In examining the interrelationship of science, technology, and society, he raises various epistemological questions to do with the nature and production of scientific knowledge. He notes the essentially social nature of science and that which is popularly known as scientific knowledge. Work in the sociology of scientific knowledge, inspired by the work of Popper and Kuhn, can be of assistance here.[13] This is particularly so in terms of the production of scientific knowledge, in part by agreements among social groupings of scientists over assumptions that are part of their everyday practice.[14] Such conventions are usually informal contacts among members of the scientific community. Within particular time frames, these conventions inform the production of what we call knowledge and science, pointing, then, to the social nature of scientific knowledge. Such an understanding demands exploration of the social relations of the technologies of disability, especially those that utilize professional and scientific discourses in constructing our knowledge of disability: "One of the consequences of the approach we are adopting is that such situations cease to appear paradoxical and become explicable in terms of the interests of the experts involved in trying to achieve certainty in conditions of uncertainty."[15] Professional knowledge systems, with their claim to objectivity and use of "the scientific method" are particularly important in defining and regulating disability and the technoscience worlds associated with it. However, the critical literature in the sociology of scientific knowledge helps to question the notion that there is one objective and agreed set of rules and criteria to which all who claim to belong to the community that is "science" adhere. As Paul Feyerabend argues, no one set of rules and procedures is universally adopted by all people claiming to be scientists,[16] an insight equally applicable to technology practitioners.

The social nature of knowledge is further explored in sociological investigation of laboratories, where scholars have studied the actual activities that take place in the laboratory, where much of what counts as science occurs.[17] Indeed, the actual materials used in scientific research and the organization of the laboratory require a special environment:

> Frequently the laboratory itself also has to be organized in a very tightly controlled way to prevent unwanted effects. Once the artificial materials are assembled in the specifically-contrived environment of the laboratory, they are subjected to experimentation using highly sophisticated instruments and techniques. Experiments, precisely because they are highly contrived, are usually hard to do. . . . Thus the process of scientific research is in large part a technical processing of artifacts in highly constrained circumstances.[18]

Such creation of specially selected environments and conditions is important with regard to the development of standards for the wheelchair and claims to the scientific and objective measurement of characteristics. Likewise, proponents of the cochlear implant, especially those utilizing professional (and medically inspired) discourses, create scientific knowledge in rigorously controlled circumstances. This is similarly the case with new communications and media technologies, and associated artifacts conceived specifically for people with disabilities. Derek de Solla Price observes that what goes on in the laboratory is more than the testing of hypotheses and theories; it is artifactual.[19] Nature is carefully shaped to make it susceptible to analysis. Turnbull, following Latour's work on laboratories, illustrates this point nicely when he points to the way in which Louis Pasteur

> developed the technique of inoculation against anthrax by making the disease conform to the simplifications and restrictions of the laboratory. . . .
> But in order that it should be effective on the farm, the farm had itself to be transformed to institute the practices of the laboratory: disinfection, cleanliness, conservation, timing and recording.[20]

This has particular pertinence for an understanding of the relations of science, technology, and people with disabilities in the examination of both the wheelchair and the cochlear implant. For example, while the wheelchair in the abstract may be theoretically regarded as an aid to mobility, it is only when the real world is designed to enable equitable access for people in wheelchairs that the wheelchair can be seen as an effective enabler. Without the necessary pavement, curbs, ramps, and funding of so-called access, the wheelchair as a system has different meanings and effects. Likewise, the world needs to be manipulated in particular ways for optimum results to be obtained with regard to the cochlear implant. In addition, that which is seen as a scientific miracle from a hearing world perspective can also be seen as foreign and threatening from a Deaf cultural perspective. Such technological systems provide exemplifications of the notion that science is not just "theory-driven" but also "technique-driven."[21]

Measurements and standards are an excellent example of the way in which modern science is always accompanied by complex social organization. Measurements need a common standard, international in scope, with each country having their own bureau to facilitate this. While wheelchairs have been made for centuries, the rise at an international level of rehabilitation engineers and other professional groupings that claim a scientific knowledge and control of the wheelchair and its prescription has in part brought about a move for a universal standard for wheelchairs. Similarly, with the cochlear implant, the setting of standards, defined by, and in the control of, particular constituencies, is seen as essential by various professional groups. As Turnbull notes, "even something as basic and transparent as measurement necessitates widespread social organization that permeates the whole society, indeed is constitutive of the society."[22]

In detailing the complex relations of science and technology, Turnbull observes that one of the great myths is that technology is simply applied science. Other myths he identifies, reflecting the critical literature, are that technology is neutral and that technology is autonomous, these both being constitutive of another much-discussed myth of technological determinism.[23] Technology may be considered in terms of artifacts (that is objects, tools, machines, and so on), practice, knowledge, and applied science. We now think of technology and science as inextricably interwoven, but technology preceded science in crucial respects. MacKenzie and Wajcman cite the water mill, the plough, and even the steam engine as some examples of "crucial inventions" that were "in no real sense the application of pre-existing science."[24] While noting that science and technology have increasingly become connected in this century, they conclude, along with other scholars, that not only is technology simply dependent on science, but technology has also contributed to science. And of course, as in the past, technology itself still shapes technology.

Various commentators have noted that the concept of technology has become so fundamental to modern life that it is difficult to analyze or challenge it. While acknowledging that technology and society are distinct concepts and entities, we assert that technology is inherently social and political, serving the interests of the status quo in society and symbolically legitimizing this society.[25] Such an approach is a particularly important premise of our perspective on digital disability, running contrary to the ideas associated with technology being neutral and autonomous and determining our lives. Rather, the digital technological systems analyzed in this book are seen to serve a predominantly non-disabled status quo, maintaining and legitimizing the situation in various ways.

In drawing upon the science and technology studies literature, we wish to point out how notions of neutral and autonomous technology are particularly important in defining and regulating disability (as is the doctrine of technological determinism). None of the literature on the wheelchair, for example, has ever dealt with the context in which wheelchairs are made, what they are made of, why they exist in their current forms, why they exist in the numbers they do, why there are variations in form and design, who controls access to the wheelchair, and who are the gatekeepers of ownership of the wheelchair. The classic history of the wheelchair written by Kamenetz ignores all these questions, taking the wheelchair as a given in a unilinear historical account of wheelchair development.[26] Underlying such accounts is the ideology of progress, where it is assumed, for instance, that those newer models are inherently better. A similar critique may be made of new media and communications technology, in which the politics of exclusion of people with disabilities, or inclusion under the rubric of accessibility, is mostly rendered invisible.

What we call, following the lead of science and technology studies scholars, "the myths" of technology, have all too often led to the writing of uncritical and one-sided histories, which have in their turn influenced scholarly and popular understandings of how technology comes about and what may be done with it in the present or future. For instance, technology is too often controlled by powerful professional interest groups in Western society. A review of the relevant literature of various professions, such as medicine and rehabilitation engineering, reveals that the wheelchair, rather than being seen as socially shaped, is considered as unproblematic, with design changes driven almost entirely by science and technology. Similarly, digital communications technologies are generally regarded as the result of the progress that is more "customer-focused."

The problem is that accounts of the development of digital technologies, like those of the wheelchair and cochlear implant, overwhelming view such technological systems as being inherently good and evidence of society's progress. Rarely is a broader perspective on the creation of technology taken, acknowledging how it is shaped by the role of professional groupings and specialized knowledges, or the politics of technological systems—such as the cochlear implant as a system that defines and regulates disability. The idea that technology is autonomous conceals the political and social contradictions and conflict associated with traditional and mobile telephones, the computer, the Internet, digital broadcasting, and other digital technologies—especially in relation to how disability is constructed with these technologies.

A common refrain of both wheelchair users and wheelchair manufacturers is that it is inevitable that the wheelchair will improve, as materials become lighter and technologies become better. Here the ideology of progress is conspicuously present, for such an understanding ignores the roles played by the state and powerful interest groups in defining the characteristics and social perceptions of the wheelchair. In the same way, users, manufacturers, and regulators, including various professionals, view the cochlear implant as improving, with much of the literature providing statistical measurements to quantify and control the technoscience world of the cochlear implant. The cochlear implant is viewed as becoming "better" over time, for example, via lighter and smaller components and via the increase in the number of electrodes it is possible to have implanted. In the case of the mobile telephone, companies argue that over time better features and functionality will be incorporated into design, and better accessories or modules tailored to the needs of people with disabilities in order to improve accessibility. But this notion of "better" is simply a measure of efficiency in attaining certain preconceived goals, often ignoring other primary social, cultural, and psychological effects.

Examples of the role of governmental and other powerful interest groups discussed in this book include the role of state- or industry-funded equipment schemes in different countries, which effectively provide the purchasing power for much disability communications equipment—for example, text telephones or particular equipment such as big-button telephones or flashing lights or dedicated software for blind people. As well, more explicit elements of governmental policy are determined by notions of how much money it is acceptable to give to people with disabilities and the power relations of people with disabilities in society. In addition, the role of professional groupings is important. The claim of medical practitioners, for instance, to have an expert knowledge of all forms of disability, and thus to know what is right and proper for people with disabilities, includes the suggestion that they certify whether people are eligible for telecommunications disability products or concessions, despite the lack of training and experience that most of them have in this area.

Just as the rise of the factory in Britain was more a managerial than a technical necessity, similarly the wheelchair, cochlear implant, and contemporary digital communications and media technologies are seen as forms of the management and regulation of people with disabilities, effectively controlling their aspirations, movements, and access to various parts of the social world. Indeed, these technoscience worlds provide a way of regulating and standardizing people with many forms of life conditions and disabilities, so that they become assembled under particular labels. These include, "wheelchair users," "hearing impaired," "hearing aid users," and "text telephone users." While the wheelchair, the cochlear implant, the mobile telephone, and the Internet are potentially liberating, they are also inherently controlling. For example, the social relations of the wheelchair as a technological system effectively control people's access in the community, the type of wheelchair they have, and their acceptance in society, and even provide a lowly platform for them to look up at "normal" people, or rather, for so-called normal people to look down upon them. The Internet may genuinely offer an opportunity for many people with disabilities to communicate with others, and not need to disclose information about their disability, to "pass" as someone temporarily able-bodied (or non-disabled),[27] yet lack of accessible websites or full use of e-mail means that people with disabilities are also systematically positioned as "other," excluded or marginalized in the friction-free supposed utopia of cyberspace too.

The wheelchair is liberating, allowing a person to get from one place to another, something that they may not otherwise be able to do unassisted. However, in a different set of social circumstances the meanings and structures associated with the wheelchair might be different, and it is worth asking whether a more liberating form of mobility would exist for people who currently use wheelchairs if they constituted some of the most powerful members of society. In the same way, the technoscience world of the cochlear implant is inherently controlling when looked at from the perspective of people being required to meet standards defined by professional and regulatory groupings before gaining access to this particular form of artifact. They must conform to norms, and are subject to a lack of power associated with not having the financial resources to control what is a multimillion-dollar and highly regulated system. Knowledge systems associated with the cochlear implant confirm the values of the hearing world and particular constructions of disability, especially those informed by medical discourse, determining what is "nice," "normal," and "natural." The perpetuation of these values is furthered by the existence and further expansion of a network of cochlear implant programs around the world. Mobile phones too have been unproblematically seen by many, including some people with disabilities, as a boon, creating new ways to communicate and offering additional security and independence. Yet as first introduced, digital mobile phones using the European GSM standard interfered with hearing aids, producing difficulties of use for hard-of-hearing people and others with hearing disabilities. The trend toward tiny mobile phones is also a mixed blessing for many people who do not have the dexterity required to press the keyboards accurately, to dial a phone number, or use other functions of a mobile phone (especially the popular short messaging services, or SMS).

Clearly, technoscience knowledge confers power upon those who control it; "technoscientists," and those who have influence and control of resources, shape the technoscience worlds of disability. This may be observed in the ways in which the laboratory has needed to be extended into the so-called real world. The introduction of Western wheelchairs into developing countries is a particularly good example of this. From various professional perspectives, the best results for the cochlear implant are also obtained in the audio laboratory, rather than in the "real world." Pressures arise to make the lived world of the implantee more like a laboratory. Indeed, the cochlear implant is only desirable, necessary, and successful within a social world that sees deafness as pathological and disabling, and is structured in accordance with this worldview. An alternative perspective, such as that provided by Deaf culture, is an example of a different knowledge system that suggests that such a technology is not inherently good.

Accounts of these clashes of values around technology were usefully deepened in a field of science and technology studies that developed in the 1980s called the "new sociology of technology." According to Stephen Hill, the new sociology of technology is "a field that seeks to identify the social shaping forces and negotiations that create technological change."[28] For instance, Pinch and Bijker attempt to develop and outline a social constructionist approach to the study of science and technology, rejecting stances that make hard-and-fast distinctions between science and technology. Instead, they note the different ways in which such terms may be used, claiming commonsense notions to be good places to start with the social study of science and technology and their interrelationship. Hence, they suggest that technology can be used to mean physical objects or artifacts, activities or processes, and knowledge. More expansive definitions of technology better suit comprehensive accounts of particular forms of technology pertinent to disability, such as the complex information and communications technologies discussed in our study. This is evident in the small but important body of work that critically considers disability and technology.[29] The social constructionist approach to technology was also greatly complicated and extended through the 1990s with important feminist work on technology,[30] and other new developments such as actor-network theory.[31]

MEDIA, CULTURE, AND DISABILITY

A critical framework, such as that outlined above, is indispensable to understanding how technology works in society. It is particularly important to explain how disability is constructed in and through technology. Regarding new media and communication technologies, there are at least further dimensions that are essential to analyze—the cultural and mediated nature of these technologies.

Fundamental to the digital, convergent, and networked nature of new media are the cultural forms they embody, carry, and represent, and the cultural changes in which they are implicated. The telephone retains its importance for communicating with others, speaking and listening, engaging in the cultural and linguistic norms and practices of conversation. Telecommunications, however, is much more expansive now than just voice telephony. It encompasses text communications (whether via e-mail or text telephones used by Deaf people and those with hearing and speech disabilities). Telephone service is provided not only by phone companies but by pay television companies who are happy to offer entertainment and information services, such as television programs, as they connect up the household. With the World-Wide Web, the Internet is not just about text e-mails; it represents the way that many people keep up to date with the news, entertain themselves, do research, enjoy erotica, listen to music, watch videos, participate in online and offline communities and subcultures. Third-generation mobile phones allow users to talk to each other, and also watch videos.

Essential to a rigorous investigation of these new cultural forms and practices is interrogating the media in which they are embedded. Communication scholars have contributed a burgeoning literature on communication practices among individuals, groups, and organizations in new media, especially the Internet. A significant literature exists on communication and disability, including the important collection *Handbook of Communication and People with Disabilities*.[32] From our perspective, we are especially interested in the ways in which media frame and produce such communicative acts and situations. Therefore we draw on traditions in critical media studies and mass communications research that emphasize the power relations in media, and that seek to account for the specific histories, audiences, and modes of different media forms, flows, spaces, and mediascapes. In doing so, we seek to bring into dialogue quite different traditions of studying media such as print and broadcast media, on the one hand, and telecommunications, on the other.

Prior to the 1990s, telecommunications was little studied in media studies, and it still remains the province of other disciplines, especially engineering, science and technology, economics, law and policy. Telecommunications continues to be a specialized field, still dominated by neoclassical economic, science and engineering, and legal treatments.[33] This neoclassical tradition has spawned many important studies,[34] but other approaches, are not well represented, tending to be neglected, overlooked, or foreclosed. Vincent Mosco wrote sixteen years ago that "the challenge to teachers of telecommunications policy is to define a new field that fits no well established discipline";[35] this task has yet to be satisfactorily accomplished.

To be sure, critique of the dominant neoclassical economic approach may be found in the work of dissenting neoclassical economists,[36] the post-Keynesians (though we are unaware if this paradigm has been brought to bear on telecommunications specifically), more extensively in the broad political economy school,[37] and in policy-oriented studies. There have been some significant and thorough treatments of social and political aspects of telecommunications and new media,[38] but these are still are in a small minority, and much of the literature often focuses on issues of access, equity, and perceived marginality, under the heading of the "digital divide."[39] Studies of the cultural implications of telecommunications are very few.

As well as bringing a critical media studies perspective to bear on telecommunications, we also focus at different stages on what has been described as the cultural dimension of media. For instance, we look at media cultures, by which we mean the cultural forms that are related to specific media forms.[40] Scholars of television have established the existence of "television cultures,"[41] which have national as well as class, sex, gender, and ethnic coordinates. Rather than people being understood as passive consumers of media, as "couch potatoes" who are addicted to media programs, the concept of media cultures suggests that consumption of media products is an active process. One example of this is the existence of subcultures around particular television programs and the variety and sophistication of the activities their members engage in.[42] The richness and complexity of such cultural activity is an important insight from the growing number of studies, which have added greatly to the appreciation of the importance of media in cultural maintenance and innovation.

Culture and media cultures are central dimensions of the construction of disability. Barnes, Mercer, and Shakespeare point out that cultural exploration of disability commenced as early as 1966,[43] noting that much of the subsequent work considers how the representation of disabled people in media, literature, film, and photography is "a primary source of disability as well as a rationalization for treating disabled people as 'deficient.'"[44] Crucial to disability activism has been cultural politics encompassing both an interrogation of disabling cultural representations[45] and the assertion of the right of people with disabilities to engage in their own cultural productions.[46] We would agree with Barnes, Mercer, and Shakespeare, that there is a much wider acceptance now that media and other cultural representations play a constitutive role in the social definition and reproduction of disability. While study of media and the representation of disability is fledgling, there are a number of helpful studies using different approaches and adopting different perspectives, whether content analysis,[47] rhetorical approaches,[48] or other approaches.[49] There are now helpful studies of disability and photography,[50] disability and film,[51] and disability and communication.[52] Similarly, while cultural studies[53] has been slow to open a dialogue with disability studies, there have been important studies by literary and cultural studies practitioners in the United States, which we have found specifically useful in drawing attention to the cultural and textual aspects of the fashioning of disability.[54] Such insights are important for understanding convergent digital media such as the media, which blur and rework the traditional distinction between "carriage"—the medium by which information is carried—and "content"—the information itself (a blurring invoked, of course, by Marshall McLuhan's dictum, the "medium is the message"). For these reasons, we adopt media and cultural studies approaches to "read" representations of disability, and to analyze discourses of disability.

With such understandings of technology, culture, and media in mind, then, in chapter two we seek to elaborate our framework of critique of new media and communications technologies by approaching the contested and famously refractory matter of disability itself.

NOTES

1. D. F. Noble, *America by Design* (Oxford: Oxford University Press, 1977), pp. xxii.

2. Judy Wacjman, *Feminism Confronts Technology* (Blackwell, U.K.: Polity; Sydney: Allen & Unwin, 1991), 162.

3. Alvin Toffler, *Future Shock* (New York: Bantam, 1974).

4. Nicholas Negroponte, *Being Digital* (New York: Knopf, 1995).

5. Bill Gates, with Nathan Myhrvold and Peter Rinearson, *The Road Ahead* (New York: Viking, 1995).

6. William Gibson, *Neuromancer* (New York: Ace, 1984).

7. Harold Innes, *The Bias of Communication* (Toronto: University of Toronto Press, 1951).

8. Walter J. Ong, *Orality and Literacy: The Technologizing of the Word* (London: Methuen, 1982).

9. There are a number of good introductions to new media technologies. For instance, see Terry Flew, *New Media Technologies: An Introduction* (Oxford: Oxford University Press, 2002); or Leah Lievrouw and Sonia Livingstone, eds., *The Handbook of New Media* (London: Sage, 2002).

10. This expression is taken from David Turnbull's book *Technoscience Worlds* (Geelong, Australia: Deakin University Press, 1991), which provides a useful introduction to the science and technology studies (STS) literature. The expression "science world" is adapted from Howard Becker's use of the term "art world" in an entirely different scholarly arena. See Howard S. Becker, *Art Worlds* (Berkeley: University of California Press, 1992); and D. W. Chambers and D. Turnbull, "Science Worlds: An Integrated Approach to Social Studies of Science Teaching," *Social Studies of Science* 19 (1989): 155–79.

11. Turnbull, *Technoscience Worlds*, 3.

12. Turnbull, *Technoscience Worlds*, 4.

13. Karl R. Popper, *The Logic of Scientific Discovery* (London: Hutchinson, 1959), and Thomas S. Kuhn, *The Structure of Scientific Revolutions,* 2nd ed. (Chicago: University of Chicago Press, 1970).

14. For example see J. R. Rouse, *Knowledge and Power* (Ithaca, N.Y.: Cornell University Press, 1987), and K. Knorr-Cetina, *The Manufacture of Knowledge: An Essay on the Constructivist and Contextual Nature of Science* (Oxford: Pergamon, 1981).

15. Turnbull, *Technoscience Worlds*, 10.

16. Paul Feyerabend, *Against Method: An Outline of an Anarchistic Theory of Knowledge* (London: New Left Books, 1975).

17. See Bruno Latour, *Science in Action* (Milton Keynes, U.K.: Open University Press) 1987; Bruno Latour and Steve Woolgar, *Laboratory Life: The Construction of Scientific Facts* (Princeton, N.J.: Princeton University Press, 1986).

18. Turnbull, *Technoscience Worlds*, 24–25.

19. D. J. de Solla Price, "Notes towards a Philosophy of the Science/Technology Interaction," in *The Nature of Scientific Knowledge. Are Models of Scientific Change Relevant?* ed. R. Laudan (Dordrecht: D. Reidel, 1984), 105–14.

20. Turnbull, *Technoscience Worlds*, 27–28.

21. Turnbull, *Technoscience Worlds*, 27.

22. Turnbull, *Technoscience Worlds*, 29.

23. Turnbull, *Technoscience Worlds*, 36.

24. Donald MacKenzie and Judy Wajcman, eds., *The Social Shaping of Technology* (Milton Keynes: Open University Press, 1985), 8–9.

25. David Dickson, *Alternative Technology and the Politics of Technical Change* (Glasgow: Fontana/Collins, 1974), 9–14.

26. See Herman L. Kamenetz, *The Wheelchair Book: Mobility for the Disabled* (Springfield, Ill.: Charles C. Thomas, 1969), and also his "A Brief History of the Wheelchair," *Journal of the History of Medicine and Allied Sciences* 24 (1969): 205–10.

27. On "passing," see Brenda Jo Brueggemann, "On (Almost) Passing," *College English* 59 (1997): 647–60.

28. Stephen Hill, *The Tragedy of Technology* (London: Pluto Press, 1988), 4. The "new sociology of technology" is a development of previous accounts of the nature of technology and especially technological change. These include classic works such as Jacques Ellul's *The Technological Society* (New York: Vintage, 1964), Lewis Mumford's *Technics and Civilization* (London: Routledge & Kegan Paul, 1934) and Herbert Marcuse's *One Dimensional Man* (London: Abacus, 1972). As well as Hill's account, other works in the new sociology of technology include MacKenzie and Wajcman, ed., *The Social Shaping of Technology* (Milton Keynes, U.K.: Open University Press, 1985), W. E. Bijker, T. P. Hughes, and T. Pinch's *The Social Construction of Technological Systems* (Cambridge, Mass.: MIT Press, 1987).

29. For instance, Katherine D. Seelman, "Science and Technology Policy: Is Disability a Missing Factor?" in *Handbook of Disability Studies* (Thousand Oaks, Calif.: Sage, 2001), ed. Gary L. Albrecht, Katherine D. Seelman, and Michael Bury, 663–92; P. Cornes, "Impairment, Disability, Handicap and New Technology," in *Social Work, Disabled People and Disabling Environments* (London: Jessica Kingsley, 1991); A. Roulstone, *Enabling Technology: Disabled People, Work and New Technology* (Buckingham, U.K.: Open University Press, 1998); P. Thornton, "Communications Technology— Empowerment or Disempowerment," *Disability, Handicap & Society* 8 (1993): 339–49.

30. A helpful piece on understanding feminist work on technology is Zoe Sofoulis, "Of Spanners and Cyborgs: De-homogenising feminist thinking on technology," in *Transitions: New Australian Feminisms*, ed. Barbara Caine and Rosemary Pringle (Sydney: Allen & Unwin, 1995), 147–163.

31. John Law and John Hassard, eds., *Actor Network Theory and After* (Boston, Mass.: Blackwell, 1999).

32. Dawn O. Braithwaite and Teresa L. Thompson, eds., *Handbook of Communication and People with Disabilities: Research and Application* (Mahwah, N.J.: Lawrence Erlbaum Associates, 2000). Braithwaite and Thompson's concluding essay, "Communication and Disability Research: A Productive Past and a Bright Future," comments that media studies of people with disabilities is "critical to the discipline's future" (513).

33. Prima facie evidence of this dominance may be provided by an inspection of the proceedings of the conferences of the leading scholarly society, the International Telecommunications Society, such as G. W. Brock and G. L. Rosston, eds., *The Internet and Telecommunications Policy: Selected Papers from the 1995 Telecommunications Policy Research Conference* (Mahwah, N.J.: Lawrence Erlbaum, 1996), and a perusal of the pages of the leading international scholarly journal, *Telecommunications Policy*.

34. For instance, see Eli M. Noam, ed., *Telecommunications in Africa* (New York: Oxford University Press, 1999), and Eli M. Noam, S. Komatsuzaki, and D. A. Conn, eds., *Telecommunications in the Pacific Basin: An Evolutionary Approach* (Oxford: Oxford University Press, 1994)

35. Vincent Mosco, "Teaching Telecommunications Policy, Critically," *Canadian Journal of Communications* 11 (1985): 51–62.

36. For example, Don Lamberton's work as evidenced in his two edited collections *Beyond Competition: The Future of Telecommunications* (Amsterdam: Elsevier, 1995) and *The New Research Frontiers of Communications Policy* (Amsterdam: Elsevier, 1999), and honored by S. Macdonald and J. Nightingale, eds., *Information and Organization: A Tribute to the Work of Don Lamberton* (Amsterdam: North-Holland, 1999) Also the work of John Quiggin, such as his *Great Expectations: Microeconomic Reform in Australia* (Sydney: Allen & Unwin, 1996).

37. Of which there are some fine studies, including, Geoff Mulgan, *Communication and Control: Networks and the New Economies of Communication* (Cambridge: Polity Press, 1991); R. E. Babe, *Communication and the Transformation of Economics: Essays in Information, Public Policy, and Political Economy* (Boulder, Colo.: Westview, 1995); E. A. Comor, ed. *The Global Political Economy of Communication: Hegemony, Telecommunication, and the Information Economy* (London: St. Martin's, 1994); Jill Hills, *The Democracy Gap: The Politics of Information and Communications Technologies in the United States and Europe* (Westport, Conn.: Greenwood, 1991); Robert McChesney, *Rich Media, Poor Democracy: Communications Politics in Dubious Times* (Urbana-Champaign: University of Illinois Press, 1999); Kevin G. Wilson, *Deregulating Telecommunications: U.S. and Canadian Telecommunications, 1840–1997* (Lanham, Md.: Rowman & Littlefield, 2000).

38. See Phil Agre and Marc Rotenberg, eds., *Technology and Privacy: The New Landscape* (Cambridge, Mass.: MIT Press, 1997); Patricia Aufderheide, *Communications Policy and the Public Interest: The Telecommunications Act of 1996* (New York: Guildford, 1999). Also Ithiel de Sola Pool's pioneering edited collection, *The Social Impact of the Telephone* (Cambridge, Mass.: MIT Press, 1977).

39. Such as S. Lax, ed., *Access Denied: Exclusion in the Information Age* (Basingstoke, U.K.: Macmillan, 2000), or Donald A. Schon, Bisch Sanyal, and William J. Mitchell, eds., *High Technology and Low-Income Communities: Prospects for the Positive Use of Advanced Information Technology* (Cambridge, Mass.: MIT Press, 1998).

40. For example, see Michael Skovman and Kim Christian Schroder, eds., *Media Cultures: Reappraising Transnational Media* (London: Routledge, 1992), and Nick Stevenson, *Understanding Media Cultures: Social Theory and Mass Communication* (London: Sage, 1995). On new media cultures, see J. Macgregor Wise, *Exploring Technology and Social Space* (London: Sage, 1997).

41. John Fiske, *Television Culture* (London: Routledge, 1987).

42. See Henry Jenkins, *Textual Poachers: Television Fans and Participatory Culture* (London: Routledge, 1992); Hamif Naficy, *The Making of Exile Cultures: Iranian Television in Los Angeles* (Minneapolis: University of Minnesota Press, 1993); Nancy K. Baym, *Tune In, Log On: Soaps, Fandom, and Online Community* (Thousand Oaks, Calif.: Sage, 2000).

43. Colin Barnes, Geoff Mercer, and Tom Shakespeare, *Exploring Disability: A Sociological Introduction* (Cambridge: Polity Press, 1999). They refer here to Louis Battye, "The Chatterley Syndrome," in *Stigma: The Experience of Disability*, ed. Paul Hunt (London: Geoffrey Chapman, 1966).

44. Barnes, Mercer, and Shakespeare, *Exploring Disability*.

45. An early example of this revisionary project is A. Gartner and T. Joe's edited collection, *Images of the Disabled: Disabling Images* (New York: Praeger, 1987).

46. For instance, see David T. Mitchell and Sharon L. Synder, *Vital Signs: Crip Culture Talks Back* (video; 48 min., Marquette, Mich.: Brace Yourselves Productions, 1996); or

Shelley Tremain, ed., *Pushing the Limits: Disabled Dykes Produce Culture* (Toronto: Women's Press, 1996).

47. John Clogston's five models of new media representations of disability—*Disability Coverage in Sixteen Newspapers* (Louisville, Ky.: Avocado Press, 1990)—were revised by Beth Haller in her "Rethinking Models of Media Representations of Disability," *Disability Studies Quarterly* 15 (1995): 26–30. See also Haller's "If They Limp, They Lead: News Representations and the Hierarchy of Disability Images," in *Handbook of Communication and People with Disabilities,* 273–88; and N. Gold and G. Auslander's "Newspaper Coverage of People with Disabilities in Canada and Israel: An International Comparison," *Disability and Society* 14 (1999): 709–31. Helen Meekhosha and Leann Dowse have sought to situate this literature, especially North American content analysis–based approaches, and call for approaches that properly comprehend gender, disability, and media, in their "Distorting Images, Invisible Images: Gender, Disability and the Media," *Media International Australia* 84 (1997): 91–101.

48. Among other studies, see: Brenda Jo Brueggeman and James A. Fredal, "Studying Disability Rhetorically," in *Disability Discourse,* ed. Mairian Corker and Sally French (Buckingham, U.K.: Open University Press, 1999), 129–35; Brenda Jo Brueggeman, "The Coming Out of Deaf Culture and American Sign Language: An Exploration into the Visual Rhetoric and Literacy," *Rhetoric Review* 13 (1995): 409–20; Kara Shultz, "Deaf Activists in the Rhetorical Transformation of the Construct of Disability," in *Handbook of Communication and People with Disabilities,* 257–70.

49. Ann Pointon with Chris Davies, ed., *Framed: Interrogating Disability in the Media* (London: British Film Institute, 1997).

50. David Hervey, *The Creatures That Time Forgot: Photography and Disability Imagery* (New York: Routledge, 1992).

51. Martin F. Norden, *The Cinema of Isolation: A History of Physical Disability in the Movies* (New Brunswick, N.J.: Rutgers University Press, 1994).

52. See "Introduction: A History of Communication and Disability Research: The Way We Were," *Handbook of Communication and People with Disabilities,* 1–14.

53. John Frow and Meaghan Morris, "Cultural Studies," in *Handbook of Qualitative Research,* 2nd ed., ed. Norman K. Denzin and Yvonna S. Lincoln (Thousand Oaks, Calif.: Sage), 315–46.

54. Noteworthy work includes Rosemary Garland Thomson, *Freakery: Cultural Spectacles of the Extraordinary Body* (New York: New York University Press, 1996); David. T. Mitchell and Sharon L. Snyder, *Narrative Prosthesis: Disability and the Dependencies of Discourse* (Ann Arbor: University of Michigan Press, 2000); Felicity Naussbaum and Helene Deutsch, eds., *DEFECT!: Engendering the Modern Body* (Ann Arbor: University of Michigan Press, 2000).

Chapter Two

Disability in Its Social Context

It is ironic to note that the very category that integrates this text, "disabled girls and women," exists wholly as a social construct. Why should a limb-deficient girl, a teenager with mental retardation, or a blind girl have anything in common with each other, or with a woman with breast cancer or another woman who is recovering from a stroke? What they share is similar treatment by a sexist and disability-phobic society. This is what makes it likely that they will be thrown together in school, in the unemployment line, in segregated recreation programs, in rehabilitation centers, and in legislation.

—Adrienne Asch and Michelle Fine, 1988.[1]

Let us stop seeing the able and disabled as normality and aberration and let us no longer set them out as two separate kinds. What will *our* discourse be?

—Henri-Jacques Stiker, 1999.[2]

So what do we mean by disability and how are we to understand it? In this chapter we explore disability as a social phenomenon. As part of this we also explore the nature of the Deaf community and debates regarding the cochlear implant as a way of illustrating the complexities and contested nature of disability. It is only when we understand the complexities of disability that we can fully grasp the way in which disability is constructed by new media.

STUDYING DISABILITY

For much of human history, knowledge about disability has been in the hands of non-disabled people. Those recognized, legitimized, or certified as knowledgeable or expert in disability have predominantly been non-disabled.[3] While this is slowly changing, even as we write, there is not a person from the disability community occupying a professorial chair relating to disability studies in an Australian university, a situation that may be starker than other Western countries but which we suspect is not too removed from the crippling groves of academe elsewhere. Just as postcolonial theorists have sought to intensify the long, slow process of decolonizing knowledge from its colonial and imperial constitution; as queer theorists have challenged the deformative effects of hetereonormativity upon our cherished notions of subjectivity and sexuality; and feminist theorists have worked to dismantle the still pervasive arrangements of patriarchy; so too are disability activists and scholars more and more systematically inventorying Western and non-Western cultures, images, texts, and practices to produce respectful, truthful, accurate, and affirmative knowledges of people with disabilities. The study of disability has entered a decisive stage, in which it has been difficult to ignore and suppress the voices and contributions of people with disabilities in knowledge about themselves. Thus two decades on from the 1981 *International Year of Disabled People* (IYDP), a new interdisciplinary field of disability studies has emerged—fragile, complex, contested, but with great richness and potential. Perhaps its most important premise, taken from the disability movement, is: "nothing about us without us." The corpus of texts and voices that makes up disability studies provides a great deal of our inspiration, yet may not be familiar to some readers. Accordingly, a short introduction to some of the main themes and debates pertinent to our book is important here.[4]

One of the key insights of the new disability studies is the social nature of disability. This is well illuminated by the classic work of Vic Finkelstein, an academic who identifies as having disability. Finkelstein posits an imaginary society where a thousand or so people, all of whom are wheelchair users, settle in a village and organize a social system to suit themselves, with its own design and building codes. At some stage a few able-bodied people come to live in the village, but they don't fit in. They are constantly knocking their heads on door lintels, and require constant medical intervention and control. Special aids have to be designed for the so-called able-bodied, now the disabled members of the village. They are given free helmets to protect their heads, and they have difficulty obtaining work because of their deviation from the norm; as a result, they become objects of charity. "In such an imaginary society," Finkelstein writes, "it would be possible for physically impaired people to be the able-bodied!"[5]

Such early thinking by disability studies scholars has been furthered in the explicit development of a social model of disability, especially by British scholars and activists.[6] One prominent exemplar, Mike Oliver, contends that

> The production of disability in one sense . . . is nothing more nor less than a set of activities specifically geared towards producing a good—the category disability—supported by a range of political actions which create the conditions to all these productive activities to take place and underpinned by a discourse which gives legitimacy to the whole enterprise.[7]

If the production of the category "disability" is no different then from the production of motorcars or hamburgers, as Oliver polemically suggests, it is then within that production process that "disablism" is to be found. Yet, the production process is not static but dynamic—it is a process of "doing." And it is this process, this "doing-production," that defines not only the moral order of the society, but also disablism. Thus, it is material discourse that defines the moral order that underpins the social, the political, and the economic—the "work of institution."[8] The social model of disability entails a distinction between "impairment" and "disability." In this theory, "impairment" is the irreducible, material, biological condition that inheres in an individual's body. Analytically, at least, it is held that this is distinguishable from "disability," something society produces or constructs. Contrary to the thinking of Margaret Thatcher's scabrous dictum that "society does not exist," disability exists only in society, and the social relations that circulate power. Impairment is pre-social, and before language and signification. Disability comes about when the individual with impairment enters into culture, and the impairment takes on a meaning.

The social model of disability has been effective in challenging the established order of disability and bringing real changes to the lives of people with disabilities. To take one example, the emphasis on the social and political construction of disability has brought about changes in the "official" conception of disability. In a society obsessed with numbers, many people will feel the need to quantify disability. What is it? What is its prevalence? And what are the associated co-morbidities? And how can we prevent and manage it? After all, disability is inherently negative, isn't it? We would suggest that such typical, dominant approaches are in sore need of being superseded. For instance, critical thinkers in the field of disability studies point out that our notions of disability are socially constituted, as are the ways we count, categorize, and survey people with disabilities. For example, most countries have based their statistical practices on the World Health Organization's approach to surveying disability, which in turn has been based on the medical model. Abberley provides a telling critique of a survey by the Office of Population, Censuses and Surveys (OPCS) in the United Kingdom. He observes that "it is a political decision, conscious or otherwise" to employ questions and an approach that locates deficit within an individual as opposed to the social parameters of disability.[9] Clearly the data on which we base our social policies, and indeed our notions of normality, may well be subject to other constructions and interpretations. New ways of collecting statistics have evolved that are more consonant with the social model.[10]

Despite its usefulness, there are difficulties and tensions in the social model theory. The impairment–disability binary is akin to the infamous sex–gender distinction in feminist theory, where "sex" is the biological bedrock, grounded in anatomy, and "gender" is the social category that produces masculinity and femininity. (Or the great binary of Marxist theory, the base–superstructure distinction, where the economic base determines superstructural forms such as law and culture.) The title of a pivotal paper by Moira Gatens, the sex–gender distinction has now been critiqued by a number of other feminist theorists.[11] In a similar vein, we note here the extensive debate on the "social model" of disability, and the work of theorists who point to some of the limitations of this approach. Our own approach is certainly informed by the social model approach. With Oliver, we wish to bring about a "paradigm shift" from one worldview of disability to another, by radicalizing the hegemony, by taking "institution, not as a reified and stable entity, but as an active process."[12] Yet we also wish to signal a critique of the social model theory.

The social model approach has developed alongside a productive tension with feminism, the importance of which for understanding disability we wish to note here. A politically and intellectually indispensable approach to understanding disability is that provided by feminist disability activists and scholars. We wish to affirm the importance of the critiques that have been mounted by women with disabilities with regard to the masculinist nature of much of what goes on in disability advocacy, disability studies, and within the academy.[13] Clearly, disability is a sexed and gendered, as well as culturally, racially, and ethnically constituted, space and category. As a group, women with disability are poorer than men with disability taken as a whole; they suffer from a continuing power imbalance with respect to men, illustrated in domestic and sexual violence, sexual harassment, lack of autonomy and control in relationships and workplaces, underrepresentation in many occupations and professions and positions of power. Gender and new media has been a topic of ongoing debate generally, but issues relating to women with disability and new media have not been widely canvassed.

When considering the fundamentally diverse nature of disability, and its determination by central categories of power such as sex, gender, race, and ethnicity, we need also consider the extraordinary global context that frames such matters. We are mindful that this book primarily considers "first-world," or wealthy, "Western" countries as its examples. Yet the politics of technology, let alone disability, are markedly more protracted and difficult when the majority of the world's population is considered.[14] As a global phenomenon, disability clearly is multifaceted. Albrecht and Verbrugge provide a sobering reminder that "global disability will be on the rise for many decades to come, fueled by population ageing, environment degradation, and social violence."[15] Crucially, the economics of disability need to be considered from this perspective.

An allied but distinct tradition to the social model theory of conceiving disability, and one in which feminist perspectives and accounts highlighting cultural difference have played an important role, is the discourse approach. Gillian Fulcher, writing within the sociological literature on education policy and disability, makes a particularly useful contribution to the understanding of the subject in her identification of four main discourses of disability—medical, lay, charity, and rights. Analysis of these discourses aids the examination of technological artifacts and systems associated with people with disabilities, such as the wheelchair and cochlear implant. In addition, Fulcher identifies an emerging fifth discourse, one associated with a corporate approach, one of the themes of which is the concept of "managing disability."[16] We would suggest that since she has written it is clear that not only is the corporatization of the management of disability increasingly important, it is clear that this operates in conjunction with the transnational forces often referred to loosely as globalization. Fulcher notes that all of these discourses "inform practices in modern welfare states," competing or combining to constitute legislative decisions and various other practices.[17]

While Fulcher's analysis is geared toward the educational situation,[18] it is pertinent to far more than this. As Fulcher goes on to observe, medical discourse dominates the social world, penetrating and informing both lay and charity discourses. Indeed, as Brissenden argues, "the social world . . . is steeped in the medical model of disability."[19] Medical, lay, and charity discourses are the traditional discourses, with medical discourse being the source of "the dominant and misleading image of disability as physical incapacity":[20]

> Medicine is the main institutionalised site for its discursive practices and the professions that "deal" with disability. Social workers, therapists, physiotherapists, nurses, teachers, borrow the logic and politics of medical discourse on disability and deploy its authority and influence to legitimise their own professional practices.[21]

With regard to medical discourse:

> A medical discourse links impairment and disability. It draws on a natural science discourse and thus on a *correspondence* theory of meaning. This theory assumes objects essentially correspond with the terms used to describe them. While this theory may have some relevance in the natural world it misconceives the social world. . . . [A] medical discourse on disability suggests to its correspondence theory of meaning, that disability is an observable or intrinsic, objective *attribute* or characteristic of a person, rather than a social construct.[22]

Through its assumption that impairment implies loss, medical discourse implies a deficit that lies within an individual, and through what Fulcher calls its "presumed scientific status and neutrality," it depoliticizes disability. Here she neglects to employ the notions of that which constitutes science and scientific knowledge. She does, however, go on to note that it is this scientific and neutral persona that presents disability as a technical issue that is beyond the exercise of power and politics. Further, medical discourse individualizes disability, suggesting that individuals have diseases or incapacities as inherent attributes. For example, this can be seen in defining people as paraplegics or diabetics or asthmatics. It also professionalizes disability, using the idea that personal troubles are a matter for professional judgments.

As Fulcher makes plain, "through its language of body, patient, help, need, cure, rehabilitation and its politics that the doctor knows best [medical discourse] excludes a consumer discourse or language of rights, wants and integration in mainstream social practices."[23] Though Fulcher only refers to consumer discourse in passing, it is worth noting that this is becoming an increasingly dominant approach used by such groups as self-help organizations and the disability movement (such as Disabled Peoples' International), not to mention its adoption (or co-option) by the state in the form of bureaus of health, human services, and so on. A consumer discourse gains importance when contrasted with the perspective of service providers. Moreover, consumer discourse has some commonalities, as well as differences, from a (human) rights discourse.

The charity ethic sits well with the medical discourse and its role in corporations that organize services outside of the welfare state. Like a number of other critics, Fulcher shows how the charity ethic defines people who are called "disabled" as needing help, as objects of pity, as dependent, and as personally tragic.[24] Likewise, it is medical discourse that influences lay perceptions of disability, perceptions informed by pity, ignorance, the charity ethic, fear, and resentment. There is a clear link here between the embedded assumptions, concepts, and powerful images in these discourses, and the discriminatory practices people with disabilities face in their everyday life. The discursive effects of people with disabilities being positioned as "other," as radically different from the norm, manifest themselves in discriminatory practices. For example, Tom Shakespeare has written trenchantly of how people with disabilities have the social and cultural function of serving as "dustbins for disavowal."[25] One of the useful things about discourse theory is that it provides a way to understand the deep social structure to such psychological attitudes.

Many authors have observed, in the words of Shapiro, that it is the "rules that constitute the meaning of disability,"[26] especially in terms of the way in which the control of one's body is central to interpersonal encounters[27] and the regulation of the welfare state's citizens. Discourse theory relates not only psyche to social structure, but also both to embodiment. Fulcher notes that "[l]ess control over one's body means others diminish the personal responsibility of the person called disabled,"[28] noting that this phenomenon stems from the paternalistic and maternalistic practices and attitudes of those who treat people with obvious disabilities as childlike and less than fully responsible. It is this recurrent theme of an uncontrolled body deviating from the autonomy permitted other citizens that appears in lay, medical, and charitable discourses, bearing out Abberley's observation that for "disabled people the body is the site of oppression, both in form and what is done to it."[29]

Discourse theory extends and complicates not only work from the social model of disability approach, but also science and technology studies, as it suggests, following the work of Michel Foucault and others, how language, culture, and discourse are not just determined by "material" reality, but actually produce "reality effects" in the real world. We note here the work of a number of disability studies scholars engaging with Foucault.[30] More recent work informed by discourse theory perspective includes that of Mairian Corker,[31] Mitchell and Synder,[32] and others.[33] While assuming the determining and shaping effects of discourses, it also emphasizes the fluid and contingent ways in which these operate. In doing so, theorists are bringing disability studies into dialogue with contemporary debates on how we understand body, identity, subjectivity, and agency, albeit quite some years after the high watermark of continental-inflected theory influence on poststructuralism and postmodernism.

WHEN CULTURE MEETS IMPAIRMENT: THE ETHICS OF THE COCHEAR IMPLANT

Examining the cochlear implant provides a way of crystallizing our reflections on disability and technology, and the way in which culture plays a crucial role in formulating knowledge, attendant ethical discourse, and the social nature of disability. Before we commence this case study, we note that in discussing disability it is important to acknowledge cultural differences, nuances, variations, and contradictions, even within Western society, let alone in other cross-cultural contexts.

Certainly the contested ethics of the cochlear implant displays this, with its ethical acceptability varying according to cultural perceptions.[34] Various worldviews and norms lead to the cochlear implant being seen to be either access to opportunity or as oppression—depending upon underlying values. In particular, the perspective of those from the hearing world, or dominant culture, may be seen to differ from the Deaf culture, which is defined in terms of sociolinguistics. It is the hearing world that sees deafness as pathological, and, as a corollary, the cochlear implant as ethical—a perspective that dominates cultural representations of and debates about this technology.[35] In contrast, Deaf culture sees it as an invasive procedure that is not necessary and is inherently unethical.[36] Such conflicting worldviews, and the knowledge systems associated with them, especially that which is regarded as "nice," "normal," and "natural," inevitably inform perceptions of whether the cochlear implant is ethical or unethical.

A cochlear implant is a device that can be embedded by surgeons behind the ear in the skull. Electrodes pass from the device into the inner ear or cochlea; approximately fifteen different types of these devices are manufactured around the world. The Australian implant has twenty-two electrodes with the recipient carrying a speech processor that receives sounds from a microphone that are analyzed and fed to a transmitting coil worn behind the ear.[37] While the nature of specific benefits is contested, the implant has been shown to provide hearing sensations for totally or profoundly hearing impaired recipients, with at least one third of recipients being able to make out a significant number of words without the additional use of lip reading.[38] The implant can be of assistance to the remainder of recipients in terms of supplementing their lip reading skills.[39]

By far the most support for the implant has come from people who are post-linguistically deafened, that is people who have acquired at least some verbal language skills and worldviews pre-deafness. For them deafness or hearing loss is a traumatic situation that is to be viewed as a disability. The implantation of the device involves surgery that can take up to five hours, which while Gibson claims it is "not . . . life-threatening,"[40] obviously has the risk to life associated with surgery. The major recorded recent complications can be seen in the medical literature to be relatively minor, involving reported incidences of postoperative infection, damage to the nerve controlling the muscles of the face, and grogginess after the operation.[41] From the perspective of the hearing world, the risks for implanting can be seen to be minimal and within other ethical parameters practiced by surgeons, especially in terms of the benefits that have been documented, such as improved lifestyle, employment, and family and social relationships.[42]

There are clear ethical implications implied in the implantation procedure. Take, for instance, the requirements of the Melbourne Cochlear Implant project that adult candidates for implantation must meet the following criteria:

1. Have a profound or total hearing loss (such that there would be no benefit achieved by the fitting of hearing aids).
2. Be postlingually deaf.
3. Have no psychiatric contraindications.
4. Have an intelligence quotient within the normal range.
5. Have no otological or X-ray findings contraindicating the implantation.
6. Have shown positive results for electrically stimulation of the promontory.
7. Be medically fit for surgery.[43]

Opposition toward the cochlear implant, however, has come from the Deaf community in a variety of Western countries. As well as the concern that it presents a threat to Deaf culture, many Deaf people feel that the technology is unethical. This view is especially strongly held because often a procedure is performed on children who are not able to exercise informed consent and are left with a surgically implanted device with attendant implications for their future orientation in the world.[44]

The Deaf culture may be seen to consist of people who are born or become deaf, use sign language as their first language, and identify themselves as being deaf while also participating in activities within the community.[45] While we draw upon literature documenting the Australian, U.K., and U.S. Deaf cultures, our remarks can be seen to apply to each distinct culture; even though the sign language differs, the sociolinguistic analysis pertains across cultures, which are also visual in their orientation. Most frequently members of the Deaf culture are born deaf. Such a perspective sees deafness as involving community, where sign language is a unique and natural way of communicating. They do not view a lack of hearing as an impairment or pathology. In terms of a sociolinguistic analysis, such a perspective contrasts markedly with dominant Western cultures—that being the perspective of the hearing world, which sees deafness as a tragedy that should be avoided or ameliorated. Members of the Deaf community in a variety of Western countries also claim marginal benefits associated with cochlear implants, given that the many recipients still need to use lip reading and/or sign language as well as services that are "special" from the perspective of the hearing world.

A particularly important question raised with regard to the ethics of the cochlear implant is: "Do parents have the right to impose pathologically unnecessary surgery on their deaf child?" Parents who come from a hearing background are often the ones who are devastated at their child being deaf, and lacking an understanding of the Deaf community,

> it may be that the parents who, regardless of the uncertainties and the risks, wish their child to have a cochlear implant are far more in need of counselling and help to accept their child's deafness than their child is in need of surgery. What deaf children need is a loving acceptance that they are deaf, and that their deafness does not diminish them as people.[46]

The Deaf culture also questions the resource allocation for the costs of a cochlear implant procedure for one person.[47] Such arguments have proposed that the money could be of far more benefit in providing support and cultural maintenance services such as telecommunications devices for the Deaf, interpreters, captioning on television, or access to secondary and tertiary education.

Certainly, given the dominance of the hearing culture and the power relations that shape norms, structures, and programs, it is difficult for parents to exercise truly informed consent. There is no veil we can hide behind to make up for a lack of experience of a social world that doesn't needlessly handicap deaf people and accepts Deafness. It needs to be remembered that from a Deaf perspective deafness is hardly pathological or a sickness, as is shown in Groce's particularly pertinent study of Martha's Vineyard in the United States, which over some two hundred years had a high incidence of hereditary deafness.[48] As the title of this work suggests, *Everyone Here Spoke Sign Language*, regardless of whether they were able to speak or hear, with sign language being the dominant form of communication. While cochlear implant programs do provide counseling of parents, and the children or teenagers, where they are of an appropriate age, before implantation, the "knowledge" that is used has been criticized from a Deaf perspective as being based upon the values of the hearing world. There are several implications of this situation for the wider area of medicine, the critical study of disability, and new media technology as sociopolitical spaces.

ETHICS, POWER, AND KNOWLEDGE

Firstly, the case of the cochlear implant bears out the idea that knowledge is socially constructed, with knowledge systems here informing that which we call ethical behavior and protocols.[49] For the most part, such a situation has not been recognized in the biomedical ethics literature, which has tended uncritically to utilize the medical model, with attendant notions of ethically acceptable interventions. In the area of ethics, while writers[50] have recognized cultural differences in terms of countries and religious beliefs, it is only recently that an analysis utilizing a sociolinguistic perspective with regard to Deafness and disability has been offered. In addition, we believe our discussion of the cochlear implant points to the social nature of ethical discourse and knowledge in the bioethics of disability.[51]

Predominantly, the experience of the Deaf community is that governments and cochlear implant programs have found their perspectives to be a nuisance or incomprehensible, which is hardly surprising, as, with few exceptions, the dominant players in these arenas have a biomedical perception of deafness as pathological, requiring medical intervention, coming as they do from the hearing world. One of the earliest and best documented examples of conflict between the worldviews of Deafness as normal and deafness as pathology is to be found in the pages of the *Medical Journal of Australia.* In 1991 controversy erupted over a number of months, especially in the Letters to the Editor column, in the wake of an article by Heather Mohay, then a senior lecturer in medical psychology in the Department of Child Health, University of Queensland. Mohay's article took as axiomatic the proposition that sign language was the natural form of communication for Deaf people, and pointed to particular problems with the cochlear implant in a generally evenhanded, even mild-mannered, article, largely informed by hearing world values.[52]

The response in the Letters to the Editor column of the journal was an impressive volume of correspondence, with a number of members of the medical and audiological professions expressing disquiet at Mohay's stance, while educators of hard of hearing and Deaf children wrote tending to support her (their position identifying special education as being desirable). In many respects this debate demonstrated the playing out of high-stake games in the attempt to control deafness and disability by particular professional groupings. The editors closed the debate with an article from Professor Gibson, director of the Children's Cochlear Implant Centre, New South Wales. Gibson's article reinforced the hearing worldview and reasserted medical dominance. For example, he argues that "postlingually deafened adults and teenagers can almost always gain from a cochlear implant. . . . In general, the longer the deafness has existed, the worse the performance."[53] He went on to put forth an "opposing view" to criticisms by Deaf groups, holding that they "are more concerned with the survival of their society—with the need for more members—than with the welfare of the children."[54] Finally, he concluded that

the final decision has to be made by their parents. The parents have to be given the opportunity to see for themselves the pros and cons of each group and to visit the different educational centres.[55]

It should perhaps be noted that there were then no educational centers in Australia dedicated to the promulgation of Deaf values as the prime component of their curriculum, making it almost impossible for parents to make such a decision in an informed way.

Two other commentators wishing to enter the lists on the debate on cochlear implant and the Deaf community, Power and Hyde, from the Centre for Deafness Studies and Research at Griffith University, experienced great difficulty in having their views published in the *Medical Journal of Australia.* Power's article was rejected, until, following further correspondence, an article appeared in September of 1992, which was significantly shorter than that originally submitted, and only accepted under the rubric of "Point of View."[56] Two things are worth noting in Power and Hyde's piece. First, they refer to the cochlear implant as "technologically impressive" as if technological artifacts exist by themselves and can be so independently evaluated. Second, both have a command of sign language and intimate connections with the Deaf community, but in order to gain entree to the pages of this professional journal, they need to trade upon their professional credentials to legitimize their version of reality and its related knowledge system. Whereas no person identifying as a member of the Deaf community participated in the debate in the *Medical Journal of Australia*, Power and Hyde conclude on its behalf:

> Members of the Deaf community wish to be seen as ordinary people who communicate in sign and other modes. They seek a greater understanding by the hearing community of their status as another realisation of the human condition. They ask that the social, educational, vocational and personal implications of this status be understood by the hearing community, especially by those advising parents of young deaf children. Greater sensitivity to these matters by those involved in cochlear implant programs would improve communication between them and Deaf people.[57]

This debate is a forerunner of others with regard to the ethics of implanting children that were subsequently played out in the international literature.[58] Starting with markedly different premises regarding disability, health, and Deafness, the conclusions have been predictable.[59] As with the *Medical Journal of Australia* controversy, the debate occurs in a cultural context where hearing views are natural and taken-for-granted, and those holding alternative perspectives labor under a heavier burden to put their case. Nonetheless, such debates, as they are, certainly underline the value-laden nature of technology and the way in which this is reflected in technology assessment and social policy.[60] Because of the differing worldviews, there will never be a total resolution of the conflict between the Deaf and hearing worlds in terms of the ethics of the cochlear implant. The Deaf community could, however, be more fully involved in the provision of information regarding life options for people and especially children who are prospective implantees, as well as in a more public debate as to how we should allocate our health care and other resources. This is particularly the case where there is little information as to the costs and benefits of pursuing particular options from a social policy perspective.

DISABILITY AND DIVERSITY

The cochlear implant case provides a resonant example of how disability is shaped through technology and culture realms. We also note that the cochlear implant has been singled out as an instance of the cyborg body—the blurred edges between human and machine at the turn of the twenty-first century (see our remarks in chapter six on the obsession of cybercultural theorists with cyborg at the expense of noticing disability). The cochlear implant is also a new media technology, mediating, as it does, communication and information. Returning to our discussion of disability, we wish to conclude this chapter with some remarks on feminist theory and also on the concept of diversity.

Feminism and cross-cultural perspectives provide a frame of reference in which to understand the rise of "diversity" as an approach. In Western countries management discourses are shifting paradigms from talk of "equal opportunity" and "multiculturalism" to the register of "managing diversity." For example, in her influential book *Diversity Leadership*,[61] Janice Dreachslin makes the case for fostering and increasing all types of diversity.

> Health care institutions that have undertaken diversity initiatives report a range of benefits including an improved customer base, improved quality of care, increased labor pool, labor cost savings, reduction in turnover, and more effective teams.[62]

In the area of health care it is immediately apparent that incorporating people with disabilities as experts in their care and management not only increases an understanding of the variety of views and experience of disability but also has enormous implications for improving quality of care. As Dreachslin notes:

> Culturally appropriate care improves customer satisfaction and quality. When clinicians have an enhanced understanding of patients' diverse cultural backgrounds and beliefs, they can better serve patients, and compliance with prescribed treatment can be improved.[63]

Within this healthcare context in the United States we see some evidence of the opportunity for cultural change through the roles of physicians, nurses, and managers with a wide diversity of disability who are able to make enormous contributions to the quality of care and rehabilitation of patients. Not only do they understand the realities, they act as vital role models, and their lives suggest that "better off dead than disabled" is a myth that needs to be exploded.

While we see the rising light of "diversity" as clearly representing another phase of managing disability, the reality is, however, that while disability tends to be mentioned in passing in the diversity management literature, as with so many other areas of practice and theory discussed, it remains at best on the periphery.[64] If mentioned at all, it is mentioned in passing. Accordingly, once we move beyond the corporate nature of the diversity cliché we can certainly see largely unrealized potential for disability to be incorporated in such an approach. However, just like the quality movement in the area of health and human services management, which also largely fails to incorporate disability as a norm, instead regarding it as a "special" consideration, this will require a conscious political decision. Just like so many approaches, a particular challenge is to move from talking *about* to incorporating the wisdom of people with disabilities as experts, something about which we are pessimistic.

CONTROLLING AND CREATING DISABILITY

As these first two introductory chapters make plain, in order to understand disability and new media, we have borrowed tools and approaches from a variety of texts, people, and encounters: from scholarly disciplines such as disability studies and science and technology studies, as well as cultural and media studies. We have also sought to acknowledge the gendered and Western nature of much of the knowledge of disability, and the way in which disability could factor into such emerging approaches as diversity management. We have also drawn upon our engagement in activism and policy debates and from our personal experiences.

In the following chapters, we use a variety of analytical lenses to examine the way in which disability is created in our everyday media environments, a taken-for-granted shaping of technology that is usually not noticed. A governing concept for us is the control of disability as a contested sociopolitical space. Disability is more than deviant bodies, challenging minds, or pitiful individuals with special needs. Societies build disability into those physical and social structures we take for granted, especially where those with power have excluded the knowledge and life-experience of those who live with disability. As a variety of writers discussed in this chapter have shown, society tends to seek to control disability, whether it be through statistics, welfare, medicine advances, or mundane technologies.

In response to this, we offer a critical stance on technology, especially the technology that is so often held up as the salvation for people with disabilities ("if only they could get the right technology, or enough of it"). At times we also point to uncritical views of disability held within the disability community. Rather than view information and communications technology as providing the all-embracing solution for people with severe disabilities, as some people who live with disability would hold, we seek to go deeper in encountering and naming the social technology that created the disability for those society chooses— often tacitly—to disable. Ours is not necessarily a Luddite perspective, at least not in its popular meaning. We do not want to smash the machines: so many of those of us who live with disability are alive because of developments in technology. However, we want to explore the political and social dimension of something that is inherently valued-laden, technology.

As we stare at the rapidly filling blank screen in our hotel room, we are reminded of the values we take for granted in the new media. Where is the benefit of a laptop screen, when vision is not the chosen form of interaction? Where is the liberation for the person who cannot read? Why do we so readily assume that all the networked technologies at our fingertips—if we have them—will transform our lives? The stark room becomes the metaphor for our complex social lives as we dig deeper to discover something as yet unnameable and perhaps even unpalatable: digital disability.

NOTES

1. Adrienne Asch and Michelle Fine, "Introduction: Beyond Pedestals" in *Women with Disabilities: Essays in Psychology, Culture, and Politics*, ed. Adrienne Asch and Michelle Fine (Philadelphia: Temple University Press, 1988), 6.

2. Henri-Jacques Stiker, *A History of Disability*, trans. William Sayers (1997; Ann Arbor: University of Michigan Press, 1999), 194.

3. Vic Finkelstein, "Emancipating Disability Studies," in *The Disability Reader: Social Science Perspectives,* ed. Tom Shakespeare (London: Cassell, 1998), 28–49.

4. There are a now a number of excellent introductions to disability studies: Lennard Davis, ed., *The Disability Studies Reader* (London: Routledge, 1997); Sharon Synder, Brenda Brueggeman, and R. G. Thompson, eds., *Enabling the Humanities: A Disability Studies Sourcebook* (New York: Modern Language Association, 2001). For commentary, see Simi Linton, "Disability Studies/Not Disability Studies," *Disability and Society* 13 (1998): 525–40; T. Titchkosky, "Disability Studies: The Old and the New," *Canadian Journal of Sociology* 25 (2000): 197–234.

5. Vic Finkelstein, "To Deny or Not to Deny Disability" in *Handicap in a Social World*, ed. A. Brechin, P. Liddiard, and J. Swain (Kent: Hodder and Stoughton, 1981), 34–36.

6. Colin Barnes, "The Social Model of Disability: A Sociological Phenomenon Ignored by Sociologists?" in *The Disability Reader*; Len Barton and Mike Oliver, eds., *Disability Studies: Past, Present and Future* (Leeds: The Disability Press, 1997); Mike Oliver, *Understanding Disability: From Theory to Practice* (London: Macmillan Press, 1996).

7. Oliver, *Understanding Disability*, 127.

8. Alain Coulon, *Ethnomethodology*, trans. Jacqueline Coulon and Jack Katz (London: Sage, 1995).

9. Paul Abberley, *Handicapped by Numbers* (Occasional Papers in Sociology No 9; Bristol: Bristol Polytechnic, 1990), 2.

10. See debate on the World Health Organization's International Classification of Functioning, Disability, and Health: Barbara M. Altman, "Disability Definitions, Models, Classification Schemes, and Applications," in *Handbook of Disability Studies*, ed. Gary L. Albrecht, Katherine D. Seelman, and Michael Bury (Thousand Oaks, Calif.: Sage, 2001), 11–68; Rachel Hurst, "International Classification of Functioning, Disability and Health,"

Disability Tribune (September 2001): 10–11, and "To Revise or Not to Revise?" *Disability & Society* 15, no. 7 (2000): 1083–87.

11. Moira Gatens, *Imaginary Bodies: Ethics, Power, and Corporeality* (New York: Routledge, 1995).

12. Coulon, *Ethnomethodology*, 73. For an exploration of the active process of "disablism" as institution, see David Wareing and Christopher Newell, "Responsible Choice: The Choice between No Choice," *Disability & Society* 17, vol. 4 (June 2002).

13. "Feminism and Disability, Part 1," special issue of *Hypatia: A Journal of Feminist Philosophy* 16.4 (2001), ed. Eva Kittay, Anita Silvers, and Susan Wendell; Susan Wendell, *The Rejected Body: Feminist Philosophical Reflections on Disability* (London: Routledge, 1996); Barbara Hillyer, *Feminism and Disability* (Norman: University of Oklahoma Press, 1993); Jenny Morris, ed., *Encounters with Strangers: Feminism and Disability* (London: Women's Press, 1999); Carol Thomas, *Female Forms: Experiencing and Understanding Disability* (Milton Keynes, U.K.: Open University Press, 1999).

14. Brigitte Holzer, Arthur Vreede, and Gabriele Weigt, eds., *Disability in Different Cultures: Reflections on Local Concepts* (Bielefeld, Germany: Transcript Verl, 1999).

15. G. L. Albrecht and L. M. Verbrugge, "The Global Emergence of Disability," in *The Handbook of Social Studies in Health and Medicine*, ed. G. L. Albrecht, R. Fitzpatrick, and S. C. Scrimshaw (London: Sage, 2000), 305.

16. Gillian Fulcher, *Disabling Policies?* (London: Falmer Press, 1989), 20.

17. Fulcher, *Disabling Policies*, 26.

18. Fulcher does not develop her analysis of the corporate approach to disability, although her later work goes on to develop the theme of managing disability through bureaucracies. Such an approach has also been taken by Christopher Newell and Judy Walker, "'Openness' in Distance and Higher Education as the Social Control of People with Disabilities: An Australian Policy Analysis," in *Research in Distance Education 2*, ed. T. Evans and P. Juler (Geelong, Victoria, Australia: Institute of Distance Education, Deakin University), 68–80.

19. S. Brisenden, "Independent Living and the Medical Model of Disability," *Disability, Handicap & Society* 1 (1986): 174.

20. Fulcher, *Disabling Policies*, 26.

21. Fulcher, *Disabling Policies*, 26.

22. Fulcher, *Disabling Policies*, 27.

23. Fulcher, *Disabling Policies*, 27.

24. A. Borsay, "Personal Trouble or Public Issue? Toward a Model of Policy for People with Physical and Mental Disabilities," *Disability, Handicap and Society* 1 (1986): 179–95; Mike Oliver, "Social Policy and Disability: Some Theoretical Issues," *Disability, Handicap and Society* 1 (1986): 5–17.

25. Tom Shakespeare, "Cultural Representations of Disabled People: Dustbins for Disavowal," *Disability & Society* 9 (1994): 283–99.

26. M. J. Shapiro, "Disability and the Politics of Constitutive Rules," in *Cross-National Rehabilitation Policies*, ed. G. L. Albrecht (Beverly Hills, Calif.: Sage, 1981), 84–96.

27. Bryan S. Turner, *The Body and Society* (Oxford: Basil Blackwell, 1984).

28. Fulcher, *Disabling Policies,* 29.

29. Abberley, *Handicapped by Numbers*, 114.

30. For instance, see contributions to Shelley Tremain, ed., *Foucault and the Government of Disability*, forthcoming, 2003.

31. Mairian Corker, "Disability Discourse in a Postmodern World," in *The Disability Reader,* 221–33.

32. David T. Mitchell and Sharon L. Synder, eds., *The Body and Physical Difference: Discourses of Disability* (Ann Arbor: University of Michigan Press, 1997).

33. Mairian Corker and Sally French, eds. *Disability Discourse* (Buckingham, U.K.: Open University Press, 1999).

34. T. P. Gonsoulin, "Cochlear Implant/Deaf World Dispute: Different Bottom Elephants," *Otolaryngology Head and Neck Surgery* 125, no. 5 (Nov 2001): 552–56.

35. Harlan Lane, *The Mask of Benevolence* (New York: Vintage, 1993).

36. See, for example, R. Nunes, "Ethical Dimensions of Pediatric Cochlear Implantation," *Theoretical Medicine & Bioethics* 22.4 (2001): 337–49.

37. For example, see: I. R. Summers, ed. *Tactile Aids for the Hearing Impaired* (London: Whurr Publishers, 1992); G. M. Clark et al., eds., *Cochlear Prostheses* (Edinburgh: Churchill Livingstone, 1990); G. M. Clark et al., "The University of Melbourne-Nucleus Multi-Electrode Cochlear Implant," *Advances in Oto-Rhino-Laryngology* 38 (1987): 1–190.

38. In terms of the difference in perspectives regarding outcomes, Crouch notes, "The evidence suggests . . . the benefits . . . in many prelingually deaf children are modest" (R.A. Crouch, "Letting the Deaf Be Deaf: Reconsidering the Use of Cochlear Implants in Prelingually Deaf Children," *Hastings Center Report* 27 [1997]:14–21).

39. For example, see Clark et al., "The University of Melbourne-Nucleus Multi-Electrode Cochlear Implant"; Clark et al., *Cochlear Prostheses*; B. Gibson, "Cochlear Implants— Some Questions Answered," *SHHH News* (February 1988): 8.

40. Gibson, "Cochlear Implants."

41. For details of complications and methods of circumventing these see B. J. Gantz, "Issues of Candidate Selection for a Cochlear Implant," *Otolaryngologic Clinics of North America* 22 (1989): 239–47.

42. A. R. Lea, *Cochlear Implants* (Australian Institute of Health Care Technology Series No. 6; Canberra: Australian Government Publishing Service, 1991), 16–22.

43. Clark et al., "The University of Melbourne-Nucleus Multi-Electrode Cochlear Implant."

44. See, for example, Michael Uniacke, "Of Miracles, Praise—of Anger—the Bionic Ear," *In Future* 6 (1987): 11–14; Ad Hoc Committee on Ear Surgery, the Greater Los Angeles Council on Deafness, *Position Paper: Cochlear Implant Surgery* (Greater Los Angeles Council on Deafness, 1985); Victorian Council of Deaf People (VCOD), *Cochlear Implant Forum Report* (Melbourne: VCOD, 1988).

45. Carol Padden and Tom Humphries, *Deaf in America: Voices from a Culture* (Cambridge, Mass.: Harvard University Press, 1988).

46. National Deaf Children's Society, England, cited in Uniacke, "Of Miracles," 13–14.

47. In 1991 it was estimated with surgery, device, and rehabilitation, the cost of the device for children ranged between $22,880 and $36,630 (in Australian dollars) (Lea, *Cochlear Implants*).

48. N. L. Groce, *Everyone Here Spoke Sign Language* (Cambridge, Mass.: Harvard University Press, 1988).

49. See, for example, T. Peach, *Confronting Nature: The Sociology of Solar-Neutrino Detection* (Dordrecht: Ridell, 1986); R. Wallis, ed. *On the Margins of Science: The Social Construction of Rejected Knowledge* (Keele, Staffordshire, U.K.: University of

Keele, 1979); F. Richards, *Vitamin C and Cancer: Medicine or Politics?* (London: Macmillan, 1991).

50. R. M. Veatch, ed., *Cross-Cultural Perspective in Medical Ethics: Readings* (Boston: Jones and Bartlett Publishers, 1989).

51. For example, see Christopher J. Newell, "A Critical Evaluation of the [National Health & Medical Research Council] 'The Ethics of Limiting Life-Sustaining Treatment' and Related Perspectives on the Bioethics of Disability," *Australian Disability Review* 4 (1991): 46–57. See also Christopher J. Newell, ed., "Bioethics and Disability," special issues of *Interaction* vol. 13 (2000), nos. 3 & 4, 2000.

52. Heather Mohay, "Deafness in Children," *Medical Journal of Australia* 154 (March 18, 1991): 372–74.

53. W. Gibson, "Opposition from Deaf Groups to the Cochlear Implant," *Medical Journal of Australia* 155 (1991): 212–14.

54. Gibson, "Opposition," 214.

55. Gibson, "Opposition," 214.

56. D. J. Power and M. B. Hyde, "The Cochlear Implant and the Deaf Community," *The Medical Journal of Australia* 157 (1992): 421–22.

57. Power and Hyde, "The Cochlear Implant and the Deaf Community," 422.

58. See H. Lane and M. Grodin, "Ethical Issues in Cochlear Implant Surgery: An Exploration into Disease, Disability, and the Best Interests of the Child," *Kennedy Institute of Ethics Journal* 7 (1997): 231–51; D. S. Davis, "Cochlear Implants and the Claims of Culture? A Response to Lane and Grodin," *Kennedy Institute of Ethics Journal* 7 (1997): 253–58.

59. See, for example, H. Lane and B. Bahan, "Ethics of Cochlear Implantation in Young Children," *Otolaryngology Head and Neck Surgery* 121 (1999): 672–75; F. A. Tellez, "Ethics of Cochlear Implantation in Young Children," *Otolaryngology Head and Neck Surgery* 121 (1999): 676; H. Lane and B. Bahan, "Ethics of Cochlear Implantation in Young Children: A Review and Reply from a Deaf-World Perspective," *Otolaryngology Head and Neck Surgery* (1998): 297–313.

60. G. J. Van der Wilt, R. Reuzel, and H. D. Banta, "The Ethics of Assessing Health Technologies," *Theoretical Medicine & Bioethics* 21 (2000): 103–15; P. Lehoux and S. Blume, "Technology Assessment and the Sociopolitics of Health Technologies," *Journal of Health Politics, Policy & Law* 25 (2000): 1083–120.

61. Janice L. Dreachslin, *Diversity Leadership* (Chicago: Health Administration Press, 1996), xi.

62. Dreachslin, *Diversity Leadership*, xi.

63. Dreachslin, *Diversity Leadership*, xi.

64. An example of diversity approach being used to discuss disability and new communication and media technologies can be found in the National Council on Disability (NCD), *The Accessible Future* (Washington, D.C.: NCD, 2001); www.ncd.gov/newsroom/publications/accessiblefuture.html [accessed 24 March 2002]. See section F, "Electronic and Information Technology as an Element of Diversity."

Part Two

NETWORKS OF DISABILITY

Chapter Three

Holding the Line:
Telecommunications and Disability

To promote . . . to protect . . . to preserve freedom and democracy, we must make telecommunications development an integral part of every nation's development. Each link we create strengthens the bonds of liberty and democracy around the world. By opening markets to stimulate the development of the global information infrastructure, we open lines of communication. . . . By opening lines of communication, we open minds. . . . Let us build a global community in which the people of neighboring countries view each other not as potential enemies, but as potential partners, as members of the same family in the vast, increasingly interconnected human family.

—Al Gore, 1994.[1]

[T]he problem is not the person with disabilities; the problem is the way that normalcy is constructed to create the "problem" of the disabled person.

—Lennard J. Davis, 1997[2]

Telecommunications networks provide the foundations for digital interactive communications, supporting a wide variety of contemporary communications and media. We know these technologies under a variety of once exotic, now familiar names: Internet, audio and video streaming, digital music in the form of MP3s, digital broadcasting, and new modes of voice and text communications. For the last twenty-five years we have seen the endless "revolution" of communication and media shaped by these digital technologies in the process of convergence. As the computer, telephone, television, radio, book, and newspaper blend together, many in the Western world, if fewer elsewhere, find that their information and entertainment, goods and services, education and health, travel and recreation reach them through a stream of ones and zeros transmitted via phone lines and radio waves.

Telecommunications has an ongoing, critical role in the exercise of power and governance within postmodern society. Telecommunications has significantly facilitated and shaped the multifaceted phenomenon we know as globalization at the beginning of the twentieth-first century,[3] something presaged by theorists of postindustrial societies.[4] With ultrahigh velocity circulation of capital and investment, postmodern finance and economy would not be possible without digital communications networks, highlighted by the disruption of the lives of many people during the highly mediated unfolding of events in New York on the eleventh of September 2001. An all too common story was of a distant relative watching the events unfold on television, then phoning or e-mailing relatives in New York to check if they were safe or to ask them what was occurring.[5]

Yet the participation of people with disabilities in globalization has been chequered, defined in terms of the dominant discourses and power relations outlined in chapter one. Disability in global telecommunications has been governed by narrow norms, left to the state in a world where increasingly the market rules. "Light-touch" regulation offers little beneficial effects, and indeed builds in disability, albeit in the name of beneficence and a nod to "rights." Benefits of globalization, such as they are, have not flowed evenly to people with disabilities. Of course, there have been the restricted forms of access enthusiastically offered by computer software and hardware manufacturers in accordance with charitable discourse. As we have globalized, we have also built in disability, based upon ableist norms. Critical scholarship informed by the lives of those who live with disability invites us to reflect upon settings, locations, discourses, and power relations, which are tacit but actually constitute a paradoxical world: one that is constantly changing but in certain respects remains the same. Accordingly, in this chapter we explore the continuing nature of disabling telecommunications.

TELECOMMUNICATIONS: THE GLOBAL CONTEXT

Strenuous efforts have been put into designating telecommunications as a responsibility of privately owned and operated companies operating across world and domestic markets. Most Western countries have restructured their telecommunications industries, allowing great competition—through a series of U.S. court decisions and finally the 1996 U.S. *Communications Act,* the 1997 *Australian Telecommunications Act,* the 1993 Canadian *Telecommunications Act,* British reforms since the mid-1980s, successive European directives, and the World Trade Organization February 1997 agreement on basic telecommunications.[6]

These developments are often referred to as "deregulation" or "liberalization" of markets. Yet, there is a novel side to such development to be found in the very complexity of the transformations required to reinvent these industries and their arrangements. Much of the guiding law and policy (such as that referred to above) is quite elaborate. Moreover, it is common for quasi-governmental bodies to be formed to enforce and embody these new market structures in what might be called networks of governance. A new notion of regulation has arisen, variously termed self-regulation, co-regulation, or "light-touch" regulation. It is now a desideratum that corporations will regulate themselves and manage a wide variety of policy matters or problems, formerly left to the state, including the problem of disability. It is proverbial that businesses are closer to the customer, and in a better position to know their desires. The vestigial role of the government bureaucracy or regulatory agency is only to set minimal rules of conduct that enable the market to perform, interfering as little as possible with its much-vaunted prerogatives. In this view, the market will be self-governing, yet what is intriguing is that the market actually takes over government of many spheres of life from the state, bearing out remarks of philosopher Michel Foucault that

> It is possible to suppose that if the state is what it is today, this is so precisely thanks to this governmentality, which is at once internal and external to the state—since it is the tactics of government that make possible the continual definition and redefinition of what is within the competence of the state and what is not, the public versus the private, and so on.[7]

One of the problems with the "light-touch" regulation is that the market is narrowly conceptualized in terms of neoclassical economics, a form of economics that conceives disability in terms of cost and deficit, as opposed to rights and consumer needs. The site for the creation and perpetuation of disability in this situation is largely the market and its associated discourse of deregulation and liberalization,[8] which are, ironically, supposed to bestow greater freedom on the individual.

This view of the market as a liberal site of lightly regulated freedom is combined in a heady mix with an equally potent myth about technology: the stubborn belief that technologies are liberating for their projected users, while paradoxically being held to be value-free. People with disabilities are often conceptualized as a *special* and indeed expensive case in point: technological solutions are held out for this potential to abolish or ameliorate the disability that is seen to lie within the individual. As we shall show, in the case of telecommunications, as much as in that of other technologies such as the cochlear ear implant, the discursive shaping of technologies proceeds via a promissory note that they will confer countless benefits upon people with disabilities. Yet this approach rests upon the model of disability as a given static deficit of an individual, as opposed to a phenomenon constituted through the very social and technological structures that are supposed to provide the salvation for those "poor handicapped people" located outside the mainstream moral community. In the case of telecommunications, now becoming a technology of the utmost significance for belonging to a persuasively digitally networked society, disability is created when telecommunications systems are designed in accordance with ableist norms—making it difficult for people with disabilities to communicate with each other, and other people in society.

ENGINEERING DISABILITY

Paradoxically the telephone was invented by Alexander Graham Bell for Deaf people, an aspect of history rarely acknowledged or reflected upon in a world where history is predominantly written using non-disabled and non-Deaf constructs.[9] Throughout the late nineteenth and the twentieth century, people with disabilities were rarely considered in the development of telecommunications. From its introduction as a communications device primarily used by business or rich domestic subscribers, the phone became part of a nation-building project in most countries, complementing cultural technologies such as the mail, press, telegraphy, radio, and eventually television.[10] Telephony as a national project was symbolized in the dominance of postal-telegraphy-telephone (PTT) organizations in most Western countries, generally owned and operated by the government along public service models, as in Europe, though regulated private monopolies also played a role in some countries, such as the United States and Canada.[11] Availability of telephone service to all the citizens within the boundaries of the nation-state was an important goal of mid-to-late twentieth-century telecommunications policy especially, and was referred to by many countries as "universal service." Despite this implicit policy of inclusion, we would argue that in fact people with disabilities were systematically excluded from this nation-building project, and the notion of citizenship it entailed.

This nation-building project in its classic phase, with its associated discourse, has now been displaced by the widespread introduction of competition and the growing technological complexity of advanced, intelligent telecommunications networks.[12] Theoretically, a person with disability is a customer to be served alongside any other, but competition in telecommunications is saddled with contradictions. Thus there are significant issues facing people with disabilities in a competitive market:

> People with disabilities are particularly vulnerable in a highly competitive market driven by rapidly advancing technology; for them the telephone network is a vital communication link but their ability to use it may be critically dependent upon the availability of telephone terminals with special features, and at affordable prices. Their needs, along with those of other groups in the community, must be taken into account as the telecommunications networks expand and develop, not out of charity but in recognition of their status as informed and discerning members of the customer base.[13]

We suggest that the introduction of competition has inaugurated what can be termed a "corporate" discourse on disability. In the corporate discourse on disability, we find now that those controlling and operating telecommunications companies seek to *manage* people with disabilities. This form of oppression is manifested in terminology of "special needs" and "special programs."[14] Based upon ableist notions, and fear of antidiscrimination legislation, telecommunications executives seek to manage disability by creating special programs that retro-fit systems designed on able-bodied norms. Accordingly, the question is never asked in the implicit and tacit values of global telecommunications who is embraced as part of the moral community and who, in a variety of ways, is excluded from the full participation in the goods of the emerging technological society. Is telecommunications one of the best examples of a society where, just like George Orwell's prophetic 1945 novel *Animal Farm,* one might say that of course all people are equal, it is just that some people are more equal than others?

TELECOMMUNICATIONS AND ACCESSIBILITY

Accessibility is often thought of as pertaining solely, or most pertinently, to disability. It has tended largely to be constructed around narrow notions of wheelchair accessibility. However, accessibility is a multifaceted phenomenon serving many groups of people. Designing pay phones so they may be used comfortably by people who use wheelchairs or scooters also benefits parents with strollers. Providing telephones with big buttons and hands-free operation assists people with dexterity or mobility problems, but may also help older people and make the phone easier to use in general. Providing text communications for Deaf people and those with hearing and speech disabilities not only makes telecommunications accessible for this group, but connects them to the network so others may communicate with them in turn. It has taken a long time indeed for accessibility to be recognized as an integral part of telecommunications, with most progress only occurring as late as the 1990s.

In the United States, the accessibility dimension of universal service received attention as early as 1982, with the *Telecommunications for the Disabled Act,* which addressed the compatibility of hearing aids with telephone instruments. This was followed up by the 1988 *Hearing Aid Compatibility Act* and the 1988 *Technology-Related Assistance Act.* However, it was the 1990 *Americans with Disabilities Act* (ADA) that was a watershed event in guaranteeing the civil rights of people with disabilities.[15] Despite what it represented, the ADA was limited in its coverage of telecommunications issues. As the World Institute on Disability (WID) points out, the legislation did not mandate access for basic or advanced telecommunications and information services or equipment.[16]

Critical of this missed opportunity and the persistence of the piecemeal approach to universal service for people with disabilities in the United States, the disability movement called for people with disabilities to be explicitly included in a new definition of universal service and telecommunications. In this sense, it could be averred that access for people with disabilities was finally recognized as an integral part of U.S. telecommunications policy in the 1996 *Telecommunications Act.* Section 255 of this act requires that telecommunications equipment and services be accessible to people with disabilities. Yet despite the greater

attention accorded to disability in the 1996 *Telecommunications Act,*[17] the seven
principles of universal service enunciated in section 254 still do not explicitly include access for people with disabilities. Even in its subsequent report and order,
the Federal Communications Commission (FCC) declined to include disability
access in the "evolving" definition of universal service, stating that it would address this in the implementation of section 255.[18]

It may be argued that the attention accorded to accessibility issues in U.S.
telecommunications can be credited to the strength of the disability movement in
that country, and cultural change symbolized by the *Americans with Disabilities
Act.* At the federal level, there has been a myriad of initiatives particularly centered on the FCC's Disability Rights Office, and its Consumer/Disability
Telecommunications Advisory Committee.[19] In the late 1990s and early 2000, the
FCC tackled quite a diverse range of accessibility issues in the area of telecommunications and new media, including mobile telecommunications, Internet, and
digital television access. One reason for this may have been that FCC Chairman
William E. Kennard, who held office during the Clinton administration, was particularly supportive of disability issues. Further, a number of experienced advocates from the disability movement were hired by the FCC, taking up senior positions in the Disability Rights Office and the Consumer Information Bureau.

In contrast, in Australia accessibility for people with disabilities was not recognized in legislation until the 1992 *Disability Discrimination Act,* and its implications for telecommunications. The legislation establishing the framework for
the introduction of limited competition in Australian telecommunications, the
1991 *Telecommunications Act,* featured a definition of universal service that
mandated the delivery of standard voice telephony service throughout Australia,
but explicitly separated the universal availability issues from universal accessibility ones. Universal accessibility, such as ensuring access for people with disabilities, was not to be provided as part of the universal service obligation. Instead, the government undertook to provide funding as one of its "community
service obligations."[20] In a time of stringent fiscal management, no such funding
eventuated for a number of years.[21]

The 1991 legislation allowed Telecom Australia (now Telstra), the govern-
ment-owned former monopoly carrier, to continue operating its own "conces-
sion" scheme to give people with disabilities access to the telecommunications
network. Telstra did not make telecommunications accessible, however, for Deaf
people and people with speech disabilities who required text telephony equipment (known in Australia as teletypewriters or TTYs). A long and at times acri-
monious battle to get Telstra to provide TTY relay services at affordable rates for
Deaf and people with hearing and speech disabilities was required before this aspect of universal service was given any attention.

Telecommunications was explicitly left out of areas named as being important
and worthy of disability standards in the Australian *Disability Discrimination Act*
1992. However, the overarching universal nature of this piece of legislation

meant that when negotiations failed, a Deaf man, followed shortly after by Disabled Peoples' International (DPI) (Australia), the then umbrella organization for people with disabilities and their organizations, successfully launched an action against the then Telecom Australia in the Human Rights and Equal Opportunity Commission (HREOC) (*Scott, DPI v Telstra*).[22] This decision caused Telecom to provide accessible teletypewriters but also eventually resulted in a change to government policy, with the requirement in the *Telecommunication Act 1997* that the functional requirements of people with disabilities be included in universal service provision. This act broadens the definition of the standard telephone service to include another form of voice communication that is equivalent to voice telephony, if voice telephony is not practical for a person with a disability.

The absence of a formal, well-articulated framework incorporating accessibility into telecommunications may also be observed in the recent history of disability in the United Kingdom. Since the privatization of British Telecom (BT) and introduction of competition, BT has continued to play a leading role in the provision of services for people with disabilities through its Age & Disability Unit, guided by its Consumer Liaison Panels. Of growing concern to BT, like other former monopoly telecommunications, was that it remained a de facto "carrier of last resort," expected to provide services for people with disabilities. In the context of U.K. universal service debates, and the implementation of the U.K. *Disability Discrimination Act*, BT expressed concern that "some would demand that BT should meet the costs, although BT was only a part of a highly competitive industry."[23] In terms of the regulatory and legislative framework, the regulator, the Office of Telecommunications (OFTEL), was charged with pursuing accessibility for people with disabilities through license conditions. Generally, OFTEL has taken the view that accessibility in the United Kingdom was being effectively met by good corporate citizenship initiatives (or lack thereof):

> The market-place was already delivering services of value to disabled customers without formal regulatory intervention, because companies wanted to be seen to be serving a group which was growing in size and commercial importance. It was not solely the financial return that made this voluntary route attractive, but also the impact on corporate reputation, brand image and customer loyalty. The *Telecommunications Act* was 13 years old and starting to creak, but it did impose a statutory duty to protect the interests of all consumers, particularly those who were disabled or elderly.[24]

This sanguine view was not shared by all people with disabilities:

> The added-value services offered by BT and other operators excluded deaf-blind customers who, as a result, were disabled rather than enabled by design. Technology which already existed was not being harnessed to improve their quality of life. It was not acceptable that needs which could not be satisfied on a commercial basis should remain unmet. Deaf-blind people expected to be able to enjoy full and equal access to the telecommunications services which technology had made possible.[25]

It should, however, be noted that OFTEL has been very important in showing leadership through its Advisory Committee on Telecommunications for Disabled and Elderly People (DIEL), a specialist body advising on disability issues, which is influential on government and industry alike.[26]

Despite important initiatives, the United Kingdom, like Australia, moved only slowly to take a systemic approach to incorporating disability access into telecommunications. It has been moved to do this principally through a tardy, reactive approach to regulation rather than taking a proactive leadership role. As in the Australian and U.S. situations, telecommunications in the United Kingdom has been affected by general policy and legislation on disability.[27] The long-awaited 1995 *Disability Discrimination Act* places a duty on service and facilities providers not to discriminate against disabled people (the terminology used by people with disabilities in the United Kingdom). Since this time, the Disability Rights Commission, an independent body set up by the government, which works to eliminate discrimination against disabled people, has played an important role in raising the profile of disability issues in telecommunications.

DISABILITY AND UNIVERSAL SERVICE

In the United States and Australia, if not so much in the United Kingdom and other countries, considering disability as part of a wider concept of universal service has been extremely important. The importance accorded to disability in universal service policies provides an instructive example of how the rights discourse on disability is eclipsed by the medical, charity, lay, and management discourses. Universal service has a long history of being associated with the provision of basic voice telephony service by a monopoly telecommunications carrier. In many countries, even economically advanced ones, this remains the standard telephone service today. The traditional definition of universal service has been tied to the universal *availability* of telecommunications, with some thought given to universal *affordability*. One of the neglected elements, however, has been universal *accessibility*: that is, are people actually able to use the handset and other equipment provided to make and receive phone calls, and thus communicate?

Not surprisingly, people with disabilities were poorly served when the conception of universal service was solely based on availability and affordability of basic voice telephone service. There has been growing public awareness of the fact that many people have been left out of universal service, and that universal accessibility *is* an important element of universal service.[28] Historically, however, most countries have not taken the accessibility dimension of universal service seriously—with the result that the right of people with disabilities to universal telecommunications service has been neither guaranteed nor delivered.

If the history of universal service has been for many people with disabilities a disabling one, to what extent has this been acknowledged by policymakers? Are governments, regulators, corporations, and communities finally refashioning universal service so that it is truly *universal*?

REMEDIAL OR INCLUSIVE UNIVERSAL SERVICE?

While legislators, regulators, and telecommunications companies increasingly grapple with disability in telecommunications, it is clear that on the whole industry and government policymakers have not rethought in a systemic way universal service as incorporating accessibility for all. All too often exhibiting a bias in policy making toward market-based solutions, government officials advocating reforms are often reluctant to champion a new conception of universal service held to cost corporations dearly. In the year 2002 we often do not appear far removed from the situation described in a 1993 study that found that U.S. Congress deliberations on universal service and disability kept returning to the question of whether equity means that everyone pays a little more so that people with disabilities have full access or that rates are kept low (as a consequence of the latter, people with disabilities must use adaptive devices designed post hoc).[29]

The disabling history of universal service weighs heavily on policy formulation. There is a persistent, indeed dominant, viewpoint that the appropriate approach to disability is "remedial" rather than all embracing. An understanding of disability is still not regarded as something that should be considered from the outset and made integral to the shaping of existing and new technologies. Instead, the status quo persists whereby disability is an issue that policymakers would prefer not to have to deal with, and are only persuaded to attend to under the pressure of general legislation that outlaws discrimination on the basis of disability.

A U.K. policy moment provides a striking example of frameworks employed by policymakers. In February 1998, OFTEL initiated a consultation aimed at identifying measures to be incorporated in the *Telecommunications Act* to complement the general disability legislation. Part of the impetus for this initiative was the requirements of the Amending Voice Telephony Directive (AVTD) of the European Economic Community. OFTEL proposed a code of practice on telecommunications access for people with disabilities that it would incorporate in operators' license conditions. OFTEL's preferred option at the outset was for a code of practice to apply to most operators consistent with what it termed the "modern view of the civil rights" of elderly and disabled people, laid out in the *Disability Discrimination Act*. In its consultation, OFTEL took a cautious approach, formulating a draft Code of Practice that essentially was a codification of existing practice and application of it to newer market entrants. OFTEL estimated the cost of implementing its draft Code of Practice as ten to eighteen million pounds—a modest sum compared to the annual turnover of the telecommunications industry. Whereas OFTEL was prepared to put a figure on the costs of its proposals, it made no such attempt to quantify or otherwise more precisely suggest the scope of the benefits. OFTEL rejected the idea of the provision or "subsidy" of textphones, as going beyond the provisions of the *Telecommunications Act*—though in its final statement, it did recognize that the high cost of textphones and similar devices is preventing large numbers of people with hearing and speech disabilities from accessing the network.[30]

It is disappointing that in this case OFTEL showed little recognition (even if notional) of the accessibility aspect of universal service. Rather it appeared to be prepared only to engage in a long overdue incremental retrofit of universal service, finally giving British people with disabilities the right to basic voice telephony, not seizing the opportunity to put them on an equal footing in new media services. Tellingly, OFTEL cordoned off its deliberations on universal service[31] from its 1998 exercise on telecommunications for people with disabilities, unwilling to put accessibility at the heart of universal service, despite platitudes suggesting the contrary—instead of seeing accessibility issues raised by people with disabilities as an opportunity to ensure more effective, efficient, and equitable telecommunications for the future. In our view, OFTEL's thinking was a vintage instance of seeing disability, and social aspects of universal service, as an expensive supplement—instead of the very heart of the matter.

MOBILE DISABILITY

One of the most significant developments in telecommunications in the last two decades of the twentieth century is the introduction of mobile telephony—a new technology, but one with its own peculiar patterns of disabling telecommunications.

One precursor of mobile telecommunications is radio telephony, mainly used by the military, ship captains, police, or emergency services. Another forerunner is citizens' band (CB) radio, especially popular in the 1970s and 1980s and romanticized in the 1977 film *Smokey and the Bandit*. Used by long-haul truck drivers, CB radios were adopted by ordinary car drivers. Mobile phones as more easily carried and portable devices began to be commercially introduced in a number of countries in the 1980s, when users cheerfully referred to their handsets as a "brick"; even then the mobile phone was difficult for many people with disabilities to hold and use. This system was based on analog technology (AMPS), which we now call first-generation mobile technology. During the 1990s digital mobile phone systems were introduced around the world, promising better voice quality and data transfer rates, more efficient use of scarce radio spectrum, and security from interception of calls. The two dominant systems implemented were the Global System for Mobiles (GSM) system (in Europe, parts of Asia, and Australia), and the Code Division Multiple Access (CDMA) system (in the United States and other countries).

By the close of the twentieth century these digital mobile phones had enjoyed extraordinary success, with ownership rates that outstripped fixed phone ownership in many countries. Success of this consumer product may be attributed to a number of factors: mobility, whereby a person may be contacted wherever they are, rather than having to wait in close proximity to a fixed phone; individualization, allowing a phone to be associated with an individual person, rather than a house, office, or other dwelling; fashion, whereby a mobile phone has very much become part of the semiotic system shaping subjectivity—the ring-tone of a phone can be programmed (taste in music can be publicly signaled), the color and look of the phone can be chosen and modified (permitting aesthetic sense, cultural values, and wealth to be displayed); mobility of data, so voice and text communications may be combined.

The rapid refashioning of telecommunications as *mobile* allows power to operate along different planes, surfaces, and, following the terminology of Gilles Deleuze and Félix Guattari, lines of flight.[32] People are now potentially easily identified as tangible individuals for surveillance or marketing (or both), at any time of the day, wherever they are—in the nation-state or wherever they are in the world (for at least those who can afford global roaming, satellite phones, or travel). An important associated development is the global positioning system (GPS) technology that allows the location of an individual to be pinpointed. This is being combined with mobile telephony in mass-market consumer applications, such as in a car that has a safety airbag inflated, triggering a courtesy call from the manufacturer's service center to the driver to see what they require. In the absence of a reply, emergency vehicles are given the location details and called to the scene.

Like other forms of telecommunications, mobile telecommunications has conferred both ability and disability. For instance, mobile telecommunications has opened up new spaces and uses of communications, formative of the lives and subjectivities of people with disabilities. Short Messaging Services (SMS) were an unexpected but significant development in second-generation mobile phones, not least for people with disabilities. Deaf people, for instance, have been able to avail themselves of SMS services as a relatively cheap, easy-to-use any-to-any communications technology for communicating with other Deaf and hearing people. Given that many people who do not have TTYs have digital mobile phones, Deaf people are able to communicate short messages more easily (albeit with great difficulty on the cramped keyboards, where a greater number of keystrokes are required).

Yet for people with disabilities, there were also significant difficulties with second-generation mobiles, intersecting with but differing from other sites of conflict. The most well-known of these is the case of hearing aid users and GSM digital mobile phones. In the early 1990s, after the new digital mobile system had been developed and was starting to be introduced commercially in a number of countries, it was revealed that this technology emitted a high level of electromagnetic interference. Such interference had the potential to cause a buzzing sound in people's hearing aids, as well as actually making the phones difficult to

use for people with hearing aids.[33] Phone companies internationally, governments, and regulators put much effort into "managing" the public outcry. In doing so, they appeared to be motivated by a concern that this new, expensive technology might not be adopted by consumers, despite widespread support from
governments. Attention was directed to the need for hearing aids to cope with
higher levels of electromagnetic emission, given the wide range of technologies
emitting such signals (not just mobile phones).

A European standard was introduced in 1990 requiring hearing aids to be im-
mune to emissions from mobile phones. Research was also conducted on removing
the source of emission further away from the hearing aid, and eventually "hands-
free kits" were designed for hearing aid users as a solution. Even this solution did
not provide assistance for many, and other tactics were required on the part of the
disability movement. In Australia, for instance, resort was needed to human rights
and antidiscrimination law in order for the matter to be successfully addressed: the
Human Rights and Equal Opportunity Commission (HREOC) conducted a public
inquiry into the matter, which resulted in a conciliation some eighteen months
later.[34] Despite such interventions and measures such as "hands-free kits," the problem remains and is only partially solved in some countries with the availability of
an alternative digital mobile technology (the second-generation digital mobile telephony technology, CDMA or Code Division Multiple Access).[35]

What effectively occurred in this case was that phone companies were forced
to contemplate a costly redesign of the technology as a whole or envisage modifications of the technology. If disability and accessibility had been an everyday
part of how companies, government departments, standards-setting bodies, and
regulators envisioned advanced telecommunications, this sort of technology de-
bacle would have been avoided. If the needs and aspirations of people with disabilities, such as those who are hard-of-hearing and use hearing aids, had been
better understood, and if they had been integrally involved in the design, policy,
and implementation process,[36] not only would the technology when introduced
have been more accessible, the corporations would have faced a better outlook in
terms of their finances, while the government and regulators would not have been
reluctantly dragged into taking some action on behalf of aggrieved citizens left
off a new digital mobile telecommunications network.

The politics of this introduction of the second-generation digital mobile
telecommunications technology are intriguing in themselves. These power relations reflect the shaping of the design and implementation of the technology by
corporate and state interests, operating in new and renovated diffuse sites of
power such as standards-setting bodies. Again, there is a sense in which people
with disabilities are not routinely conceived as consumers or citizens, their exclusion coexisting with new techniques and forms of governmentality.

At the end of the 1990s, the wireless access protocol (WAP) was introduced, one
of a number of developments under the rubric of 2.5 G (generational) mobile
phones. This was the forerunner of "always on" mobile telecommunications, pro-

viding text and Internet communications and e-commerce for users. Features of the Internet such as finding information, purchasing services, receiving news, or conducting transactions are found on WAP-enabled mobile phones, though take-up of services was slow in 2000–2001. More hyped than WAP has been so-called third generation (3G) mobile technology, promised to bring broadband capabilities, such as interactive video. This is the Universal Mobile Telecommunications System (UMTS), working across terrestrial and satellite networks and providing very fast Internet access for a stationary terminal (though less when the terminal is moving). In 2000, spectrum for 3G mobile was fetching exorbitant sums in Europe and the United States, though by the end of the year lower prices were being offered.

One may see 3G mobile as a juggernaut of the values we find inscribed in technology, a totem also of governmentality. In this technology may finally be realized the dreams of video communication found in utopian science-fiction and futurology for decades. We would emphasize the potential of 3G mobile to improve the lives of people with disabilities, but indicate fundamental conditions of exclusion. Shipley and Gill note that 3G mobile might facilitate "remote location and guidance (giving enquirers personal information on how to reach their destinations, with the service centre pin-pointing their locations automatically)" and "remote interpretation for deaf [sic] people, by Sign Language or Lip-speaking (as soon as visual displays of adequate size and definition are available)."[37] However, they also identify problems: operators of 3G have huge sums to recoup due to the cost of spectrum, licenses, and infrastructure, and may wish to focus upon the most profitable sectors, thus neglecting people with disabilities and other groups perceived as "disadvantaged"; the wireless transmission technology used with 3G may also cause problems of interference and noncompatibility with hearing aids (due to use of TDMA, the problem with GSM mobile phones, in conjunction with the CDMA system); the continuing trend toward smaller mobile phones is not helpful for many people with disabilities; network-based facilities like automatic answering, voice-mail, and call progress announcements are not helpful for blind people or people with vision disabilities; many Internet-based applications are visually oriented, so exclude blind consumers.[38] Shipley and Gill call for the establishment of a "culture of inclusion" in the design and standards-setting process, and telecommunications industry more generally, and the establishment of a forum for discussion of inclusion and accessibility issues with industry, in order that "[d]isabled and elderly people are enabled to participate in the benefits of 3rd generation mobile communication systems from the outset, as discriminating consumers but not discriminated against."[39]

GOVERNING DISABILITY

Mobile telecommunications have often been considered as constituting a value neutral device while at the same time being a technology of freedom for people with disabilities. On the other hand, mobile telephony has been critiqued for excluding people with disabilities. What we wish to explore is the way in which mobility of communications is a technology of normalization, in the terms of Foucault's theory.

Foucault argues that the development of bio-power—or the power over life—has the effect of the "growing importance assumed by the action of the norm, at the expense of the juridical system of the law."[40] Far from representing the view that law ceases to be important, Foucault's argument is that law is increasingly invested with norms and operates more and more as a norm.[41] This is an important insight in the case of telecommunications in which, as we noted above, there has been a consolidation and redrafting of key legislation, and also a shift in law from reliance on statutes and courts, to industry self- and co-regulation. Some of the features of this new landscape may be shown in an Australian case, which has clear parallels elsewhere.

There have been a number of significant struggles and legal cases worldwide in which access to telecommunications for people with disabilities has been achieved.[42] A landmark instance in Australia is the *Scott, DPI v Telstra* case, discussed earlier in this chapter. As we have noted, the victory in the Scott case was extremely significant in terms of defining telecommunications access in Australia as a human right, and as a clear legal precedent that helped to enshrine the principles of the *Disability Discrimination Act* in the *Telecommunications Act 1997*.

However, there is a sense in which the "victory" in this case had as its corollary a significant implication for how disability was constructed. For instance, following the Scott case, disability was effectively conceived in such a way that Deaf people, who in Australia had largely avoided identifying as having a disability, were required to utilize the notion of disability and its regulatory power to gain some form of functional access to the telecommunications system. In effect, a rule by the Australian HREOC was a strong affirmation of human rights, yet it also served to manage or govern disability in two crucial ways. Firstly, it required the establishment of a special scheme to complement the status quo, as opposed to changing the status quo so as to incorporate deviant bodies. Secondly, its practical impact was to promote a focus upon one form of disability and to foster the "divide-and-conquer" attitude often taken when medicalized notions of disability are contrasted with each other, again in terms of the extra cost of disability—without looking at the problem of how those costs are derived, or how disability is constituted. Evidence of the pathological body[43] was pivotal to the determination of the case, and was manifested also in the scheme Telstra established to give effect to the ruling.[44]

This broad operation of regulation of disability demonstrated in such legal cases is evident in mobile telecommunications. When the issue of the accessibility of second-generation mobile telephony for hearing-aid users brought public outcry, the matter was then managed in a range of a quasi-governmental, governmental, and corporate forums. This brought only a partial and dilatory resolution to the matter, and also required, at least in Australia, the intervention of the human rights body, which convened a hearing on the issue in 2000. The HREOC hearing had the effect of shutting down critiques of the regulatory and technological systems, those systems that operate with the requirements of governmentality. Resistance to the normalizing operation of the law was thus discouraged.

It could be argued that governmentality, as Foucault conceives it, operates through digital communications systems to encourage the proliferation of mediated communications, producing the citizen as consumer, whose information may be monitored, captured, and analyzed, and who will be "always on," and thus available for marketing opportunities in subtle ways. Within this system of digital governmentality, disability is created as the objectified other. Those with disability lack the full attributes and claims of personhood. For example, the consumer of telecommunications is often a person who buys things on behalf of people with disabilities, rather than the person with disability doing so herself— something justified on the circular grounds that their disability precludes them from doing it themselves.

DISABILITY AND ACTIVE CITIZENSHIP

A related aspect of governmentality evident in disability and telecommunications is that of citizenship. Here we find the work of Nikolas Rose helpful as it elucidates the sense in which we inhabit a society in which power is not centered simply in a state or in transnational corporations, but in a network of loosely connected arenas and sites in which self-activating citizens are required to play a role in constructing and policing zones of circumscribed autonomy and freedom.[45] This calls out in turn for an active, sophisticated citizenry; indeed such a concept of citizenship is constructed in the discourse of competitive telecommunications. Active citizens are expected to do the work of making choice, competition, and new networked technologies possible. They are expected to be consuming mobile telecommunications in all its myriad forms, downloading special ringing tones from the Internet, avidly using short text message services, having an interest in video broadband telephony.

Thus we see much evidence of the rise of the consumer-citizen, something fostered through state-sponsored legislation and regulation. The role the consumer-citizen is expected to play is that of a self-propelling, engaged agent in the considerable work involved in being free to choose, as well as participating in the reworking of governance under the rubric of industry self-regulation mentioned above. In telecommunications we find evidence of Rose's gloss on the new ways in which "advanced liberal forms of government" rest upon the "activation of the powers of the citizen":

> Citizenship is no longer primarily realized in a relation with the state, or in a single "public sphere," but in a variety of private, corporate and quasi-public practices from

working to shopping. The citizen as consumer is to become an active agent in the
regulation of professional expertise. . . . Even in politics . . . the citizen is to enact his
or her democratic obligations as a form of consumption.[46]

There are ways in which people with disabilities, and the disability movement,
are being called upon, or required to become,[47] active consumer-citizens. People
with disabilities are asked to be involved in making their own "choices" about the
products and services they receive, and also, at another level, to be involved in
the formulation of state and corporate policy.

In telecommunications, people with disabilities have very much been asked to
be active agents in regulation in a range of macro- and micro-arenas. To take one
example, the introduction of competition in telecommunications has been accompanied by a rhetoric of "customer-focus," calling for consultation with consumers, inviting consumer representatives to sit on advisory boards or panels.
These consultative fora have assumed greater importance because they have
taken up some of the regulatory and policy-formulation roles previously played
by the state and its agencies. In Australia, for instance, an industry self-regulatory
body has been established by the telecommunications industry, the Australian
Communication Industry Forum, which is responsible for developing regulation
in areas previously governed by the government and industry, and also for initi-
ating regulation in areas not previously subject to any state or self-regulation.
This is an interesting example of the manner in which governmentality is being
extended, under the guise of a discourse of deregulation and self-regulation.

The Australian Communication Industry Forum established a specific Disability
Advisory Body to manage and govern the disability sector via the language of consultation. This is a body positioned as distinctly marginal and subordinate to the Industry Forum's managerial structure and decision-making processes. Like those
other Australian regulators (such as the Australian Communications Authority), the
main board of the Industry Forum still does not have people with disabilities present, though it has made serious efforts to break with consultation techniques based
upon non-disabled norms. That is, in this selective worldview the realities of disability are not represented, and this is reproduced in consultative, participatory, and
decision-making mechanisms.[48] From a disability perspective, we can only suggest
that quality and democracy have a non-disabled face in terms of the consultative
and participatory processes employed in industry self-regulation. We would seriously question the quality and democratic nature of consultative and participatory
processes employed in industry self-regulation as well as the substances of the outcomes they deliver.[49]

TRANSNATIONAL INTERSECTIONS: COST 219

In the example of the Australian Communications Industry Forum we see governmentality operating at a national level to create and manage disability. These

new modes of power may also be observed at a transnational level in telecommunications, for example in the case of the decade-long European COST 219. COST is a framework for scientific and technical cooperation in Europe. It allows coordination of national research at a European level, resulting in "actions" including basic and precompetitive research as well as activities of public utility. Since its inception, organizations and institutes from COST signatory countries have played a central role, but from 1989 non-COST countries, especially from Central and Eastern European countries, have also been able to participate in individual COST actions, if there is a justified mutual interest. Each country involved has complete freedom of participation according to their national research priorities. A special feature of all COST actions is the complete freedom of participation by each country involved according to national research priorities. With the participation of at least five, COST countries sign a Memorandum of Understanding—which governs the joint aims, the type of activity to be pursued, the terms of participation and compliance with sovereignty and if necessary, with intellectual property rights—and an action can then commence. COST funding covers only the coordination expenses of each action and reimburses the travel costs of the national delegates of the European Economic Area.[50]

Spanning 1986–1996, COST 219 collected information about existing telecommunication and teleinformatics with respect to elderly and disabled people, as well as about ongoing research and development in the field. It promoted the study of the practical needs of disabled people and the elderly and evaluated the future possibilities of information technologies.[51] COST 219 was followed by the 1996–2001 COST 219bis, with the main objective of increasing

> availability of telecommunication services and equipment so that they are accessible also to elderly people and people with disabilities. These services and equipment should be designed so that the special needs are taken into account. Alternatively they could also be made adaptable to meet the required needs. In cases where neither of these can be achieved the Action will aim to establish appropriate supplementary services and equipment. The aim is therefore to make sure that the "Design for all" concept in one form or another is taken into account when dealing with telecommunications and teleinformatics.[52]

It brought together parties with an interest in disability and technology to work over a long-term period. Those involved included representatives from government, industry, large and well-resourced disability organizations (some whose origins lie in bodies organized around charitable and disease-specific conceptions of disability, and some whose origins lie more in rights-discourse), and technology consultants. COST 219 and COST 219bis, as their publications and proceedings bear out, have played an important role in early on raising issues for people with disabilities with respect to convergence. In a sense, they are an example of what can be termed an "epistemic community," a transnational grouping of a range of stakeholders who together devise new forms of knowledge and become influential.[53] Thus COST 219 and its successor raise the profile of disability in telecommunications and new media,[54] and at a deeper level are also involved in helping to shape disability in technology. However, both are also intimately involved in governmentality and disability, with distinct limits of its imagining of people with disabilities and their needs. We detect, for instance, a strong focus on physical and sensory disability. There is a sense here of the technique, as epistemology, providing a solution to what is conceived as the problem of physical and sensory disability. And yet, paradoxically, in so doing it helps to create the problem of disability. By contrast, intellectual disability is not so often focused upon in discussions of technology, as the record of the COST 219 and 219bis activities shows.

For all its considerable achievements, the COST 219 and 219bis work bears the imprint of the disabling history of telecommunications, and the genuine difficulties of breaking with this. There is commendable use of an Advisory Committee of people with disabilities and older people to guide the COST 219bis work, but there is a sense in which people with disabilities and their representative organizations remain "advisors" as opposed to "shapers"—with the role of the technical expert still positioned as most powerful. The work of COST 219bis has produced a number of insightful and helpful analyses of issues of accessibility and disability in telecommunications and new media,[55] but the organizations and individuals presenting these papers at its summary 2001 conference overwhelmingly appeared to be representatives of technology specialists, industry, and traditional disability organizations—with a minority of people with disabilities and their advocates on the conference program. Legitimate questions are raised here about the politics of who controls and shapes the technology. These questions become even more difficult when considering the input of people with disabilities into industry-dominated standards-setting processes, as COST 219bis members themselves note:

> COST 219bis members involved in standards work report that one of the challenges is that de facto standards are often created by industry consortia and are mainly used at the discretion of manufacturers and service providers. This means that there is little opportunity for any consumer input . . . even if the processes for consumer participation are improved in the formal standards development, there is still a need for strong legislative and regulatory processes to ensure that industry make use of these standards.[56]

BEYOND DISABLING TELECOMMUNICATIONS

Sadly, the juggernaut of disabling telecommunications rolls on. Lessons about the incorporation of disability into first- and second-generation mobile telecommunications have been scarcely registered in the design and rollout of third-generation mobile telecommunications. This is but one example indicating that dominant, concentrated centers of power with respect to disability still remain in telecommunications.

In this light, we hypothesize that disability and governmentality have a two-fold character, that they are in a double bind. Like other deviant bodies in society, we find disability to be located on the margins of telecommunications. Disability is constituted as an "add-on," and people with disabilities inherently require "special solutions." Well-intentioned efforts to understand and address needs of people with disabilities have created a complex apparatus of practices to manage and govern disability: special equipment funds; special modifications to technology; specific entitlements for people with disabilities, or certain groups of people with disabilities; separate consultative bodies.

Since disability has finally been given some limited recognition in telecommunications, very often disability representative bodies and people with disabilities as individual consumers are expected to play an extremely proactive role in articulating their needs and expectations, and thus educating telecommunications companies. Thus disability may be read in the light of a more general trend to "active citizenship" elicited by contemporary forms of governmentality that Rose identifies, with its own specific modalities of this relating to the power relations of disability. At the same time it is important to acknowledge that people with disabilities are paradoxically often ignored or overlooked as "active citizens," perhaps still lingering on the margins of the governable. Indeed, people with disabilities are routinely not regarded as full citizens, as physical deficit is translated into lack of moral worthiness. No better illustration can be found than the lack of discussion of disability as a mainstream political issue in Western societies. Disability is generally not felt to be central to questions of how a society is constituted and how it is governed, nor is disability very often raised in the context of now-popular discussion of the reinvigoration of civil society. We note here the implications for an understanding of society of how President Franklin D. Roosevelt sought to hide his disability while in office—as if the body politic could not be ruled or led by someone with a disabled body. In Australia, disability was systematically rendered invisible in a national Constitutional Convention, and other debates, on whether the country should become, however belatedly, a republic.[57]

Central to the realignments of roles and responsibilities of state and corporations, public and private sectors, is the complexity entailed. This poses real difficulties for people with disabilities seeking to intervene powerfully into these new and old but recast arenas. Social movements and nongovernmental organizations are at a distinct disadvantage because of the time and resources needed to attend innumerable committee meetings and public consultations, analyze documents, and prepare submissions. Governments and businesses are much better placed to finance their involvement in the various stages of such processes, and so tend to predominate.

Contemporary notions of citizenship assume ability to access and use a range of communications technologies, as suggested by visions of e-government. What then of many people with disabilities who are excluded from the communications they may require to be admitted to the ranks of cybercitizens, as defined by dominant norms? They are of course active citizens, but do their activities count? When you are a person with multiple speech and communication disabilities for whom the communications system is not viable at all, how are you expected to participate as an active citizen in the process of governmentality? Uptake of text technology, which is supposed to replace telephones, has been notoriously low within the speech-impaired community. We would suggest in part that this is because the text telephone (or teletypewriter or telecommunications device for the Deaf, depending on national context) is a cultural artifact of the Deaf community, and has been imposed by narrow non-disabled norms upon the speech-impaired community, many of whom have multiple physical disabilities as well.[58]

When one draws lessons from the disability literature and practice, it is clear that freezing entitlement to accessible telecommunications at the level of voice telephony creates new dimensions of disability. New technologies may finally catch up with communications capabilities of human beings. Interactive video (broadband and narrowband), for instance, promises to allow Deaf people to communicate in their own language, sign language. Accordingly, accessible telecommunications policies should ensure that new technologies are empowering rather than confining for people with disabilities. In addition to serving the needs of people with disabilities, disability may provide exemplary paradigms for other users. The present frameworks for telecommunications—even in their reformed versions—are not adequate for incorporating the needs of *all*, not just those with disability. Disability, as a valuable limit-case, suggests new policy processes for governments and corporations that provide better perspectives on questions of digitization and converging new media.

NOTES

1. U.S. Vice President Al Gore, *Opening Speech,* International Telecommunications Union, First World Telecommunications Development Conference, Buenos Aires, Argentina, 21 March 1994. www.iitf.nist.gov/documents/speeches/032194_gore_giispeech.html [accessed 24 March 2002].

2. Lennard J. Davis, "Introduction," in Lennard J. Davis, ed., *The Disability Studies Reader* (New York: Routledge, 1997), 9.

3. Manuel Castells, *The Information Age,* 3 vols. (Oxford: Blackwell, 1996–98).

4. Daniel Bell, *The Coming of Post-Industry Society: A Venture in Social Forecasting* (New York: Basic, 1973).

5. For instance, see Dion Dennis, "The World Trade Centre and the Rise of the Security State," Event-scene 9, *Ctheory: Theory, Technology and Culture* 24.3 (2001) www.ctheory.com; Anna Munster, "Net Affects: Responding to Shock on Internet Time," in *Politics of a Digital Present: An Inventory of Australian Net Culture, Criticism and Theory,* ed. H. Brown et al. (Melbourne: Fibreculture, 2001; www.fibreculture.org/

publications.html), 9–18. For an earlier discussion of world media events, see McKenzie Wark, *Virtual Geography: Living with Global Media Events* (Bloomington: Indiana University Press, 1994).

6. See William H. Melody, ed., *Telecom Reform: Principles, Policies and Regulatory Practices* (Copenhagen: Lyngby University Press, 1997); M. Jussawalla, ed., *Telecommunications: A Bridge to the 21st Century* (Amsterdam: Elsevier, 1995).

7. Michel Foucault, "Governmentality," in *Power*, ed. James D. Faubion, trans. Robert Hurley et al., *The Essential Works 1954–1984* (London: Allen Lane The Penguin Press, 2000), vol. 3, 221. A concept developed in Foucault's later work, governmentality describes the way that the power in the liberal and neoliberal democratic state is exercised by increasingly pervasive systems of governance. Power thus far exceeds the boundaries usually ascribed to the state, and penetrates deep into the spheres of everyday life and personhood (such as health, sexuality, the body, and so on). For illuminating glosses, see Colin Gordon, "Governmental Rationality: An Introduction," in *The Foucault Effect: Studies in Governmentality with Two Lectures by and an Interview with Michel Foucault*, ed. Graham Burchell, Colin Gordon, and Peter Miller (Chicago: University of Chicago Press, 1991); and Mitchell Dean, *Governmentality: Power and Rule in Modern Society* (London: Sage, 1999).

8. John Braithwaite and Peter Drahos, *Global Business Regulation* (Cambridge: Cambridge University Press, 2000).

9. Just as with Bell's own role in "oralism"; see Douglas C. Baynton, *Forbidden Signs: American Culture and the Campaign against Sign Language* (Chicago: University of Chicago Press, 1996). For an excellent introduction to critical histories of disability, see Paul K. Longmore and Lauri Umansky, eds., *The New Disability History: American Perspectives* (New York: New York University Press, 2001). Little of the literature on telecommunications and history has explored disability. For example, Ann Moyal's important book *Clear across Australia: A History of Telecommunications* (Melbourne: Thomas Nelson, 1984) in no way documents the experience of people with disabilities or even raises issues of disability in telecommunications.

10. Benedict Anderson, *Imagined Communities* (London: Verso, 1983). For a critique of Anderson, and a discussion of nationalism and communications technologies, see Manuel Castells, *The Power of Identity*, vol. 2 of *The Information Age* (Oxford: Blackwell, 1997), 27–32.

11. Among many histories see Gerald W. Brock, *Telecommunication Policy for the Information Age: From Monopoly to Competition* (Cambridge, Mass.: Harvard University Press, 1994) and Kevin G. Wilson, *Deregulating Telecommunications: U.S. and Canadian Telecommunications, 1840–1997* (Lanham, Md.: Rowman & Littlefield, 2000).

12. For example, see Robin Mansell, *The New Telecommunications: A Political Economy of Network Evolution* (London: Sage, 1993).

13. John Gill and Tony Shipley, *The Impact of Telecommunications Deregulation on People with Disabilities: A Review for COST 219bis by the UK Group* (London: Royal National Institute of the Blind, 1997), www.stakes.fi/cost219/DISASTER.HTM [accessed 15 March 2002].

14. Though jarring to some, or outmoded to others, oppression is the appropriate descriptor of the power relationship, and a concept still used extensively. See Paul Abberley, "The Concept of Oppression and the Development of a Social Theory of Disability," *Disability, Handicap & Society* 2 (1987): 5–20.

15. Stuart N. Brotman, *Extending Telecommunications Service to Americans with Disabilities: A Report on Telecommunications Services Mandated under the* Americans with Disabilities Act *of 1990* (Washington: Annenberg Washington Program, Northwestern University, 1991).

16. WID, *Telecommunications and Persons with Disabilities: Building the Framework* (Oakland, Calif.: WID, 1993), 25.

17. For an evaluation of how accessibility fared with the intensification of competition, see *Market Monitoring Report on Accessible Telecommunications* (U.S. Architectural and Transportation Barriers Compliance Board [Access Board]: Washington, D.C., 1998), www.access-board.gov/telecomm/marketrep/index.htm [accessed 25 March 2002].

18. FCC, *Report & Order in the Matter of Federal-State Joint Board on Universal Service*. 97-157 (CC Docket No. 96-45) (Washington, D.C.: FCC, 1997), section III, 53, and IV, 84.

19. The Consumer/Disability Telecommunications Advisory Committee was established by the FCC in November 2000. For information see www.fcc.gov/cib/cdtac/welcome.html.

20. "Community service obligations" was a part of a rhetoric that developed through the late 1980s and early 1990s as a way of separating social aspects of service provision from narrowly commercial ones. The concept was deployed in a number of industries, especially utilities, where governments were seeking to privatize, corporatize, or commercialize service delivery. For example, see Peter B. White, *Community Service Obligations and the Future of Telecommunications in Australia: Final Report* (Melbourne: Commission for the Future, 1989); and Bureau of Transport and Communications Economics, *The Cost of Telecom's Community Service Obligations* (Canberra: Australian Government Publishing Service, 1989).

21. Gerard Goggin, "Universal Service: Voice Telephony and Beyond," in *All Connected: Universal Service in Telecommunications*, ed. Bruce Langtry (Melbourne: Melbourne University Press, 1998), 78–105.

22. Michael J. Bourk, *Universal Service?: Telecommunications Policy in Australia and People with Disabilities*, ed. Tom Worthington (Canberra: Tomw Communications Pty Ltd, 2000); also available at www.tomw.net.au/uso.

23. Brian Perrett, BT Age & Disability Unit, *May I Use the Phone?: A Seminar Held by the COST219 UK Group on Wednesday 9th July 1997, Summary of Proceedings* (London: Royal National Institute of the Blind, 1997; www.stakes.fi/cost219/DDASUM.HTM [accessed 15 March 2002]).

24. Christine Farnish, Consumer Director, OFTEL, *May I Use the Phone?* See also Office of Telecommunications (OFTEL), *Telecommunications Services for People with Disabilities: Consultative Document* (London: OFTEL, 1998) www.oftel.gov.uk [accessed 15 March 2002], section 12.

25. Graham Hicks, SENSE, *May I Use the Phone?*

26. A good example of the work of DIEL (OFTEL) is their publication *Communicating with Customers Who Are Disabled—A Guide for Telecom Companies* (London: OFTEL, 2001); www.oftel.gov.uk/publications/consumer/gpm0901.htm [accessed 14 February 2002]. More information on DIEL is available at www.acts.org.uk/diel.

27. See Colin Barnes, *Disabled People in Britain and Discrimination: A Case for Anti-Discrimination* (London: Hurst & Co., 1991), and his "Institutional Discrimination against Disabled People and the Campaign for Anti-Discrimination Legislation," in *Critical Social Policy: A Reader,* ed. D. Taylor (London: Sage, 1996), 95–112.

28. For instance, see Ian R. Wilson and Gerard Goggin, *Reforming Universal Service: The Future of Consumer Access and Equity in Australian Telecommunications* (Sydney: Consumers' Telecommunications Network, 1993).

29. F. G. Bowe, "Access to the Information Age: Fundamental Decisions in Telecommunications Policy," *Policy Studies Journal* 21(1993): 765–74.

30. OFTEL, *Telecommunications Services for People with Disabilities: Statement* (London: OFTEL, 1998); www.oftel.gov.uk [accessed 5 September 1999].

31. Office of Telecommunications (OFTEL), *Universal Telecommunications Services* (London: OFTEL, 1997); www.oftel.gov.uk [accessed 5 September 1999].

32. Gilles Deleuze and Félix Guattari, *A Thousand Plateaux: Capitalism and Schizophrenia*, trans. Brian Massumi (Minneapolis: University of Minnesota Press, Minneapolis, 1987).

33. E. Burwood and R. Le Strange, *Interference to Hearing Aids by the New Digital Mobile Telephone Systems, Global Systems for Mobile (GSM) Communications Standard* (Sydney: National Acoustic Laboratories, 1993).

34. HREOC, *Inquiry on Mobile Phone Access for Hearing Aid Users* (Sydney: HREOC, 2000); www.hreoc.gov.au/disability_rights/communications/communications.html [accessed 11 November 2001].

35. Tony Shipley, *Interference and Electro-Magnetic Compatibility* (London: Royal National Institute of the Blind, 2000), www.tiresias.org/reports/emc.htm [accessed 15 March 2002].

36. Patrick Roe, ed., *Guidelines-Booklet on Mobile Phones: A COST 219bis Guidebook* (Brussels: COST 219bis, Commission of the European Communities, 1999).

37. Tony Shipley and John Gill, *Call Barred?: Inclusive Design of Wireless Systems* (London: Royal National Institute of the Blind, 2000); also available at www.tiresias.org/phoneability/wireless.htm.

38. Shipley and Gill, *Call Barred?* 8–10.

39. Shipley and Gill, *Call Barred?* 28. While Shipley and Gill's critique is helpful, here we would question the assumption that "inclusion" as a reflex is always good, wishing instead to problematize a too-ready acceptance of social order that creates inclusion as a necessity too neatly and coercively assimilating difference and disability.

40. Michel Foucault, *History of Sexuality: An Introduction* (London: Allen Lane, 1979), vol. 1, 144.

41. Dean, *Governmentality*, 188.

42. WID, *Report Card on Telecommunications Accessibility* (WID: Oakland, Calif., 1998).

43. Felicity Naussbaum, and Helene Deutsch, eds., *DEFECT!: Engendering the Modern Body* (Ann Arbor: University of Michigan Press, 2000).

44. On this, see Bourk, *Universal Service?*

45. Nikolas Rose, *Powers of Freedom: Reframing Political Thought* (Cambridge: Cambridge University Press, 1999).

46. Rose, *Powers of Freedom*, 166.

47. In the work of the Marxist philosopher of subjectivity, Louis Althusser, this process of being called upon, or required to become, consumer-citizens could be termed "interpellation." See Louis Althusser, *Lenin and Philosophy, and Other Essays*, trans. Ben Brewster (London: New Left Books, 1971). A sophisticated, revisionary account of this is provided in Judith Butler's *The Psychic Life of Power: Theories in Subjection* (Stanford, Calif.: Stanford University Press, 1997).

48. Christopher Newell, "Disabling Consultation? A Report Card from the Disability Sector," *Communications Update* 145 (1998): 13–14.

49. Here we share the concerns of the consumer movement worldwide regarding the adequacy of and compliance with co- and self-regulatory codes of practice and standards. For an Australian critique, see Helen Campbell, "Choosing Telecommunications?: Consumers in a Liberalised, Privatised Telecommunications Sector," *Media International Australia* 96 (2000): 59–68.

50. The COST Homepage may be found at www.cordis.lu/cost/home.html [accessed 1 December 2001]. COST publications on telecommunications include: S. von Tetzchner, ed., *Issues in Telecommunication and Disability* (Brussels: COST 219, DGXIII, Commission of the European Communities [CEC], 1991); Patrick Roe, ed., *Telecommunications for All* (Brussels: COST 219bis, CEC, 1995); Jan-Ingvar Lindström, ed., *Universal Services Issues* (Brussels: COST219b, CEC, 1998).

51. Bob Allen, ed., *Complete but Not Finished: The Final Report of COST 219* (Brussels: COST 219, CEC, 1997); www.stakes.fi/cost219/COSA120.html [accessed 15 March 1997].

52. See "COST 219bis," www.stakes.fi/cost219/COSA120.html [accessed 1 December 2001]. The predecessors of COST 219bis may be found in the COST Technical Committee Telecommunication dating back to 1985, which aimed to continue the work started by the Nordic Telemedel initiatives in 1979.

53. Braithwaite and Drahos, *Global Business Regulation.*

54. For example, Ad van Berlo, ed., *Design Guidelines on Smart Homes: A COST 219bis Guidebook* (Brussels: COST, Commission of the European Communities, 1999), www.stakes.fi/cost219/smarthousing.htm [accessed 15 March 2002].

55. See Patrick Roe, ed., *Bridging the Gap? Access to Telecommunications for All People* (Brussels: Commission of the European Communities, 2001), www.tiresias.org/phoneability/bridging_the_gap/ [accessed 15 March 2002].

56. Gunela Astbrink, *Participation by People with Disabilities in Telecommunications Standards-Setting Processes in Europe,* consumer discussion paper prepared for Consumers' Telecommunications Network *International Standards Project* User Workshop, Global Standards Collaboration Forum (GSC7), Sydney, September 2001, www.ctn.org.au/internationalstandards.htm [accessed 15 March 2002]. Astbrink refers here to comments made in Roe, *Bridging the Gap.*

57. Christopher Newell, "Debates Regarding Governance: A Disability Perspective," *Disability and Society* 13 (1998): 295–96.

58. J. Owens et al., *Telecommunications Needs of People with Communication/Speech Difficulties* (Geelong, Australia: Deakin University, 1998).

Chapter Four

Disability on the Digital Margins: Convergence and the Construction of Disability

Most people on earth will eventually have access to networks that are all switched, interactive, and broadband.

—Frances Cairncross, 1998[1]

While Americans with disabilities can all too often be counted on the have-not side of the information and information access equation, the reasons and remedies for this exclusion are not so well or widely understood. . . . As isolating as these limitations are, their impact is all the more frustrating because they are largely needless. If design principles and technological capabilities did not exist for making our [electronic and information technology] accessible to persons with disabilities, regrets might be in order. However, such techniques for the most part do exist and can usually be implemented at little cost, with minimal disruption to industry, commerce, and other technology users. Questions thus arise about why such enhancements are not more widely utilized and what can be done to bring about their use.

—U.S. National Council on Disability (NCD), 2001[2]

INFORMATION MANIA

The 1990s was the decade when information and communications services took central stage in debates over economic and social development. Terminology varied from country to country: Information superhighway was *the* buzz word in the early to mid-1990s, with its European coinages such as *infobahn* or *infostrada*; "information society" reappeared, though it is a word with an older lineage;[3] the term "information infrastructure" was popular among elite decision makers and the electronically informed. According to the Organization for Economic Cooperation and Development (OECD):

63

Underlying the concept of "information infrastructures," "information superhighway," "information society," etc. is the common concept of the need to develop and diffuse broadband communications technologies.[4]

While there has been much talk about the disappearance and scaling back of the role of the state in the last decades, governments still play an important role in constructing, regulating, and creating markets, communities, and social identities. With the vogue for information superhighways, national governments around the world took up positions on the construction of the technological systems of new media. Quite a number of Western governments sought to fashion a consensus on how the state, corporations, schools, universities, and nongovernmental organizations would together create a utopian future through information superhighways, as can be seen in a brief survey.

PROJECTING THE DIGITAL NATION

The United States policy on the information superhighway was released in September 1993, *The National Information Infrastructure: Agenda for Action*.[5] President Bill Clinton had established the Information Infrastructure Task Force in 1993 to articulate and implement his administration's vision for the National Information Infrastructure (NII). The United States projected its vision to the world at large, proposing a Global Information Infrastructure. As enunciated by Vice President Al Gore in Buenos Aires in March 1994, this global vision revolved around five principles: encouraging private sector investment, promoting competition, providing open access to the network for all information providers and users, creating a flexible regulatory environment that can keep pace with rapid technological and market changes, and ensuring universal service.[6] These were adopted in the International Telecommunications Union's "Buenos Aires Declaration on Global Telecommunication Development for the 21st Century." As the most powerful country in the world, the United States spent a great deal of effort further trying to promote its views, as elaborated in its 1995 report entitled *The Global Information Infrastructure: Agenda for Cooperation*.[7] (When electronic commerce took over as the vogue word from information superhighways, the U.S. government issued its 1997 report, *A Framework for Global Electronic Commerce*.)[8] Universal service was an early focus of National and Global Information Infrastructure deliberations: the U.S. NII Task Force included a Telecommunications Policy Committee, with a Working Group on Universal Service, to "ensure that all Americans have access to and can enjoy the benefits of the National Information Infrastructure."[9]

The universal service agenda provided an opportunity for disability issues to be raised, but once again these were not taken as seriously as they should have been—or properly incorporated into a vision of information superhighways for all.[10] In large part, it was left to the disability community to pose questions and suggest strategies, for instance as in the NCD's 1996 report *Access to the Information Superhighway and Emerging Information Technologies by People with Disabilities*. This report noted potential advantages and disadvantages of the national information infrastructure.

Advantages

For people with disabilities, NII provides all the advantages provided to everyone else, plus some special ones. The special advantages include the following:

- Drastically increasing the ability of individuals with some types of disabilities (including visual, hearing, physical, and cognitive/language impairments) to access and use information.
- Decreasing the personal isolation that individuals experience because of restrictions in their ability to move about, communicate, or get together with others sharing their interests or situation.
- Allowing individuals to interact with others in a way that makes their disability invisible or irrelevant.
- Allowing convenient access to educational and medical services.

Disadvantages

Anyone who cannot afford or who cannot physically access and use NII will be at a severe disadvantage. Inaccessibility poses a special risk for individuals with disabilities. If access depends on third-party developers' ability to create special interfaces, people with disabilities are likely to always be left six to twelve months behind. In addition, multimedia trends pose difficulties for individuals with visual impairments, and pointing and gesture interfaces are difficult for individuals with physical impairments. Voice input can create problems for both individuals with hearing impairments and those with physical/speech impairments if no alternate input options are provided.[11]

In Europe, the European Commission (EC) commissioned the May 1994 Bangemann Report, *Europe and the Global Information Society: Recommendations to the European Council*, followed up by the implementation document *Europe's Way to the Information Society: An Action Plan*.[12] The Bangemann Report recognized the potential social challenges in the global information society: "The main risk lies in the creation of a two-tier society of have and have-nots, in which only a part of the population has access to the new technology, is comfortable using it and can fully enjoy its benefits."[13] Accordingly, it recommended that "[f]air access to the infrastructure will have to be guaranteed to all, as will provision of universal service, the definition of which must evolve in line with the technology."[14] However, the report also presented the information society as something desirable and necessary, and thus important to ensure adoption, rather than resistance, by the populace: "There is a danger that individuals will reject the new information culture and its instruments."[15] Therefore, it also proposed a widespread program to secure consent: "A great deal of effort must be put into securing widespread public acceptance and actual use of the new technology."[16] Although disability was not prominent in early European information society documents, it did soon receive attention subsumed under general social and cultural issues.

In November 1994, the British government issued a White Paper entitled *Creating the Superhighways of the Future: The Potential of Broadband Communications*.[17] The disabled are mentioned in chapter two of the White Paper, identified as potential beneficiaries of broadband communications:

> Home shopping, banking, education, travel and theatre/cinema booking, directories, classified advertising and bulletin board/exchange of information services are also all likely to develop over communication networks in the next few years. Disabled people, or those who have difficulty in using traditional telecoms services, may find these especially valuable.[18]

The remainder of the report deals with the roles of government and the regulatory framework with respect to broadband communications, and does not again mention disabled people. The concept of the social is itself only mentioned twice more, most substantively in chapter five, under the rubric of universal service, where the government's potential responsibility is preemptively circumscribed: "At present, with broadband services still at an early stage of development, it would be premature to try to assess the extent to which new services will become widely available on a commercial basis, and the economic and social consequences of such development."[19] A rhetorical emphasis on the benefits of technologies for people with disabilities is coupled with an omission of specific measures to affirmatively imagine people with disabilities as an integral part of information superhighways. Unsurprisingly it was the disability community and movement that pressed for proper consideration of the issues.[20]

In Australia, the federal government established the Broadband Services Expert Group, and directed its Bureau of Transport and Communications Economics to undertake a large, interdisciplinary study, the Communications Futures Project.[21] We see yet again that people with disabilities were given passing mention, then systematically sidelined from information superhighway discussions—with even fewer initiatives from government, industry, or the disability community than in larger countries to give disability issues due consideration.

A DIVIDED HIGHWAY?

In the mid-1990s, communications technologies were constructed discursively, institutionally, and politically as "new" and "broadband." Yet technologies have been constructed as "new" or "high-tech" for a number of decades at least, encoded symbolically as central to social, economic, and cultural changes.[22] In the excitement about information superhighways (and other "information" cognates), previous nation-building projects involving media and communications technologies[23] were displaced and reshaped by national and international discourses on convergent interactive digital technologies, with attendant anxiety regarding globalization. There is quite a paradox evident in these directions:

> at a time when virtually every government in developed countries is embarking upon greater privatization, deregulation and liberalization of their communications industry, and withdrawal from their traditional roles, most governments have been constructing national communications development strategy plans. . . . These national development plans tend to be highly technologically deterministic, centered on the urgent development of high-capacity information infrastructure, and generally with only sketchy attempts at cost-benefit analysis or analysis of its social impact.[24]

We share the criticisms of such writers of the inflated visions of the "information superhighways" of the mid-1990s. We would also point to the importance of questions of who controls, influences, and benefits from "information" and "superhighways." Unsurprisingly, it soon became apparent that the developments gathered together under the banner of "information superhighways" would be substantially controlled and shaped by the state in conjunction with corporate and international business interests.[25]

The metaphor of "superhighway" is instructive, as many have critically noted, metaphors being very important to the shaping of reality and to understandings of technology.[26] The highway was shaped by that technological system that is the motor car. This has arguably shaped much of the social reality we call cities. For one to use and participate in cities effectively, affordable access to and control over a car is vital. Poor people, who have to rely on basic public transportation, do not fare as well. People with disabilities, those who are linguistic minorities, or those who are rurally isolated are not well served by the socially constructed technological systems that are modern cities.

There is a deeper critique to be made of the "information superhighway" discussions, apparent when one considers that the "information" referred to in the phrase is not given, but socially constructed. One example of how this occurs is in the case of ASCII (American Standard Code for Information Interchange), which became a default standard binary code for information and the exchange of text. E-mail still relied on the ASCII standard into the twenty-first century, occasioning frequent problems with elaborately formatted e-mail. Yet the discourse on information superhighways neglects the politics of how ASCII rose to dominance. In the story of ASCII is sketched the history of globalization of an American character code that suits dominant corporate interests and exerts pressure for other protocols to conform.[27] A particularly interesting and related case study here is found in the debate associated with text communication for Deaf people and people with disabilities in the United States and Australia. Whereas Baudot, previously used for telex machines, used to be the standard for text phones, ASCII

became the default. The disability community, especially Deaf representative organizations and their allies, needed to organize globally from 1994 to 1997 to
achieve international standardization of telephony, which would allow older,
Baudot-based teletypewriters and newer ASCII-based devices to communicate
with each other. This was followed by work on international technical standards
on accessibility to multimedia systems and services. The setting of standards—
whether devised by proprietary, commercial organizations or national and international standards bodies—is crucial to the shaping of disability.

Concern grew during the 1990s regarding a yawning chasm between what
were termed the "information rich" and "information poor," in a society where
the control, influence, and definition of "information" increasingly confers
power, early on raised by Reinecke and Schultz:

> If ability to pay is the criterion for who participates in what has been described as the
> new information order, access to new telecommunications services will be restricted.
> The demarcation between information rich and poor will become almost precisely
> that between the economically rich and poor. No better reason for that has been ad-
> vanced than it is the wish of companies and individuals in the private sector to make
> money from information technology.[28]

Anxieties about the growing rift between the "information rich" and "information poor" were registered in obligatory mentions of the matter in official policy
documents and in a growing literature. The issue became known by the shibbo-
leth of the "digital divide," a term that seems to have been coined in the United
States. By the end of the twentieth century, a minor discussion on the "digital divide" sat side-by-side with a major discussion on how to accelerate development
and deployment of information and communications technologies. A number of
useful and comprehensive reports on the "digital divide" were published, with
policymakers and researchers exhibiting great solicitude for the fate of those
stranded in the interstices of the network.[29] A major international aid initiative in
2001 on the part of the Western, developed countries, sponsored by former U.S.
President Clinton, sought to bring the benefits of computers and networks to developing countries.

Not wishing to question the worthiness of such initiatives, however, we point to
the rather intractable existence of poverty alongside great wealth, of people with
access to new digital technologies alongside people without even payphones, of
Internet and text messaging cultures blossoming alongside realms of homelessness
and hunger. Manuel Castells has provided comprehensive evidence for the proposition that the "rise of informationalism in this end of millennium is intertwined
with rising inequality and social exclusion throughout the world."[30] Castells documents how the "selective triage of informational capitalism," results in a "sharp
divide between valuable and non-valuable people and locales" and the creation of
social exclusion in the form of a "new world, the Fourth World . . . made up of
multiple black holes of social exclusion throughout the planet."[31] While Castells's

theory of the information age is much debated, his work certainly provides a warrant for questioning the bona fides of Western governments intent on ushering in free market information capitalism with only a thin patina to palliate enduring inequality and lack of power sharing of digital technologies. Disability may well have its roots in Castells's Fourth World, straddling some of the black holes of social exclusion to be found in rich and poor countries. In any case, people with disabilities remain systematically excluded from interactive digital communications, even while receiving consolatory attention in policy discussion.

DECISIONS AND DECISION MAKERS

A major context for understanding the public conversations on "information superhighways" in the mid-1990s is the politics of decision making: the question of who was put forward as representative of the public, and who was routinely privileged and authorized as a decision maker.[32] We have made plain our view that the shaping of the granted notion of "information superhighway," and its synonyms, has been in accordance with social and corporate forces that do not have the interests of the majority of people, especially marginalized citizens or residential consumers[33] at the forefront. Confirmation of this may be found in an examination of the membership of boards of inquiry, working groups, management, or policy agencies charged with the planning and management of emerging information services. As a truism, people who have the life experience of being from a non-English-speaking or minority-language background; of having a disability, of living in a rurally isolated location, or of being a woman are not well represented in such sites of power. This comes as no surprise: in the United Kingdom, a study of media and telecommunications content services and products found that of a total of ninety "gatekeepers" (members of decision-making boards of U.K. regulators) a slight majority were male, but only four members (4 percent) were not white, approximately 80 percent appeared to live in London, and a quarter were educated at Oxford or Cambridge University; eight of the eleven bodies were chaired by men, and all chairpersons were white.[34]

Nonetheless, in the planning of most Western governments during the 1990s, fundamental concepts of access and equity for all residential consumers were certainly being left by the wayside. As we have noted, in a number of different countries governments established committees to provide advice on policy responses to questions raised by convergent new media, and "information superhighways." In Australia, for instance, the Broadband Services Expert Group (BSEG) was established to "inquire into issues relating to the delivery of broadband services to homes, schools and businesses." The membership was to include twelve people from "diverse backgrounds."[35] Yet, such diversity was evidently in the eye of the beholder, as only one was a woman and there was no representation of community, consumer, or public interest groups.[36] Critics argued that at the time government lacked a commitment to fostering wide participation in decision making around communications technologies. Indeed, the shortcomings of the BSEG Interim Report confirmed these fears. The Interim Report was based on select invitation-only consultations with limited community participation. It tended to be enthusiastic about the possibilities that the technology would unleash and vague about what sort of policy directions were appropriate for government to take. The Interim Report was limited in its coverage of consumer and social policy issues, being characterized by general statements that did not take the social and cultural dimensions of technology seriously. The BSEG's Final Report was something of an improvement, taking on board criticisms; however, serious flaws remained evident.[37]

What then of the participation of people with disabilities in such decision-making bodies? Without wishing to peremptorily assume whether or not someone has disability, it is clear that very few people known to identify with disability, or who were acting as official representatives of people with disabilities, were chosen as representatives to inquire into and make recommendations on information superhighways. While such bodies may actually be quite useless or lacking in any real practical effect, they are important in the symbolism of power. Questions of who is the *best* or most *important* or *relevant* person to be chosen for such a committee reveal something significant about the character of a society, and its governance.[38] In this sense it is clear that people with disabilities are not seen to be important actors in government or corporate power relations; there is an expectation that they are acted upon, rather than being powerful agents in their own right—or needing to be accommodated by the state or communications industry. As well as the lack of representation in positions of power and authority on information superhighway policy and decision-making boards, also of concern were the limited opportunities and resources afforded to consumers to participate in such governmental discussions. Such limited consultation effectively excludes the interests of many residential consumers, especially those without access to the resources to participate in such urban-based forums, and is of concern, given that the deliberations of the group will play a key role in government policy making. Members of marginalized groups such as people with disabilities are not well represented in the high echelons of management and policy making due to social barriers, and people with disabilities in general come from much lower socioeconomic background, predominantly relying upon pensions and benefits.

It is the systematic exclusion of the life experiences of such residential consumers that has led to the construction of a restricted discourse of emerging information services, where the vision leaves many people, who cannot inform, influence, access, or afford such services, by the wayside. Such a situation builds upon the already existing inequality and lack of services for all in the telecommunications arena.

OFFICIAL AND "REJECTED" KNOWLEDGE

Lack of participation in powerful decision making on new communications and media technologies exacerbates an already fraught politics of knowledge for people with disabilities. The context of much research on new media technology has been narrowly commercial for some time. Telecommunications companies, potential carriers, and service providers from telecommunications, media, advertising, computing, and publishing industries conduct market research and form strategic alliances at regional, national, and international levels. A problem with such market research is that it can perpetuate inequality via the use of norms that have marginalized those who do not have as good control of social resources as others. For example, the views of people on the margins with communication and intellectual disabilities, and those from a non-English-speaking background, often are poorly represented in telephone and other traditional market research survey methodology. In short, people on the margins are often not the research subjects, especially in market research. Further, the methodologies used exclude them, and thus they are not included in the samples. Hence, their information is effectively missing from the knowledge that is constructed.

Acutely aware of the shortcomings of commercial market research, and in need of rigorous knowledge, many governments primed themselves for debates on the information superhighway by commissioning research. In Australia, for instance, the Bureau of Transport and Communications Economics (BTCE) undertook a large-scale Communications Futures Project, which aimed to gain an understanding of the broad range of issues related to emerging information and communication services and technologies, particularly in relation to the behavior of large-market participants. In this case, the establishment of a major potential source of independent research and analysis on new communications technologies was laudable—and all the more important given the increasing paucity of public domain research and information on competitive markets around the world. In response to early criticism the bureau's researchers made efforts to include some representatives of residential consumers in their discussions. However, the focus of the project still reflected the dominant view of the new digital technologies in which the market is assumed to hold an unrivalled power.

Such an approach is seriously flawed in terms of the assessment of how residential consumers' dynamic needs and interests may be assessed and met by emerging communication technologies—yet remains all too common. Certainly, there has often been little or no recognition that the needs and aspirations of many consumers are not well achieved or realized through competitive telecommunication arrangements. Often this neglect on the part of influential contributors to policy debates takes on a triumphalist tone, merely asserting the gains of competition without a willingness to engage in detailed assessment of criticism. To rectify this, we suggest that a great deal of work is needed if governments and providers are effectively to understand and address the needs and aspirations of the diversity of the full range of consumers and citizens—a task not made easier when markets are conceptualized in narrowly commercial terms.

THE ROAD AHEAD

Throughout the 1990s, as we noted in chapter 3, many governments held the view that telecommunications competition would bring such "information superhighways" into being, and that the need for guiding government policy or regulation would be progressively lessened. Yet such a view, informed by neoclassical economic frameworks, takes little account of the behavior of corporations and governments being shaped by noneconomic social factors. For example, it is only recently that senior managers in many telecommunications corporations around the world recognized minority or cultural grouping in nations in which they were doing business as important customers. In English-speaking countries, telecommunications managers were slow to recognize barriers for their non-English-speaking background customers, let alone see them as potentially profitable. Likewise, predominantly non-disabled legislators, advisers, and telecommunication managers still do not view the lack of access by Deaf people and people with speech and multiple disabilities as a market opportunity, rather as an economic liability.[39]

In such a context, there will continue to be many people, especially people with disabilities, now and in the future who may have only limited access to the emerging technologies. This is glaringly obvious, and ritually pointed out, if not seriously tackled, in the case of much of the developing world. Further, such citizens are likely to have only limited influence over the definition of such services provided by media and communications corporations. The incorporation of self-articulated consumer needs, desires, and aspirations, including those of members of marginalized social groups, is also needed for an information-rich superhighway for all. An active state will be essential to ensure that the needs and interests of all citizens, including those with disability, are met. However, there is little evidence of this occurring, as governments exhibit timidity in the face of transnational corporations.

As Offe comments, while governments tend to support consumer welfare because of consumer votes, particularly with regard to essential services such as telecommunications, the limits of a government's ability to promote the interest of residential consumers in its policy are clear: it runs the risk of companies withdrawing their economic activity and so must ensure that no "unreasonable" demands may be imposed on the manufacturers and suppliers.[40] The most spectacular example of this logic was the case of the Multilateral Agreement on Investment (MAI), which would have made governments extremely wary of enacting policy disadvantageous to companies, who then would have considerable rights to seek compensation. It was heartening for those committed to democratic governance that a world groundswell against the MAI saw this defeated, for a time at least.[41]

It may also be noted that manufacturers and suppliers are increasingly identifying "consumer issues" where taking account of these may increase profitability. This is seen in the segmentation of markets that were thought of as a much broader market of residential consumers. One of the problems here, however, is that some markets will be identified as much more lucrative than others depending on the monetary consideration and conceptualization of the market. Many large telecommunications companies, especially those with some residual government ownership, control, or obligations, are in even more complex situations than that of mere supplier or carrier, "just another business" as the adage has it—former monopoly carriers such as British Telecom, the United States AT&T, Australia's Telstra—as there still remains an expectation that a higher level of social responsibility and service to all citizens remains as a central goal. Yet these dominant telecommunications corporations—largely still responsible for delivery of universal service in most countries—have also adopted market segmentation approaches.

For example, it is likely that people in their thirties and forties who are residents of areas with higher socioeconomic status will be a much eagerly sought market for home based multimedia, employment, information, and recreation services than people in lower socioeconomic areas with high unemployment and less disposable income. Such a marketing approach has shaped stances in the gay and lesbians communities in richer countries in the 1990s whereby sections have encouraged the construction of themselves as significant consumers, and thus communities with economic power. These trends have been contested, with dissenting gay and lesbian commentators and activists arguing that this marginalizes other gays and lesbians, such as those spending money on AIDS-related expenses, who are less significant in economic terms as consumers.[42]

Another important aspect of Offe's work is his analysis of how consumer interests may be better promoted in contemporary societies, showing that the integration of the spheres of consumption and production in an "autonomous" sector may help to break up the power of the individual and collective imperative of wage-labor and "full employment," which presently enables the industrial sector to insulate itself against consumer and use-value interests.[43] This is an important consideration with regard to information superhighways, given the redefinition of paid and unpaid work in households and the increase in paid work practices such as telecommuting, and is likely to have particular implications for people with disabilities given their underrepresentation in traditional paid workforces.

As we have suggested, a substantial number of consumers and citizens, such as people with disabilities, will not fall into the lucrative markets identified by private interests. The definition and delivery of information services will inevitably be influenced by such markets. Yet, consumers as a group are more likely to be better served by a universally accessible infrastructure that is morally and legally accountable to the general public, as opposed to the situation provided by private interests driven by shareholders' profits to the exclusion of the common good. In conjunction with this, a dynamic notion of universal service in terms of geographical availability, accessibility, affordability, technological standards, and social participation will be necessary. Further, the involvement of consumer interests will be necessary in defining and controlling what the information should be and how it is to be packaged and transported. In addition, the changing nature of residential consumers, and citizens more broadly, will need to be recognized. Certainly, the nature of consumption of emerging communication services and the types of "consumers" themselves are likely to be markedly different in ten years' time, compared with the present.

The global nature of information and communications technologies and the hegemony of international markets and transnational interests raise issues for consumers in general. It is not just the interests of ordinary and marginalized residential consumers that are at stake. Indeed, consumers in all countries face a challenge to devise a social fabric and the provision of public goods so as to ensure that new media will be to the benefit of all rather than predominantly transnational interests. Consumers and citizens will need to organize more effectively at national and international levels in the future in the face of narrowly defined markets and decreased government regulation. Such work will also need to be informed and shaped by alternative, critical knowledges.

CONSUMER RESEARCH: AN AUSTRALIAN EXPERIMENT

In this regard, it is fundamentally important for people with disabilities, as well as other groups, to have the economic, institutional, and conceptual space and independence to conduct their own sustained reflection and research on converging communications technologies. This independence is likely to lead to different constructions of knowledge and discourse, and to suggest a different set of cultural practices, compared with that currently dominating industry and government policy making and research. A useful case study of an attempt to articulate consumer-based knowledges may be found in Australia in 1994.

The Australian Telstra Consumer Consultative Council (TCCC) initiated a wide-ranging consultation on new communications technologies.[44] These consultations involved research conducted on new communications technologies by consumer groups, research institutions, and academic researchers.[45] This research covered topic areas pertaining to a diverse range of groups: women, low income people, consumers with disabilities, older people, aboriginal people, people from non-English-speaking backgrounds, rural and remote consumers, youth, and "technically advanced households and individuals." Significantly, with two exceptions, such research involved providing resources to organizations for, and of, the groups mentioned, to enable them to organize their own research. In the case of low income people research was undertaken by the Australian Council on Social Service, and for the emerging social grouping of "technically advanced households and individuals" (which was not an already organized "community of interest"), the Consumers' Telecommunications' Network (itself a coalition of consumer organizations) employed a consultant.

Within a very tight time-frame organizations contracted with Telstra to organize research and consultations within their constituency or population group regarding such areas as the nature and size of the population group, existing use of telecommunications and information technology, likely future developments/changes for the population group, barriers to the use of new computing and telecommunications technology services, and how new developments could meet needs of the population group (as articulated by them). These questions were addressed in light of a discussion paper prepared by Telstra, with consumer input, to aid informed discussion regarding the emerging social and technological systems. Essential to this were people who had both a technical knowledge and an understanding of the complex social relations of technology.

The research was supervised via a committee comprised of representatives from Telstra and consumer representatives. Both parties brought research experience to bear, and consumer representation included academic, social, and action research experience, which was offered to assist groups conducting research, and of which there was some take-up by several groups. In addition to the population groups mentioned, papers were also commissioned on such topics as privacy and security, occupational health and safety, content regulation, fair trading, impact on family and social relations, and universal service. While the content of these other papers was not necessarily from the perspective of residential consumers, it provided an important aid to informed discussions by consumer and other interest groups.

Indeed, the combined research also provided a starting point for a seminar series jointly organized by the Telstra Consumer Consultative Council & Telstra Regional Consumer Councils, Consumers' Telecommunications Network (CTN), and the Small Enterprise Telecommunications Centre (an organization representing small business users of telecommunications). Seminars in each state and territory of Australia sponsored by Telstra and the BSEG provided a forum for residential consumer and small business representatives to have some input into how broadband services might be defined.[46] In addition, the paper pertaining to people with disabilities was made available on the South Australian–based Bulletin Board "Common Ground," regarding disability issues, and feedback from participants was included in the evaluation.

Interestingly enough the outcomes of the research and seminars showed that residential consumers and small business shared similar concerns regarding access to and affordability of the emerging technologies. Key recommendations included: that a redefinition of delivery of universal service be undertaken, extending it to take into account technological change, and that this be periodically reviewed, with input from a "wide range of groups"; that disadvantaged groups be consulted concerning specific projects intended to be of assistance to them, and that funding of such programs become part of "the basic obligation of government, carriers and service providers"; that basic "no frills" equipment be available from service providers and equipment suppliers (for instance, modems at reasonable cost), to ensure access to new telecommunications services, and that this be designed for ease of use and to prevent "rapid obsolescence"; that the government establish consultation mechanisms; with respect to industry that formal and informal consultation processes need to occur at all levels of product development and service provision; and that priority be given to social research into the uptake and impact of new telecommunications technologies.[47]

This research, consultations, and the resulting recommendations indicate how different knowledges can be constructed, compared with existing dominant knowledge, given appropriate mechanisms. Such research can be successful, even when conducted in partnership and funded by an interested corporation. Here the provision of resources allowed residential consumers to organize and research for themselves effectively, to share their experience and formulate policy recommendations. This goes some way toward redressing the inequitable situation where consumer groups make up the vast majority of the population, yet their life experience and needs are routinely rejected by companies and government policy making.

Many of the population groups represented were typically represented negatively in dominant discourses, such as lacking in command of English (in the case of people from non-English-speaking background or those who are Deaf), abilities (people with disabilities), or living too far from urban centers (rural and remote dwellers). This research project gave them an opportunity, within obvious limits, to organize research for themselves around future policy questions and imagine ways in which future social and technological systems could be of real assistance for them, via providing an inclusive communications systems, and identifying barriers to this achievement for them. Overwhelmingly, the picture that emerged showed that these groups, which account for a significant proportion of the population, lay outside the dominant discourse of telecommunications. This discourse, and its accompanying definition of markets and policy processes, has incorporated negative conceptions of such populations; indeed it has rejected the knowledge that these population groups propose. This consumer knowledge may be dismissed as "uninformed" or "ignorant," which shows a lack of understanding that all people bring knowledge to such encounters. However, we would suggest that rejection of that which does not fit narrow norms or expectations may give rise to such terminology.

There is a lack of acknowledgment of the life circumstances of people with disabilities in all stages of research and policy development. The situation continues in the creation and perpetuation of "special needs" as a recurring feature of policy to the present day. We would argue that it is narrow norms and knowledge that exclude and create "special needs," resulting in "rejected knowledge."[48] Simply put, such rejected knowledge is either not recognized by dominant knowledge systems and discourses, or is reinterpreted in policy exchanges, in ways that are in accordance with dominant knowledge. For example, for years people regarded by dominant knowledge to be "disabled" have been held to have special and ex-ceptional needs in terms of voice-dominated telephony, with scant regard given to alternative accounts that it is such dominant knowledge, manifested in techno-logical systems, which creates disability. In this way, knowledge about disability has been constructed in an oppressive manner that rejects alternative accounts. From this perspective there is a clear danger that the government and telecom-munications industry were leaving the concerns and knowledge of some groups of residential consumers, particularly those marginalized groups, "by the road-side"[49] in the development of knowledge on new communications technologies.

POLICY AND KNOWLEDGE
CONSTRUCTION IN TELECOMMUNICATIONS

The research produced for the 1994 Australian "Have Your Say" seminars, to-gether with the accompanying national consultation under the auspices of the BSEG, produced a body of material that complements and cuts across the official broadband policy outcomes. In policy exchanges, "consultation" represents a repertoire of techniques or even an arena where different forms of knowledge are hybridized, prioritized, and synthesized by different actors. Policy is also consti-tuted over longer time periods by ongoing research and development of knowl-edges. This context of how policy draws on knowledge and research is an im-portant one for considering the construction of disability in telecommunications.

One starting point for understanding how policy is produced is the recognition that there are definite margins and centers established in the canons of such com-munications and information research. A 1995 review of literature relating to telecommunications competition and residential consumers concluded that there existed

> a near invisibility of literature written from the perspectives of residential consumers and small businesses, in much of the "official" literature on telecommunications. Pub-lications by consumer, community and public interest organizations are more difficult to obtain and are published in more ephemeral forms due to cost and time constraints. . . . They are rarely considered, reviewed or commented on in academic, corporate or government publications. In this sense they are marginal to the policy making circuits that exist between academic institutions, corporations and governments.[50]

In 2002, we would suggest that the situation is little different, and that forms of knowledge developed by residential consumers, not least those of people with disabilities, are still to a large extent rejected by policy makers, or at least ren-dered marginal:

> there is little consideration of consumer or social issues in the formal evaluation of telecommunications policy, especially in relation to structural adjustment. There is a

need for greater research and analysis of these issues, particularly using social science and public policy approaches.[51]

On an empirical level, data on the effects of telecommunications policy on residential consumers is lacking in most countries, and on a methodological level, commonly used frameworks remain inadequate for understanding such data. As we have argued, narrow economic efficiency approaches dominate research and policy, and equity, while social and consumer dimensions are neglected. This has direct implications for how disability is understood, and how people with disabilities are inserted into policy making.

Disciplines and interdisciplinary endeavors actually shape the object of their study. It is no surprise that the empirical impoverishment of the policy and research discourses on residential consumers in telecommunications is matched by methodological and theoretical shortcomings. The identification and social situation of researchers also has an effect on the constitution of the object of study, and the knowledges produced. This has been theorized by researchers using an ethnographic approach to study information and communications technologies in the home.[52] In the course of their study, Silverstone, Hirsch, E. Morley, and D. Morley attempted to treat the families they were researching as "partners" rather than "subjects." This called for greater reflexiveness in the researchers' own "ethnographic self-knowledge" in allowing comment on the research process by the researched.[53] Indeed, the transformation of the power relations of research has been a feature not only of contemporary reflexive ethnography, humanities, and social sciences research, but also of disability studies.[54] Conceiving of research as a dialogue between the researchers, with their peculiar social mores and interests, and the researched, who bring their values to the exchange, is a useful step toward recognizing the value-laden nature of telecommunications, and generating different forms of knowledge. This is demonstrated in Ann Moyal's landmark national survey of women's telephone use in Australia, in which a "qualitative, ethnographic methodology was selected which assumed the nature of 'a dialogic approach' . . . contiguous with female-gendered communication patterns."[55]

Of course, such a methodology itself produces a particular sort of knowledge, which like other forms of knowledge is related to its institutional setting. Most researchers are embedded in institutional contexts such as corporations, universities, research institutes, government departments, or research organizations, although a few resourceful individuals exist in the role of "independent" scholars. A recurring theme in literature on the epistemology of telecommunications policy research is the need for funding independent of industry, government, and other agenda to foster innovative, critical research.[56] The locus for this critical research is generally thought of as the university. While it is undoubtedly true that universities have a central role to play in fostering a critical intellectual climate in telecommunications, as in other areas of societies, there are other institutions and settings that also foster critical research.

A fundamental premise of the research conducted by many organizations in the disability and consumer movements is to allow other researchers, with different institutional locations and knowledge systems (such as that of the "disability movement"), to produce knowledge in the telecommunications arena. A prime aim of this strategy is to encourage people with disabilities to elaborate knowledges about their own telecommunications usage. It also allows these researchers to generate knowledge about other peoples' usage of and discourses on telecommunications.

There are a number of difficulties that need to be explored with this model. There is the fear that such research will merely be "self-reporting," and will not involve proper critical research on the groups involved. This is a danger shared by institutional locations, such as government and corporate research that is often "self-reporting," in the sense of uncritically investigating aspects of its own behavior and not adequately analyzing important social and consumer issues. The standard of research is raised as a concern. Practices of academic transmission of knowledge drawing on quality measures such as peer reviewing offer safeguards in relation to ensuring that good research techniques are used, and that researchers frame their work with respect to the relevant literature in an area. Yet the deployment of these techniques has not been adequately examined, leading one commentator to suggest, for instance, that "the study of peer review is in its infancy."[57] A particularly important question in relation to peer reviewing is: "Who are the 'peers' in a particular area?" Mostly, they are other academics, who are held by established disciplines or knowledge systems to be experts in the field that the study has situated itself in. This leaves the question of whether other experts should be consulted with or comment on a study, as well as the difficult question of what constitutes expertise itself.[58] For instance, researchers proposing to investigate an area could be asked to communicate with other researchers and consumer and community groups that represent or have an interest in that topic. This can promote a broader approach to a topic than narrow academic specialization might generally require. It does not, however, acknowledge particular expertise by members of such community and consumer groups, who increasingly may also use the tools of academia in the engagements.[59]

Further productive relationships can, and should, be fostered between university and research institutions and consumer and community groups to lift the definition and profile of social issues in telecommunications. Such relationships could include "mentoring," whereby academic-based researchers are funded to provide research expertise to consumer and community groups, which due to time, funding, and resource constraints lack the ability to conduct high-quality research projects on an ongoing basis. Exchanges of researchers, and institutional links, would further enhance the already blossoming relationships between consumer and community groups and the academic community over the past few years. These relationships have been due in no small part to the value that both sides place on independent critical research.

Whereas large corporations, the telecommunications industry, and governments are able to "buy in" expertise by commissioning, for example, consultancy advice on economic issues or market research, consumer and community groups do not have the money required and often rely heavily on voluntary or donated work. Further, the perspectives of these groups do not often fit readily with the knowledge base of established market researchers or neoclassical economists, whose views are approved by the telecommunications industry. Researchers with alternative views and understanding of residential consumer issues are few and far between, because these do not tend to be the lucrative areas for specialization.

DIFFERENT KNOWLEDGES

In a discussion of the construction of disability in relation to informationalization, and the theories of Castells, Bob Sapey has argued that "informationalisation has been destructive of the *legitimising identities* of industrial societies, in particular patriarchy, but *resistance identities* are developing and manifesting themselves through new social movements."[60] At this historical conjuncture, Sapey suggests, "disabled people may have the opportunity to develop *project identities* which legitimize and shape the future impact of technology."[61] Sapey's remark helps us to understand the interventions of people with disabilities into the "forces which construct disablement"[62] in the information age.

In the context of the information age, knowledges of residential consumers can be seen to be an emerging interdisciplinary, indeed transdisciplinary, endeavor, with their own contradictions and conflicts. Such knowledges are likely to grow in significance with changes still being brought by competition and convergence. People with disabilities are another significant group, who at times identify as residential consumers, at other times as citizens, and at other times—though not as often as they might—identify as business people, managers, or policy or decision makers. Just like residential consumers, people with disabilities need to be able to produce their own knowledges regarding such developments and emerging consumer needs and desires,[63] and to enter into policy exchanges with government, industry, and other groups, especially consultation and advocacy in the relation to competition in essential services, such as telecommunications and energy industries.[64] Society at large will benefit if economic, institutional, and conceptual space and independence is given to all citizens, and their particular groupings and communities, to conduct their own sustained reflection and research on the emerging communications technologies. This is important given the way in which the knowledge of people with disabilities can be seen to be rejected by dominant knowledge, which is informed by narrow notions of economics and markets. Such subaltern knowledge can make an important and yet currently undervalued contribution to policy exchanges, and help shape the emerging social and technological systems that are becoming today's and tomorrow's norms.

NOTES

1. Frances Cairncross, *The Death of Distance: How the Communications Revolution Will Change Our Lives* (London: Orion Business Books, 1998), xi.

2. National Council on Disability (NCD), *The Accessible Future* (Washington, D.C.: NCD, 2001).

3. According to Manuel Castells, the information society and similar terminologies were all "originated in Japan in the mid-1960s—*johoka shakai* in Japanese—and transmitted to the West in 1978 by Simon Mora and Alain Minc (in their *L'Informatisation de la société* [Paris: La Documentation française, 1978])" (*The Rise of the Network Society*, vol. 1 of *The Information Age* [Oxford: Blackwell, 1996], 21).

4. OECD, *Information Infrastructure Policies in OECD Countries* (Paris, OECD: 1996); www.oecd.org/dsti/iccp/iip.html [accessed 15 February 2002]. Our attention was drawn to this quotation by Dianne Northfield's helpful *The Information Policy Maze: Global Challenges—National Responses* (Melbourne: RMIT, 1999), which provides an overview of the information infrastructures policies adopted in a number of countries (see especially chapter 2, "Approaches to Navigating the Maze: National Information Strategies," 36–112).

5. Information Infrastructure Taskforce, *The National Information Infrastructure: Agenda for Action* (Washington, D.C.: Department of Commerce, 1993); www.ibiblio.org/nii/toc.html [accessed 15 February 2002].

6. See Brian Kahin and Ernest J. Wilson III, eds., *National Information Infrastructure Initiatives: Vision and Policy Design* (Cambridge, Mass.: MIT Press, 1997).

7. *The Global Information Infrastructure: Agenda for Cooperation* (Washington, D.C.: National Telecommunications and Information Administration, 1994); www.ntia.doc.gov/reports/giiagend.html [accessed 15 February 2002]. For associated documents, see www.iitf.nist.gov/index-old.html [accessed 15 February 2002].

8. *A Framework for Global Electronic Commerce* (Washington, D.C.: Department of Commerce, 1997); www.iitf.nist.gov/eleccomm/ecomm.htm [accessed 15 February 2002].

9. *The National Information Infrastructure*, www.ibiblio.org/nii/NII-Task-Force.html [accessed 15 February 2002].

10. Despite initiatives such as Federal Communications Commission (FCC), *Building Bridges to the Information Superhighway: Annual Report of the Disabilities Issues Task Force* (Washington, D.C.: FCC, 1996).

11. NCD, *Access to the Information Superhighway and Emerging Information Technologies by People with Disabilities* (Washington, D.C.: NCD, 1996); www.ncd.gov/newsroom/publications/superhwy.html (15 February 2002).

12. High-Level Group on the Information Society, *Europe and the Global Information Society: Recommendations to the European Council (Bangemann Report)* (Brussels: European Commission, 1994); www.medicif.org/Dig_library/ECdocs/reports/Bangemann.htm.

13. *Europe and the Global Information Society*, chapter 1.

14. *Europe and the Global Information Society*, chapter 1.

15. *Europe and the Global Information Society*, chapter 1.

16. *Europe and the Global Information Society*, chapter 1.

17. Department of Trade and Industry, *Creating the Superhighways of the Future: The Potential of Broadband Communications* (London: HMSO, 1994); www.archive.official-documents.co.uk/document/dti/dticmd/ [accessed 15 February 2002]. For a

discussion of the British policy experience see P. Goodwin, "British Media Policy Takes to the Superhighway," *Media, Culture & Society* 17 (1995): 677–89; William Dutton et al., *The Information Superhighway: Britain's Response: A Forum Discussion* (Policy Research Paper 29; Programme on Information and Communications Technologies, Economic and Social Research Council: London, 1994).

18. *Creating the Superhighways*, paragraph 21, chapter 2.

19. *Creating the Superhighways*, paragraph 76, chapter 5.

20. For instance, see the July 1996 special issue of the *New Beacon* magazine, published by the U.K. Royal National Institute of the Blind (RNIB). The RNIB also established an Information Superhighway Project. See also Sally Rosenthal, "Adrift on the Information Highway: Confessions of a Wannabe Computer Nerd," *Electric Edge: Web Edition of the Ragged Edge* (Sept/Oct. 1997), www.ragged-edge-mag.com/sep97/net.htm [accessed 1 February 2002].

21. Bureau of Transport and Communications Economics, *Communication Futures Project: Final Report* (Canberra: Australian Government Publishing Service, 1995). For accounts of Australian broadband policy, see "Communication Futures in Australia," special issue of *Prometheus* 14, 1 (1996); special issue of *Media Information Australia* "Superhighway Blues," 74 (1994); and Trevor Barr's *New Media.com.au* (Sydney: Allen & Unwin, 2000).

22. For discussion of earlier periods of technology enthusiasm, see: W. H. Dutton, J. G. Blumer, and K. L. Kraemer, *Wired Cities: Shaping the Future of Communications* (Boston: G. K. Hall & Co., 1987); Carolyn Marvin, *When Old Technologies Were New: Thinking about Electric Communication in the Late Nineteenth Century* (Oxford: Oxford University Press, 1990).

23. Benedict Anderson, *Imagined Communities* (London: Verso, 1983).

24. Barr, *New Media.com.au*, 169.

25. A range of theorists were quick to point this out, especially those in the political economy school, such as Dan Schiller, *Digital Capitalism: Networking the Global Market System* (Cambridge, Mass.: MIT Press, 1999), as well as many other media and communications scholars, such as McKenzie Wark, "What Does Capital Want?" *Media Information Australia* 94 (1994); also the writers in Dayan Kishan Thussu, ed., *Electronic Empires: Global Media and Local Resistance* (London: Arnold, 1998).

26. See Harmeet Sawhney, "Information Superhighway: Metaphors as Midwives," *Media, Culture & Society* 18 (1996): 291–314, and "Dynamics of Infrastructure Development: The Role of Metaphors, Political Will and Sunk Investment," *Media, Culture & Society* 23 (2001): 33–53. See also Y. Malhotra, A. Al-Shehri, and Jeff J. Jones's 1995 paper "National Information Infrastructure: Myths, Metaphors and Realities" www.brint.com/papers/nii/ [accessed 1 February 2002], where they ask, "What alternative perspectives are suggested by some other metaphors?"

27. Work was conducted through committees of the European Telecommunications Standards Institute and the International Telecommunications Union. See Gunnar Hellström, "Standardization of Text Telephony," www.omnitor.se/english/standards [accessed 15 March 2002].

28. I. Reinecke and J. Schultz, *The Phone Book: The Future of Australia's Communications on the Line* (Melbourne: Penguin, 1983), 232. An influential early piece is Graham Murdock and Peter Golding, "Information Poverty and Political Inequality: Citizenship in the Age of Privatised Communications," *Journal of Communications* 39 (1989), extending

their earlier "Unequal Communications Access and Exclusion in the New Communications Marketplace," in *New Communications Technologies and the Public Interest*, ed. Marjorie Ferguson (London: Sage, 1986), 71–83.

29. Of a voluminous literature, see National Telecommunications and Information Administration (NTIA), *Falling through the Net: Defining the Digital Divide* (Washington, D.C.: 1999) www.ntia.doc.gov/ntiahome/fttn99/contents.html [accessed 20 June 2000]; Wendy Lazarus and Francisco Mora, *Online Content for Low-Income and Underserved Americans: The Digital Divide's New Frontier* (Santa Monica, Calif.: The Children's Partnership, 2000), www.childrenspartnership.org/ [accessed 20 June 2000]; Donald A. Schon, Bisch Sanyal, and William J. Mitchell, eds., *High Technology and Low-Income Communities: Prospects for the Positive Use of Advanced Information Technology* (Cambridge, Mass.: MIT Press, 1998).

30. "The Rise of the Fourth World: Information Capitalism, Poverty and Social Exclusion," chapter 2, *End of Millennium*, vol.3, *The Information Age: Economy, Society and Culture* (Oxford: Blackwell, 1998), 165.

31. Castells, *End of Millennium*, 165, 161, 164.

32. On the question of who occupies positions of power see R. F. Drake's "The Exclusion of Disabled People from Positions of Power in British Voluntary Organisations," *Disability and Society* 9 (1994): 461–80.

33. The term "residential consumer" is hardly unproblematic, especially given the changing nature of the technological systems under discussion. Further, the distinction between work carried out in places of business and consumers at home (residential consumers) will increasingly become blurred. We retain the term "residential consumers," however, because of the importance of recognizing distinct issues for consumers who lack the influence and control of corporate and business use, yet identify needs and aspirations which are not found in the dominant discourses of communications and information technologies.

34. Appendix 2, "The Gatekeepers: Who Regulates Media Content," Richard Collins and Cristina Murroni, *New Media, New Policies: Media and Communications Strategies for the Future* (Cambridge: Polity Press, 1996), 199–200.

35. Broadband Services Expert Group, *Networking Australia's Future*, Interim Report (Canberra: Australian Government Publishing Services, 1994), 1.

36. By comparison, the United States Advisory Council on the National Information Infrastructure at least included public interest groups. It is, of course, possible that such representation may only be token, as the purpose of the council was to "facilitate private sector input to the Information Infrastructure Task Force" (*Information Infrastructure Task Force*, 21).

37. BSEG, *Networking Australia's Future: Final Report* (Canberra: Australian Government Publishing Service, 1994).

38. The work of Pierre Bourdieu is helpful here, as it points to the role social and cultural capital play in the reproduction of society's power arrangements. See Pierre Bourdieu and Jean-Claude Passeron, *Reproduction in Education, Society and Culture*, trans. Richard Nice, 2nd ed. (London: Sage, 1990); and Pierre Bourdieu, *Distinction: A Social Critique of the Judgement of Taste*, trans. Richard Nice (Cambridge, Mass.: Harvard University Press, 1984).

39. Gerard Goggin and Christopher Newell, "Crippling Competition: Critical Reflections on Disability and Australian Telecommunications Policy," *Media International Australia* 96 (2000): 83–94.

40. Claus Offe, *The Contradictions of the Welfare State*, ed. John Keane (London: Hutchinson, 1989), 223. Interestingly, the notion of "reasonable" is key in equity and discrimination legislation in most jurisdictions.

41. James Goodman and Patricia Ranald, eds., *Stopping the Juggernaut: Public Interest Versus the Multilateral Agreement on Investment* (Sydney: Pluto Press, 2000).

42. A. Gluckman and B. Reed, "The Gay Marketing Moment," *Dollars and Sense* (1993): 18.

43. Offe, *Contradictions of the Welfare State*, 237.

44. Now the Telstra Consumer Consultative Council (TCCC). Established in 1989, the TCCC is an innovative forum for Telstra (formerly Telecom Australia) to consult with consumer and community groups on issues affecting residential consumers.

45. This research was published as Linda Adamson et al., *Planning for an Information Society: Population Group Discussion Papers and Policy Issue Discussion Papers* (Melbourne: Telecom Australia, 1994).

46. Jane Elix and Jane Lambert, *Final Report: "Have Your Say" National Seminar Series on Future Communications Technologies: Issues and Opportunities* (Sydney: Community Solutions, 1994).

47. Elix and Lambert, *Final Report*, 11–17.

48. See E. Richards, *Vitamin C and Cancer: Medicine or Politics?* (London: Macmillan, 1991); R. Wallis, ed., *On the Margins of Science: The Social Construction of Rejected Knowledge* (Keele, Staffordshire, U.K.: University of Keele, 1979).

49. Gerard Goggin and Christopher Newell, "Reflections from the Roadside: Residential Consumers and Information Superhighways," *Media Information Australia* 74 (1994): 34–41.

50. Gerard Goggin and Claire Milne, "Literature Review: Residential Consumers and Australian Telecommunications 1991–94," in Trish Benson, ed., Consumers' Telecommunications Network, in *For Whom the Phone Rings: Residential Consumers and Telecommunications Competition,* ed. Trish Benson (Sydney: Consumers' Telecommunications Network, 1995), 28–29. The inaugural issue of the important journal *Telecommunications Policy* opens with an editorial by Lawrence H. Day expressing the hope that it will serve to bring together in an on-going dialogue both policy researchers, on the one hand, and decision makers and policy analysts in government and industry, on the other. Day announces that "[s]pecial efforts will also be made to involve in the debate the groups of telecommunications users, industrial and governmental, in whose names many policy developments are undertaken. Users are seldom given adequate opportunity to express their views, and every effort must be made to guarantee their inclusion in this new forum" (L. H. Day, "Telecommunications Policy: Teamwork," *Telecommunications Policy* 1 [1976]: 2). Unfortunately this statement does not acknowledge residential consumers as important end users of telecommunications, although twenty years on we are better able to make such distinctions.

51. Goggin and Milne, "Literature Review," 29.

52. R. Silverstone, E. Hirsch, E. Morley, and D. Morley, "Listening to a Long Conversation: An Ethnographic Approach to the Study of Information and Communication Technologies in the Home," *Cultural Studies* 5 (1991): 204–27.

53. Silverstone et al., "Listening to a Long Conversation," 222.

54. For example, see J. Morris, "Personal and Political: A Feminist Perspective on Researching Physical Disability," in *Debates and Issues in Feminist Research and Pedagogy:*

A Reader, ed. J. Holland and M. Blair with S. Sheldon (Philadelphia: Clevedon; Adelaide: Multilingual Matters, and Milton Keynes, U.K.: Open University, 1995), 262–72; M. Oliver and C. Barnes, "All We Are Saying Is Give Disabled Researchers a Chance," *Disability and Society* 12 (1997): 811–13.

55. Ann Moyal, "The Gendered Use of the Telephone: An Australian Case Study," *Media, Culture and Society* 14 (1992): 52. See also Moyal's "The Feminine Culture of the Telephone: People, Patterns and Policy," *Prometheus* 7.1 (1989): 5–31.

56. See W. H. Rowland, "American Telecommunications Policy Research: Its Contradictory Origins and Influences," *Media Culture and Society* 8 (1986): 159–82, and "The Traditions of Communication Research and Their Implications for Telecommunications Study," *Journal of Communication* 43 (1993): 207–17.

57. B. W. Speck, *Publication Peer Review: An Annotated Bibliography* (Westport, Conn.: Greenwood, 1993); K. A. Hansen, "Bibliographies and Scholarly Communication," *Journal of Communication* 44 (1994): 63.

58. See R. E. Rice, C. L. Borgman, and B. Reeves, "Citation Networks of Communication Journals, 1977–1985: Cliques and Positions, Citations Made and Citations Received," *Human Communications Research* 15 (1988): 256–83. Also Tony Becher, *Academic Tribes and Territories: Intellectual Enquiry and the Cultures of Disciplines* (Milton Keynes, U.K.: Open University Press, 1989).

59. On the relation of activist to academic, see Penny Germon, "Activists and Academics: Part of the Same or a World Apart?" in *The Disability Reader: Social Science Perspectives,* ed. Tom Shakespeare (London: Cassell, 1998), 245–55.

60. Bob Sapey, "Disablement in the Informational Age," *Disability and Society* 15 (2000): 634.

61. Sapey, "Disablement in the Informational Age," 634.

62. Sapey, "Disablement in the Informational Age," 634.

63. For example, see Fredric K. Schroeder, "Research and the Organized Blind Movement," *Braille Monitor* 44.8 (August/September 2001), www.nfb.org/BM/BM01/BM0108/BM010807.HTM [accessed 15 March 2002]; and the response by Geerat J. Vermeij, "Research and the Blind," *Braille Monitor* 45.2 (March 2002), www.nfb.org/bm/bm02/bm0203/bm020305.htm [accessed 15 March 2002].

64. Consumers' Telecommunications Network, *Voices in the Market: Consumer Consultation and Advocacy in an Era of Competition* (Sydney: CTN, 1995).

Part Three

New Mediations of Disability

Getting the Picture on Disability: Digital Broadcasting Futures

No one anticipated that the members of an average household would watch the screen some six hours a day, while in poor homes television would become a substitute hearth, glowing constantly day and night. Few people foresaw that television, more than any other force, would provide the unifying images that would define the national experience and consciousness. Television marched into America's living rooms and took over for 50 years. . . . Television took us to Dallas and made John F. Kennedy into a national icon. It took us to the moon. It awakened us to the horrors of war in Vietnam. . . . But now its time is over. The television age is giving way to the much richer, interactive technology of the computer age.

—George Gilder, 1992[1]

Beside frustration while watching television and videos, many people who are blind or visually impaired feel "left out" because they miss information that sighted people easily get in this culture where television and films play such a large part. . . . So-called "water cooler" discussions play a large part in adult social interaction, and similar types of discussions may play an even larger role in the lives of children and teenagers; being unable to participate fully limits interactions and can negatively affect one's self-concept.

—John Simpson, 1999[2]

Television is a central medium of communication and entertainment in the lives of billions of people. Nearly ubiquitous in households in wealthy countries, it is widely watched in poor countries and has become synonymous with modernity and modernization. The impact of television cannot be underestimated. In economic and financial terms, it is a huge manufacturing and entertainment industry across the world. In cultural terms, it is directly and intimately connected with political and economic arrangements, and with how people conduct their everyday lives. It is kingmaker, town crier, and confessor. In postmodern theories of culture television has become a harbinger of hyperreality—shaping reality in persuasive, concrete ways, as Jean Baudrillard argues in his scandalous study of the way that the coverage of the Gulf War was only available to most people as mediated, televisual representation.[3] And yet for many people with disabilities, television has been a difficult to see or hear, impossible to watch or listen to, absent cultural technology. The traditional broadcasting paradigm of television only fitfully included large numbers of people with disabilities. Indeed we can see that increasingly TV as a sociopolitical space has disabled people, but because of its dominant understandings and power relations we located the blame with deviant individuals we know as disabled.

At the beginning of a new millennium, nearly everything about television is up for grabs. The role of traditional government (or public service) broadcasters is under threat, and rapidly transforming.[4] Commercial free-to-air television stations are scrambling to preserve their revenue sources as competition for advertising from Internet and multimedia sources intensifies. Cable (pay) television companies are feeling the strain too, with subscriber demands for new services and popular movies and programs being spread thin across more and more delivery options. Community or public access television enthusiasts are straining to maintain their programming on limited resources while arguing for access to spectrum and new digital technologies.[5] And the most serious challenge faced by existing television companies is the introduction of digital television. Like other communications and media technologies, digitization provides an arena in which crucial questions will be fought out: Who will have television licenses? Which standards will be adopted? How much will consumers pay for television sets, set-top boxes, programs, and services? Which companies or individuals will control or make money from digital television?[6] Will the result be more choice, or just more confusion?

Yet lost in the smoke of battle over digital television are crucial questions for people with disabilities. With its greater technical sophistication and possibilities, digital television offers the potential to redress barriers to access for people with disabilities—belatedly ushering them into the television age and, hopefully, putting them in the box seat for the new interactive television experience promised by proponents of digital television. In this chapter, then, we consider the question of television's digital future. Will it be disabling or enabling—or both?

In the first part, we examine a significant recent example of how people with disabilities have been represented on traditional television. We analyze the television representation of one of the most important media events—sport—and in particular, the 2000 Sydney Olympic games, alongside its poor cousin, the Paralympics. Following from this discussion of the cultural dimension of television, in the second part of the chapter we consider how disability is being constructed in the all important (re)construction of television for the third millennium, and its second century, in debates over the introduction of digital television. In the concluding part of the chapter, we explore the implications of this two-sided screening of disability in television and what it means for notions of cultural citizenship.

DISABLING MEDIA REPRESENTATIONS OF OLYMPIC PROPORTIONS

While there are a few helpful studies of media and the representation of disability, television studies, in common with much of media and cultural studies, remains relatively untouched by analyses of disability[7]—whereas the field has at least partially engaged with critical theory on categories such as class, gender, race, colonialism, and sexuality. It is such an approach that we have in mind as we turn to how the 2000 Olympics and Paralympics were televised.

By and large, mainstream media neglected to report the biggest Paralympics ever, the 2000 Sydney Paralympics—at least in the lead-up to those games. Sydney Paralympics organizers faced a number of difficulties in gaining coverage. Early on, the organizers faced the prospect of paying the networks to televise the Paralympics, as happened with the 1996 Atlanta Paralympics. Organizers held negotiations over a two-year period with Channel 7, which in one proposal requested that the Paralympics underwrite them for $3 million in case of a shortfall in advertising revenue. Finally in February 2000, a collaboration for host broadcaster between Sydney-based television facilities company Global Television, and the production company, All Media Sports (AMS), was announced.

It was only in March 2000 that the Australian broadcaster for the Paralympics was finally announced—the Australian Broadcasting Corporation (ABC), along with the Channel 7 network, the initial domestic broadcaster, which promised to "complement" this coverage with a highlights package broadcast daily on its pay-TV channel, C7. The Australian ABC had previously broadcast the 1992 and 1996 Paralympics, and committed itself to broadcasting a minimum of sixty minutes of daily highlights of the games in the early evening (before prime time), with repeats, updates, and new segments in a further forty-five minute broadcast late each night (after prime time). After some further negotiation, the ABC decided to present a live broadcast of the opening and closing ceremonies. Despite it being a rather lackluster affair (at least for some), there was actually substantial media and television viewer interest in the Sydney Paralympics. The Paralympic opening ceremony was broadcast live in Australia on the ABC (as was the closing ceremony), and was the highest-rated program in 2000 outside the three commercial networks—attracting more than 2.5 million viewers, the thirty-fourth-most-watched program for the year.

Aside from the opening and closing ceremonies, the rest of the Paralympiad was obviously not deemed of sufficient entertainment or information value, prior to the event, to be accorded the same "live" event television coverage as its Olympic counterpart. A Channel 7 spokesperson explained that

> We have had a good relationship with [the Sydney Paralympic Organising Committee] SPOC regarding the coverage of the Games, however we were also aware that we

could only offer limited air-time to the broadcast. This agreement with ABC is ideal.
. . . We will continue to support the Paralympics Games through our daily highlights
package on C7 and with Seven's ongoing sponsorship of Paralympian Donna
Ritchie.[8]

There was at least one sign that Channel 7 may have regretted its "limited air-
time" position. Earlier on in the Paralympics, they were taken to task for sneak-
ing a camera into an event, without gaining permission. Channel 7 management
quickly apologized, claiming this breach of ABC and the host broadcaster's rights
was due to the isolated, misinformed actions of a particular camera operator.

It may be argued that the 2000 Paralympics marked a watershed in understanding and representation of disability in our society. Certainly, it is one of the
few times ever that one was able to switch on a substantial number of hours of
television in which a diversity of people with disabilities, from a range of cultures, were represented. Some have certainly suggested that such coverage by a
wide range of television programs, and in other media also, including regional
media, contributes to the questioning of stereotypes of people with disabilities. In
the aftermath of the Olympics there surged a wave of national self-congratulation
and celebration of the renewal of sociality and civility in Sydney itself. Similarly,
the Paralympics received plaudits for its spiritually uplifting character, for the efforts and achievements of its athletes. Perhaps because of the proximity of the
two events, many of the media genres and themes used for the Olympics were invoked in covering the Paralympics: profiles, flash quotes, post-events interviews,
postcoital speculation on Paralympic village promiscuity, outing of drug cheats.
There were not inconsiderable attempts to apply similar media practices in a non-
patronizing way to Paralympic events. And yet, after the Paralympics, it was media business as usual, in many ways.

We would question the extent to which the Paralympics represented a "break"
from the media episteme of disabling representations,[9] the prehistory of Paralympics. In the first place, it is the very hermetic separation between the
Olympics and Paralympics, the cordoning off of elite non-disabled sporting bodies from their "other," disabled ones, which is the visible sign that little has
changed. Despite the efforts made by many in the media to emphasize the "same-
ness" in the coverage accorded to the Paralympians, it is clear that the representation of disabled sport was, and remains, cast as fundamentally inferior to that of
the Olympics. Further, as some have observed in letters to the editor of newspapers, the celebration of the willpower and heroics—in short, the "supercrip"
status—of Paralympian athletes is the flipside of another phenomenon: namely,
the unstated criticism of, or at least the avoidance of the life experiences and circumstances of, those people with disabilities who are not able to or do not wish
to aspire to the brief fame of the elite athlete. Many people with disabilities are
not able to compete in sports, or do not fit the narrow biomedical categories used
to classify Paralympic events. This was evidenced in Channel 7's sponsorship of

one Paralympian, without sponsoring athletes with disabilities in general, or recognizing at all the social nature of disability.

Within the discourse of the valorization of certain bodies, and even certain disabled bodies, in the cynosure of sporting excellence and national pride, as exemplary citizens, Paralympians ran a poor second; or rather, they ran outside the Olympic arena. We were able to find only two instances of explicit or iconic representation of disability in the opening ceremony, a theater in which the nation was very much being narrated. The first of these was a short sequence in which sign language accompanied the chorus of a song. The second was the image of legendary Australian athlete Betty Cuthbert in a wheelchair, one of the six famous Australian female athletes who ran a lap around the stadium as the privileged final torch bearers, in honor of one hundred years of women's participation in the Games. The wheelchair is the most often recognized signifier of disability, and in this case, Cuthbert was pushed by, and subject to, her fellow Australian athlete Raelene Boyd, rather than propelling herself or using an electric chair. It appears that no attempt was made to ensure that a disability-friendly equivalent of running occurred—or that they moved together in solidarity. Through the remainder of the Games, there was only one other significant moment featuring Paralympians—a women's and men's wheelchair event, which was shown during prime time on channel 7.[10]

DISABILITY AND OLYMPISM: JOKE OR TRAGEDY?

Not for the first time, disability was pushed to the very margins of the Olympics, evacuated nearly completely, and only allowed to reappear in the Paralympics. Yet there was a significant, near obsessive other representation of disabilities in the Olympics television coverage. On Australian television, this manifested itself in that most important part of commercial television—the advertisements were geared to non-disabled viewers, selling (presumably non-disabled) audiences to (putatively non-disabled) advertisers, by denigrating people with disabilities. Three ads with representations of people with disabilities played continually during the two weeks of the Olympics.

The first of these was an ad for the Australian Hahn brand of beer. The ad featured a narrator observing and commenting on the clumsy mishaps of a master brewer. The brewer is pictured dancing with his wife, but letting her go on a whirl, and so she slams into a pillar. Then a friend is shown leaving the building, as the brewer has fixed his wheelchair. The chair accelerates out of control and flips its occupant over a stack of boxes, causing a slapstick-style accident. The final sequence is the narrator presiding over a beer tasting, praising the brewer for his exquisite taste.

An ad for another Australian beer, Toohey's, also revolved around a humorous portrayal of disability. It opens with a scene where a man looks into his fridge to find some dog food, without any luck. He reluctantly puts the leash on his small dog and takes it for a walk to the store. Passing the local pub, the man is invited in by a friend to have a drink. However, the sign on the door reads "No dogs allowed." To get around this proscription, the fellow dons dark glasses and pretends he is blind. Fronting the bar, he requests a schooner (large glass) of beer. The barman looks at him askance, and points out that "no dogs are allowed." The man responds that this is a "guide dog." Sceptically, the barman replies that guide dogs are usually "German shepherds or Labradors." To which, we get the punch line: "What have they given me then?" The man's friends laugh uproariously, while the barman smiles to his colleague and pulls the man a beer.

A third ad, also on high rotation during the Olympics, was more ambivalent in its representation of disability. This was an ad for McDonald's, set in a retirement village or nursing home. The older people depicted are sick of the quality of their food. After the main meal has been finished, they put their scheme in action. This involves checking that the coast is clear, and sending one of their number, an intrepid older woman, off on her scooter to McDonald's. Once she is at McDonald's she uses a mobile phone to take everyone's order, and then returns with the food.

These three ads each in their own way take a more or less traditional approach to disability as an easily recognizable joke. The Hahn beer ad draws on slapstick or burlesque conventions. That a man in a wheelchair is flipped over like a cartoon is presented as a laugh, and otherwise, quite unremarkable (much like the woman who is flung into the pillar). That someone who apparently has full sight might impersonate a blind man harks back to one of the oldest gags in the history of that precursor to television, the movies. Martin F. Norden has pointed out that the earliest representations of disability in motion pictures were turn-of-the-twentieth-century comedies about mendicants who pose as blind or physically disabled people in order to boost their begging prospects.[11] That a woman in a scooter is the mock hero of a gently comic plot by older people to sneak out to McDonald's for better food is benign, by contrast with the first two ads. Yet, even in this ad there are problems: there is not really a representation of reality of someone on a scooter, in terms of the way this technology affords extra mobility, allowing someone to get on or off. Albeit in an ad of short duration, the woman is depicted as confined to the scooter, or to a chair—not as moving independently at all.

Disability, then, is nigh invisible in television coverage of the Olympics, and the Olympics itself. Where it is present in the ads that frame the sporting action, disability is caricatured and mocked. Ads designed to get attention actually do represent those exceptions to the wonderful, non-disabled glorious, ideologically laden norms celebrated on our TV screens, as in the series of ads for Westpac, an Australian bank, that contrasted the feeble athletic efforts of the family members of athletes with the sporting prowess of the heroes themselves: "I don't how he/she does it!" These ads also reinforce the exceptional elite nature of Olympians by contrasting them with the mere mortals who are their parents or siblings. Similar in a sense, but more offensive and derogatory, are these disability-as-butt-of-the-joke ads, where a putatively non-disabled viewer is invited to have a laugh over the heads of people with disabilities. The structure of the humor here is revealing, as it is predicated on the otherness of disability and aging to all that glamorous sporting action. From disinterest to saturation coverage through to ads, the Olympics and the Paralympics are important examples of how the ableist construction of disability through dominant modes of television is still largely uncontested.

Against such a backdrop of traditional broadcast television disinterest in or disabling representation of people with disabilities, it is significant that the most comprehensive, informed, and sympathetic television coverage of the Paralympics, and disability generally, came from a new medium: the Internet. As the exemplar of a convergent, network digital media, the Internet has already been identified as a source of considerable challenge to the broadcast television paradigm.[12] Television and media are huge, globally integrated industries, and nowhere is the huge scale and scope of this better demonstrated than by the enormous sums of money involved in sport,[13] the pinnacle of which is the Olympics.[14] Broadcast rights for the Olympics are the subject of great contest and controversy, and once secured they are jealously guarded from any infringements. In the 2000 Olympics, the Olympics broadcast rights holder NBC vigilantly fought any attempt by nonauthorized parties to place information, pictures, or footage on the Internet. NBC itself had concentrated on television coverage—lackluster and little-watched in the United States due to the difficulties with the time-difference—and made little effort to provide any information on a more time- and location-independent not to mention increasingly popular medium, namely, the Internet. Neither NBC (for lack of innovation and foresight) nor other broadcasters, website, or Internet providers (for lack of ownership of rights, and justified fear of prosecution), seriously used the Internet to broadcast the Olympics. Innovation in this area came from elsewhere: the Paralympics.

The Paralympics is exempt from International Olympic Committee (IOC) rules banning moving pictures being shown on the web. Thus over one hundred hours of the Paralympics were web cast live—a first for the Olympics and Paralympics. Internet coverage was provided by U.S.-based We Media Inc., the operator of We Sports, an online sports network for people with disabilities. Coverage included live streaming video, real-time audio, and "extensive" coverage of the entire event through their website.[15] As well as video coverage of the games, We Sports provided breaking news, athlete profiles, full results, and summaries. Such coverage was doubly significant given the almost hysterical, and quixotic, proscription of Internet broadcasting by the Olympics organizers in order to protect the right of television broadcast rights holders.[16]

DIGITAL DISABILITY TV

Having considered the representation of disability on TV, we would now like to go beyond the scenes and screens to the construction of disability in digital television. Although a relatively new technology, digital television has had a checkered history already in the number of Western countries where it has been introduced. Fundamental policy decisions in relation to digital television in different jurisdictions have been typically a behind-closed-doors affair, with little scope for genuine citizen involvement in the making of these crucial decisions.[17] At center stage have been issues of access to new digital technologies in the television area and promotion of competition to redress oligopolistic domination. In all of this an especially crucial area of television culture has been very much overlooked in mainstream public debate: access to existing and future television offerings for people with disabilities.[18]

One of the key arenas in which these issues have been fought out is captioning standards. Captioning of television programs allows the audio component of a television broadcast to be displayed as text on the screen to assist Deaf people and people with hearing disabilities to follow the program. There are two main types of captioning: closed and open. The Federal Communications Commission (FCC) has noted that the first use of captions in the United States was in the early 1970s in an "open" format, transmitted with the visible video picture so that they appeared to all viewers. To minimize objections to captioning, the Public Broadcasting Service proceeded to develop closed captioning.[19] Closed captioning requires a decoder, and the captions are normally positioned at the bottom of the screen beneath the speaker. The captions are timed to synchronize with speech, and may include descriptions of sounds, laughter, and music. By contrast, open captions do not require a decoder and are permanently displayed on screen. (Subtitles are similar to open captions, but only cover the text, not any additional audio information.) Closed captioning has been available in a limited way for some years on analog television: in the 1970, the FCC granted PBS a number of authorizations to conduct experimental transmissions using closed captioning, and in 1976, adopted rules that line twenty-one of the vertical blanking interval was to be primarily used for the transmission of closed captioning.[20]

The first significant legislative recognition of captioning occurred with the 1990 *Television Decoder Circuitry Act*. To put this into effect, the FCC developed regulations requiring all television broadcast receivers with screen sizes thirteen inches or larger that were manufactured or imported on or after July 1, 1993, to be capable of receiving and displaying closed captions. These rules also specified relevant technical standards for reception, and also for captioning data carried on cable television systems. While the technology was available from the early 1990s onward, there was no requirement that programming need be captioned— apart from all federally funded public service announcements (mandated in the 1990 *Americans with Disabilities Act*). Available captioning until the mid-1990s relied on the voluntary efforts of program makers and broadcasters, but insufficient programs were broadcast with captions.[21] In light of foreshadowed legislative proposals, the FCC gave notice of an inquiry in 1995. The FCC requested comments on a number of pertinent issues, including the capacity of digital television to carry captioning and the role of the free market forces in promoting the availability of closed captioning. The FCC gathered submissions and information, but the inquiry was superseded by the sweeping telecommunications reforms heralded by the 1996 *Telecommunications Act,* which included significant disability accessibility measures. The 1996 *Telecommunications Act* amended the 1934 *Communications Act* with the aim of ensuring that video services were accessible to people with hearing and visual disabilities. While there had been a significant increase in the amount of video programming with captioning since the 1990 *Television Decoder Act,* it was Congress's concern "to ensure that all Americans ultimately have access to video services and programs particularly as video programming becomes an increasingly important part of the home, school and workplace."[22] The promulgation of the 1996 *Telecommunications Act* gave sharper focus to captioning issues, with directions to the FCC to inquire into the accessibility of video programming to individuals with hearing and visual disabilities.[23] As a result, the FCC adopted rules and implementation schedules to ensure that video programming is accessible via closed captioning to persons with hearing disabilities. In April 2000, the FCC adopted rules to require broadcasters, cable operators, and other multichannel video programming distributors to make local emergency information that they provide to viewers available to persons with hearing disabilities: "The FCC concluded that critical aural information that affects the safety of viewers must be made available to persons with hearing disabilities."[24]

In addition to audio captioning, the other key issue regarding people with disabilities and digital television is that of video description. Video description is the description of key visual elements, inserted into natural pauses in the audio of the programming. The purpose of video description is to make television programming more accessible to the many Americans who have vision impairment. It has developed from audio description, which developed from the 1970s and early 1980s onward as a means of providing for blind and vision-impaired people a verbal description of live theater, art works or museums, sport and other public events, or movies.[25] In the early 1980s there were pioneering efforts in the United States to provide description of broadcast television and video. One of the main providers, WGBH's "Descriptive Video Service,"[26] was established in 1986, and the other, "Narrative Television Network (NTN),"[27] started in 1988.[28] Similarly to captioning, digital television offers new possibilities for video description to be incorporated as an everyday part of television viewing. The enhanced transmission and reception capabilities of digital television mean that extra audio channels can be provided to carry the video description data for those listeners or viewers who desire it. Understanding the importance of digital television for people with disabilities, WGBH's National Center for Accessible Media (NCAM) undertook a number of innovative measures to ensure that technical standards, equipment, and policies were in place to enable the video description capabilities of digital television to become a reality.

The FCC adopted rules regarding video description in July 2000 (though two of the commissioners dissented in part, and issued separate statements).[29] Notice of the proposed rulemaking was given in a press release by FCC Chairman William Kennard, who rhapsodized over attending a screening of *Star Wars*, with video description, in Seattle.[30] Kennard pointed out that people "with visual disabilities watch television in similar numbers and with similar frequency to the general population," and that the issue of disabilities cannot be an afterthought—especially as an estimated eight to twelve million Americans have visual disabilities and thus will directly benefit from video description. Among other things, the FCC order required affiliates of the top four commercial broadcast TV networks in the top twenty-five TV markets to provide fifty hours per calendar quarter of prime-time and/or children's programming with video description. Similar requirements apply also to multichannel video programming distributors (of a certain size and market). Petitions for reconsideration of this rule and order have been subsequently made. On the one hand, cable television stations and motion picture organizations sought to question the FCC's authority to make such rules, as well as the basis for the decision. On the other hand, the National Federation of the Blind (NFB) submitted that the measure should go further: information scrolled across the TV screen must also be described, not just some entertainment programs.

While the NFB took this position regarding the provision of essential information, interestingly it took a different stance on descriptive video and entertainment. It joined with industry groups to oppose a move by some blind citizens, and the FCC in its rulemaking, to make video description of all entertainment compulsory: "The National Federation of the Blind has supported descriptive video, but it has consistently opposed the notion that audio-described films and television programming should be required by law."[31] According to NFB President Marc Maurer:

> We believe that prime-time TV entertainment and movies are presentations of artistic talent. We believe it is highly desirable to describe them so that the blind, along with the sighted, may enjoy them. However, we think freedom of expression should permit the artist (if the artist is particularly boneheaded) to leave the description out. . . . We have taken this position because we recognize that, for every accommodation demanded, a price will necessarily be paid in money, in acceptance of the blind in the greater society, in the influence blind people can have, and in good will.[32]

Captioning and video description have entered policy domains in the United States, and through the efforts of the disability movement and its supporters in particular, some significant steps have been taken to build accessibility into digital television. It comes as no surprise that unfortunately these efforts have taken quite a fight. Commercial media companies, equipment suppliers, and standards bodies have gone some way toward registering the needs and preferences of people with disabilities. However, many people with disabilities still did not have access to television and video programming. As a result, disability advocates have needed to build a case through detailed organizing, research, and intervention in state and federal regulatory processes, as well as in Congress also—with considerable achievements as a result. The role of the state in providing guidance and strictures on minimum standards for the marketplace has been important. One of the paradoxes in this, for U.S. political history, is that such state intervention took place under federal Republican as well as Democratic governments, at a time when the prevailing mood and ideology of both political parties was a stated bias against an active state. Nonetheless the United States enjoys certain advantages as the most wealthy, powerful country, where leaders in policy, communications and information technology, and manufacturing industries are headquartered. To gain a fuller sense of the difficulties and paradoxes of the construction of disability in digital television, it is worthwhile to briefly compare developments in the United States with a smaller country. We will use Australia, as an example well-known to us. Australia also has many advantages, as a wealthy member of the Organization for Economic Cooperation and Development, but it is a country that increasingly is a "technology-taker" rather than "maker" (despite its science and technology potential and achievements), with a smaller economy—thus the shaping of disability in its technology circuits is useful to observe.

In Australia, the government established a review of captioning standards, as one of nine reviews arising from the original July 1998 decisions on digital television,[33] considering whether there is a need for amendments to the 1992 *Broadcasting Services Act*. Commencing in January 1999, the review has been considering the issue of captioning standards in the *Broadcasting Services Act*. Captioning has been dealt with since 1992 as part of the self- or coregulatory arrangements. The Federation of Australian Commercial Television Stations Code of Practice has committed licensees to try to increase the amount of closed captioned programming. There is some evidence that this has been successful: the Seven Network captioned 85 percent of its prime-time programs in 1998; it also decided to provide captioning for much of the Olympics; and live unscripted programs such as budget speeches, election coverage, and current affairs are routinely captioned, as are live sporting events.

As part of the government's digital television policy, it moved to consolidate captioning by providing for the determination of standards in relation to the captioning of television programs for the Deaf and hearing impaired.[34] Two primary objectives were set out in relation to captioning:

> As far as is practicable, commercial and national television broadcasters should provide a captioning service for television programs transmitted during prime viewing hours (defined as between 6–10.30 pm);

As far as is practicable, broadcasters should provide a captioning service for television news programs and television current affairs programs, transmitted outside
prime viewing hours.

Following a first round of submissions by interested parties, the government issued an Options Paper.[35] The main argument concerned the cost of substantially
increasing the amount and type of programs captioned. The relevant section of
the *Broadcasting Services Act* called for "public interest considerations to be addressed in a way that does not impose unnecessary financial and administrative
burdens on providers of broadcasting services."[36] This clause provided a cue for
broadcasters to cite cost as one of the reasons why the captioning standard needs
to be phased in. For example, regional station WIN TV argued that partial captioning of just news announcers' introductions to each story combined with
graphics would "enable the hearing impaired to obtain a substantial flavour of the
news story involved."[37] It also pleaded for the possibility of the general exemp-
tion whereby digital television did not need to be available in country areas until
2004 to be extended further with respect to captioning. Yet claims that captioning
would substantially increase the cost of local news are put in context by figures
in the government's Options Paper showing that the cost of captioning in the
Southern New South Wales regional market would be about $600,000 against a
profit in 1997–1998 of $26.1 million. The government broadcaster, the Australian
Broadcasting Commission, took the opportunity to note that its present levels of
captioning were dependent on specific funding from the government.

For their part, disability groups and captioning providers were very critical of
the government's Options Paper. On behalf of the Australian Association of the
Deaf, a submission by Phil Harper pointed out that in fact the U.K. and U.S. governments were phasing in captioning of *all* programs. Similarly to the Australian
Caption Centre (ACC), the main provider of captioning in Australia, Harper argued that "there is no evidence that we are aware of any difficulties in captioning
programs," and that there "can seriously be no argument to support any difficulties broadcasters have with 'live unscripted programs, sport and news updates.'"[38] The ACC noted that it had sufficient time to plan for the 1 January 2001
implementation date, provided television networks finalized their captioning
arrangements a few months before this.[39]

Despite such arguments, the government did not heed the desires of the audiences, instead acceding to the wishes of the broadcasters. Its regulation requires
closed captioning for all prime-time programs, and for TV news and current affairs programs at any time these screen. The government did not mandate captioning for live sport or other live unscripted programs.

Apart from the limited nature of Australian government captioning policy decisions thus far, one of the more curious features of these decisions on digital television is that they did not at that stage cover pay television, and while they do
apply to multichanneling by publicly owned broadcasters (and in the future, com-

mercial broadcasters), other potential future developments in the digital broad-casting realm have not been well thought through. Yet these are areas where captioning is not substantially being provided, and which remain unaddressed, and unregulated, at the time of writing. We conclude that the Australian government's policy position of captioning in digital television was very much a reactive response. The government wished to extend captioning to digital television, but conceived this very much in terms of addressing existing gaps in basic television service—programming that most other Australian citizens have enjoyed during the 1990s at least. Ironically, the medium where "public" choices have to be made because of spectrum—that is, broadcast and digital terrestrial TV—has provided a less energetic response to issues of disability than the apparently greater freedom afforded by the Internet, as we discuss in chapter six. It seems that it is not just the "Wild West" character of the Internet that has generated some interest in accessibility and disability. Pay TV has done even less than heavily regulated broadcast television—it has simply reconstructed the inaccessibilities in multi-channel television that public policy has agonizingly moved to try to address in limited-channel free-to-air television.[40]

We reflect that one of the major problems with policy making on communications and media in Australia is that the specialist government policy arms—especially the Department of Communications, Information Technology, and the Arts—and the regulatory bodies—especially the Australian Communications Authority and the industry self-regulatory body, Australian Communications Industry Forum—do not take disability seriously at all. They lack skilled and experienced staff, especially those with direct knowledge and experience of living with disability, and so provide little leadership themselves. Disability also languishes at the margins of civil society and political life, and so is not taken seriously by government, parliamentary representatives, and the two main political blocs, the Liberal and National party coalition and the Australian Labor Party. Rather than the Australian Communications Authority—a similar, though also rather different, counterpart to the U.S. FCC—playing a leadership role in disability and communications in Australia, it is left to the under-funded and under-staffed Human Rights and Equal Opportunity Corporation to handle such issues, through its disability commissioner. We note that a similar phenomenon may be observed in other jurisdictions, such as Canada, where the Canadian Human Rights Tribunal handed down an important ruling urging the Canadian Broadcasting Corporation to consult with Deaf people and people with hearing disabilities on captioning:

> Like many people, Henry Vlug enjoys watching television. Unlike the majority of Canadians, however, Mr. Vlug cannot hear the audio portion of television programming as he is Deaf. At issue in this case is whether the Canadian Human Rights Act requires that the Canadian Broadcasting Corporation make all of its English language network and Newsworld television programming accessible to the deaf and hard of hearing.[41]

In drawing contrasts on digital television and disability in different countries, we do not assume that there is a straightforward sense in which one country is "ahead" or "in front" of the others. That is, we do not see accessibility for people with disabilities in digital television as something in which a straight line can be drawn across a graph to represent progress. In their rule making, more or less culturally sensitive and disability-aware as they might be, regulatory institutions, even ones with relatively more informed cultures such as the FCC, are still engaged in a process of constituting disability. In the case of closed captioning or video description, the FCC, akin to counterparts in other countries, defines what "access" for people with disabilities is, and, as a corollary, what benefits the technology might confer upon them. In doing so, such agencies do not engage with a number of other dimensions of disability. Try as they might, they may encompass further dimensions of disability, but will never be able to overcome it. Rather, the process of creating, deploying, defining, signifying, and resignifying the technology is a thoroughly social one—in which disability will always be created, enmeshed in a set of social relations of power. At the end of the day we choose in public policy and commercial decisions whether to build disability into our emerging television. Thus it is apparent that in many Western countries, the corporate interests, and negative notions of disability discussed in chapter one, still see disability incorporated into new technologies such as digital TV.

DIY DISABILITY

The construction of disability on digital television, briefly previewed in the preceding argument, has direct implications for what is often called "cultural citizenship." By cultural citizenship we refer to the right and opportunity of citizens to participate in the cultural life of a society. Television, video, and radio are important media for the conduct of everyday life and for access to information and entertainment.[42] These are media in which culture in its diverse contemporary forms is reproduced, created, and transformed, in which culture unfolds and happens. Ironically, one of the implications of the lack of video description or closed captioning in television is that the blind television viewer is potentially unable to properly appreciate, or enjoy, the gag in ads like the Toohey's ad (the man with the dog pretending to be blind to enjoy a beer).

Cultural citizenship is a complex, much-debated topic, but one of considerable significance for life in the contemporary world. Cultural citizenship has been rethought from the perspective of postmodern subjectivity and media forms. A useful example of such a recasting of cultural citizenship is leading television theorist John Hartley's notion of the "Do-It-Yourself-Citizen" (DIY citizen). Hartley proposes that "citizenship" is no longer simply a matter of a social contract between a state and subject, no longer even a matter of acculturation to the heritage of a given community; DIY citizenship is a choice people can make for themselves. . . . they can change a given identity, or move into or out of a repertoire of identities. . . . there's an increasing emphasis on *self*-determination as the foundation of citizenship.[43]

For Hartley, the DIY citizen engages in the "practice of putting together an identity from the available choices, patterns and opportunities on offer in the semiosphere and the mediasphere."[44] How do we learn this "difficult trick of 'suiting yourself,' as it were, while remaining locked into various actual and virtual, social and semiotic communities"?[45] Well, the screen's the thing: "Television audienceship provides the training ground."[46] In Hartley's view, television and media generally are crucial, because they produce the public sphere and its publics; the media play a role as a pervasive institution in circulating ideas analogous to that played by the church in medieval times.[47] So if we accept, with Hartley, that television is central to the mediated public sphere, especially because it teaches cultural citizenship, where does disability fit in?

Let us consider the DIY citizen in the light of the representation of disability on television, as, for example, in the ads shown during the Olympics discussed earlier. In the case of the Toohey's beer ad, we can now see that the new age Toohey's man grabs an "off-the-shelf-style" on the way to the pub: the DIY blind man kit. The semiotics of beer is quite significant for cultural studies, as Hartley shows elsewhere with a reading of beer bottle tops and the representation of indigenous culture,[48] so perhaps these beer ads should give us pause. When we review Hartley's notion of DIY citizenship via the optic of disability, we encounter a number of questions that deserve further exploration, not least issues of the appropriation and misappropriation of disabled identity. Postmodern and poststructuralist approaches to disability have much to offer, pointing as they do to the fluidity of identity and the possibilities for opening up new ways to imagine disability. The challenge, excitement, but also confusion of such new directions is signaled by the editors of a collection on disability, art, and culture, who describe disability as a "farrago of contradictory effects, in which there is no outside."[49] It is possible that cultural identity could well be just as radically decentred and decontextualized for people with disabilities watching the Olympics, and using television in all sorts of aberrant ways. At this stage of television's history, however, it does seem to us that the politics of DIY are rather different for many disabled citizens than they are for beer-drinking man (as in the Toohey's ad). It may be easier for some citizens (non-disabled ones, for instance) to have the freedom to assume identities and citizenship possibilities, and fully engage in the DIY postures, than others (people living with disabilities). The politics of identity and citizenship still too often place people with disabilities in less expansive, well-resourced positions compared to their non-disabled counterparts. Not all citizens have equal resources, opportunities, or secure positions from which to exercise the prerogatives of DIY citizenship.

To illustrate our point, let us consider another possible version of the DIY citizen: a Spanish basketballer with intellectual disability. A celebrated case during the 2000 Paralympics was the selection of Spaniards who apparently did not have intellectual disabilities, by national sporting selectors—allegedly to improve the team's overall performance. These Spaniards pretending to be disabled played in the national basketball team and shared in a gold medal victory. The incident came to light through the efforts of one of those selected, Carlos Ribagorda, a Spanish journalist, who wished to reveal this imposture of officials selecting non-disabled athletes and who published an article in the Spanish magazine *Capitol*, which was subsequently picked up by the London *Times* and then quickly caused a worldwide outcry. In response, the International Paralympic Committee suspended the whole category of athletes with an intellectual disability, of whom there were 244 competing in the 2000 Paralympics.[50]

There is a paradox here common to undercover work and entrapment: some athletes with disability are therefore pilloried for their alleged DIY imposture—while a journalist blowing the whistle wins gold. Some people are just pretending to be disabled, gaining special treatment and unfair advantage, and are labeled a "cheat." Who is allowed to identify, indeed "qualify," as someone with disability is strictly policed by non-disabled norms, a disciplinary arrangement of power with a long genealogy. To use Hartley's terms, television and media generally in the Spanish Paralympian case are certainly playing the role of citizenship educators, "teaching" populations who their others "are" in this instance—those who do not stay within the ordained bounds of disability stereotypes. The conclusion we draw is that citizens with disability have their DIY bricolage much more tightly constrained than many of their non-disabled counterparts.

Disability, we suggest, poses troubling questions for cultural citizenship in a digital future. As a starting point, we certainly agree with O'Regan and Cunningham on the need to "structure screen services for both majoritarian and minoritarian populations in the interest of equity, access and the acquisition of social and cultural capital."[51] There is a further opportunity here too, as our societies contemplate television after broadcasting. Such a rethinking of central media forms affords a chance, or raises an imperative perhaps, to recast cultural citizenship. Here disability poses a threshold question for the adequacy of any such concept of citizenship, cultural or otherwise. As the moral philosopher Alasdair Macintyre argues, "how we stand in relation to the plight of the presently disabled turns out to be a measure of ourselves and of our own moral education or miseducation . . . a verdict on us."[52] This is as true behind, on, and in front of digital television screens as it is elsewhere. The question is whether or not critical accounts of disability continue to lie discarded on the cutting-room floor. This is a question not just posed by digital broadcasting but another technology with which it is converging—the Internet.

NOTES

1. George Gilder, *Life after Television* (New York: Norton, 1992), 22–23.

2. John Simpson, *When a Word Is Worth a Thousand Pictures: Improved Television Access for Blind Viewers in the Digital Era* (Melbourne: Blind Citizens Australia, 1999), 25.

3. Jean Baudrillard, *The Gulf War Did Not Take Place*, trans. Paul Patton (Sydney: Power Publications, 1995). See also Baudrillard's *"L'esprit du terrorisme," Harper's Magazine* 304, no. 1821 (February 2002): 13–18; and other contributors to this issue discussing the events of 11 September 2001.

4. William Hoynes, *Public Television for Sale: Media, the Market and the Public Sphere* (Boulder, Colo.: Westview, 1994); Horace Newcomb, ed., *Television: The Critical View,* 6th ed. (New York: Oxford University Press, 2000); Michael Tracey, *The Decline and Fall of Public Service Broadcasting* (Oxford: Oxford University Press, 1998); Jan Wieten, Graham Murdock, and Peter Dahlgren, eds., *Television across Europe* (London: Sage, 2000).

5. Deirdre Boyle, *Subject to Change: Guerrilla Television Revisited* (New York: Oxford University Press, 1997); Laura R. Linder, *Public Access Television: America's Electronic Soapbox* (Westport, Conn.: Praeger, 1999); Dave Rushton, ed., *Citizen Television: A Local Dimension to Public Service Broadcasting* (London: John Libbey, 1993).

6. See Chris Forrester, *The Business of Digital Television* (Oxford: Focal Press, 2000).

7. A pioneering study is Lauri E. Klobas, *Disability Drama in Television and Film* (McFarland & Company, 1988). Also see a study conducted by the British Broadcasting Commission's Disability Unit: Guy Cumberbatch and Ralph Negrine, *Images of Disability on Television* (London: Routledge, 1992).

8. Sydney Paralympics Games Organising Committee, "ABC [Australian Broadcasting Commission] to Host Paralympic Games," press release, 13 March 2000.

9. On representation, see David T. Mitchell and Sharon L. Synder, "Representation and Its Discontents: The Uneasy Home of Disability in Literature and Film," in *Handbook of Disability Studies*, ed. Gary L. Albrecht, Katherine D. Seelman, and Michael Bury (Thousand Oaks, Calif.: London: Sage, 2001), 195–218.

10. For an extended discussion of media representation of the Paralympics, see our "Crippling Paralympics?: Media, Disability and Olympism," *Media International Australia* (2000) 97: 71–84.

11. Martin F. Norden, *The Cinema of Isolation: A History of Physical Disability in the Movies* (New Brunswick, N. J.: Rutgers University Press, 1994).

12. See Bruce W. Owen, *The Internet Challenge to Television* (Cambridge, Mass.: Harvard University Press, 1999).

13. David Rowe, *Sport, Culture and the Media* (Buckingham, U.K.: Open University Press, 1999).

14. M. de Moragas Spà, N. K. Rivenburgh, and J. F. Larson, *Television in the Olympics* (London: John Libbey, 1995).

15. We Media, www.wemedia.com [accessed September–October 2000].

16. K. Needham, "Who Needs Tickets When the Web Serves Up Front Row Seats?" "Olympics Historic Edition," *Sydney Morning Herald*, 16–17 September 2000, 11.

17. For discussion of these issues in relation to Australia see Terry Flew and Christina Spurgeon, "Television after Broadcasting," in *The Australian Television Book*, ed. Graeme

Turner and Stuart Cunningham (Sydney: Allen & Unwin, 2000), 69–85; Jock Given, *The Death of Broadcasting?* 2nd ed. (Sydney: University of New South Press, 2002).

18. Here we would note one signal contribution, Tom O'Regan and Stuart Cunningham's useful discussion of people with disabilities and television under the rubric of "marginalised audiences" in their "Marginalised Audiences," in *The Australian Television Book,* 201–12.

19. FCC, *Notice of Inquiry, in re Closed Captioning and Video Description of Video Programming,* MM Docket No. 95-176, FCC 95-484, paragraph 3; www.fcc.gov [accessed 2 December 2000].

20. FCC, *Notice of Inquiry,* MM Docket No 95-176, paragraph 4.

21. At the time of the announcement of the inquiry, the FCC believed that approximately 70 percent of broadcast network programming was closed captioned, including nearly 100 percent of broadcast network prime-time programming, and nearly 100 percent of nationally broadcast public television programming. However, on available information only 4 percent of basic cable programming and 35 percent of premium cable programming were captioned (FCC, *Notice of Inquiry,* MM Docket No 95-176, paragraph 13).

22. FCC, *Report in the Matter of Closed Captioning,* paragraph 4.

23. FCC, *Implementation of Video Description of Video Programming: Report and Order,* MM Docket No. 99-339 (Washington, D.C.: FCC, 2000); www.fcc.gov (2 December 2000).

24. "FCC Orders Increased Accessibility of Video Programming to Viewers with Hearing Disabilities," Press release, April 13, 2000 (Washington, D.C.: FCC); www.fcc.gov [accessed 2 December 2000].

25. Simpson, *When a Word Is Worth a Thousand Pictures,* 29.

26. WGBH homepage is at: www.wgbh.org.

27. Narrative Television Network homepage is at: www.narrativetv.com.

28. Simpson, *When a Word Is Worth a Thousand Pictures,* 31–32.

29. FCC, *Implementation of Video Description of Video Programming: Report and Order.*

30. William Kennard, *Notice of Proposed Rulemaking on Video Description,* 18 November 1999, FCC (Washington, D.C.: FCC); www.fcc.gov [accessed 2 December 2000].

31. Marc Maurer, "From the President's Mail Basket: Reflections on Descriptive Videos," *Braille Monitor,* 41.5 (May 2001), www.nfb.org/BM/BM01/BM0105/bm010506.htm [accessed 15 March 2002].

32. Maurer, "From the President's Mail Basket." The 2000 NBF convention in Atlanta, Georgia, passed a resolution calling upon the "Federal Communications Commission to modify its currently proposed and narrowly focused mandate for descriptive video in favor of one that would prioritize making important on-screen textual information universally available to America's blind television viewers through a standardized audio format" ("Recent NFB Resolutions Concerning Descriptive Video," *Braille Monitor,* 41.5 [2001]).

33. For the Australian context of digital television, see Productivity Commission, *Broadcasting Inquiry: Final Report* (Melbourne: Productivity Commission, 2000); Julian Thomas, "It's Later Than You Think: The Productivity Commission's Broadcasting Inquiry and Beyond," *Media International Australia* 95 (2000): 9–18.

34. Department of Communications, Information Technology and the Arts (DCITA), *Review into the Captioning Requirements of the* Broadcasting Services Act 1992: *Issues Paper* (Canberra: DCITA, 1999); www.dcita.gov.au [accessed 15 November 2000].

35. DCITA, *Review into the Captioning Requirements of the* Broadcasting Services Act

1992: *Options Paper* (Canberra: DCITA, 1999); www.dcita.gov.au [accessed 15 November 2000].

36. Section 4 (2), *Broadcasting Services Act* 1992.

37. WIN TV, *Review into the Captioning Requirements of the* Broadcasting Services Act 1992: *Options Paper: Submission* (Wollongong, Australia: WIN, 1999); www.dcita.gov.au [accessed 15 November 2000].

38. Australian Association of the Deaf (AAD), *Review into the Captioning Requirements of the* Broadcasting Services Act 1992: *Options Paper: Submission* (Sydney: AAD, 1999); www.dcita.gov.au [accessed 15 November 2000].

39. ACC, *Review into the Captioning Requirements of the* Broadcasting Services Act 1992: *Options Paper: Submission* (Sydney: ACC, 1999); www.dcita.gov.au [accessed 15 November 2000].

40. Our thanks for Jock Given for this point.

41. *Henry Vlug and Canadian Human Rights Commission and Canadian Broadcasting Corporation*, Reasons for Decision, Canadian Human Rights Tribunal, T557/1500, 15 November 2000.

42. Toby Miller, *Technologies of Truth: Cultural Citizenship and the Popular Media* (Minneapolis: University of Minnesota Press, 1998).

43. John Hartley, *Uses of Television* (New York: Routledge, 2000), 178.

44. Hartley, *Uses of Television*, 178.

45. Hartley, *Uses of Television*, 178.

46. Hartley, *Uses of Television*, 178.

47. John Hartley, *The Politics of Pictures: The Creation of the Public in the Age of Popular Media* (London: Routledge, 1992).

48. John Hartley and Alan McKee, *The Indigenous Public Sphere: The Reporting and Reception of Aboriginal Issues in the Australian Media* (Oxford: Oxford University Press, 2000).

49. Susan Crutchfield and Marcy Epstein, eds., *Points of Contact: Disability, Art, and Culture* (Ann Arbor: University of Michigan Press, 2000), 9.

50. Owen Slot, "More Paralympic Cheats Than Originally Feared," *The (Melbourne) Age*, Monday 5 February 2001.

51. O'Regan and Cunningham, "Marginalised Audiences," 211.

52. Alasdair Macintyre, "The Need for a Standard of Care," in Leslie Pickering Francis and Anita Silvers, eds., *Americans with Disabilities: Exploring Implications of the Law for Individuals and Institutions* (New York: Routledge, 2000), 86.

Chapter Six

Blind Spots on the Internet

[W]e can use the computer to do all sorts of wonderful things which can assist individuals who have various disabilities. At this point, the computer still looks like a "good guy". But that's only half of the story. Let's look at the other half— where computers have the very great potential of creating new barriers and widening the gap between disabled and able-bodied people rather than helping the disabled individual overcome these gaps.

—Gregg C. Vanderheiden, 1983[1]

As we move towards a highly connected world, it is critical that the Web be usable by anyone, regardless of individual capabilities and disabilities. . . . The W3C is committed to removing accessibility barriers for all people with disabilities—including the deaf, blind, physically challenged, and cognitive or visually impaired. We plan to work aggressively with government, industry, and community leaders to establish and attain Web accessibility goals.

—Tim Berners-Lee, 1997[2]

STORIES AND BLIND SPOTS

The Internet has been one of the fast-growing communications technologies in recorded history. Though it has its origins in U.S. military research in the 1960s, the Internet did not really come into its own until the 1990s, when its staggering growth swept all before it. The invention of the World-Wide Web in 1989 made the Internet much easier to use, bringing together different information transfer systems (file transfer protocol; search engines such as Archie and Veronica; and programs such as telnet, chat programs, and even e-mail). Combined with the adoption of point-and-click graphic user interfaces and mice for IBM PC-based computers, the Internet could by early 1990s be accessed without the requirement

that users learn text-based applications or acquire a knowledge of the Unix operating system. Consequently, the exponential growth of the Internet as a mass,
any-to-any medium from the early 1990s onward in more developed countries
saw the World-Wide Web became synonymous with the Internet, and widely regarded as accessible for most people who could afford to use it.[3]

Throughout much of its history to date, the Internet has been seen as something
of a utopia, something different—cyberspace—where normal limitations can be
transcended, and new freedoms found. A number of recurring themes and common myths will be familiar from debates on the Internet.[4] The Internet as zone of
utmost freedom, peopled by hackers and libertines, and well-nigh impossible to
regulate. The Internet as space of online communities. The Internet as a cornu-
copia of information and communication possibilities. Many people still believe
that the Internet remains, and should remain, a site of Jeffersonian individualism:
"In fact, life in cyberspace seems to be shaping up exactly like Thomas Jefferson
would have wanted: founded on the primacy of individual liberty and a commitment to pluralism, diversity, and community."[5] Where "information wants to be
free" (Stewart Brand),[6] and where open-source code[7] still stands a chance against
the monolithic digital overlords such as Bill Gates's Microsoft. The rise of the Internet as a mass medium has put into question some of these myths of the Internet, and they have been put under further strain by the emergence of the com-
mercialized and bureaucratized Internet.[8] Fostering visions of e-commerce and
new economy, business has staked its claim to the net. Regulators have sought to
make the Internet safe for the family, or, at least, through censorship and filtering
software, make the family better able to police and regulate some of its members
(usually children) on the Internet. Schools, universities, and adult education have
become web-based, and access to government information and services now
takes e-government forms.

What is striking about the history of the Internet, its contemporary forms, and
future visions, is that disability is both highly visible and curiously invisible in
its digital landscapes. The official story of many corporations is that the needs
and desires of people with disabilities are incorporated into planning for online
services, in line with business's new enthusiasm for using digital technology to
meet customers' needs and so making more money. "Touch Your Customers,"
Bill Gates says in his enthusiastic primer on how business can use a "digital
nervous system,"[9] but many people with disabilities are in the curious position
of being either untouchable or manhandled, or both by turns. The new myth of
the Internet is that people with disabilities are special beneficiaries of the Internet, and that their needs have been taken care of by technology designers, policymakers, and service providers. While the Internet has brought changes to the
lives of many people with disabilities, they have also been firmly kept in the
margins online or just left offline. More subtly too, the Internet has also ushered
in new dimensions of control.

It is this revisionary story we seek to tell in this chapter. Firstly, we look at the discourse on body and identity on the Internet, and how disability figures, and is figured. Secondly, we turn to the history of computing and disability, for a brief overview of how disability has been constructed in information technology. Thirdly, we take up the matter of one of the apparently more successful and well-known aspects of Internet accessibility for people with disabilities—the Web Accessibility Initiative.

NET BODIES

A great deal has been written on subjectivity and identity on the Internet, especially exploring the premise that identity can be freely assumed or invented on the Internet.[10] Writers remain fascinated with the formation of subjectivity in spaces like multiuser spaces (such as the MOOs and MUDs, which were forerunners of chatrooms), with their ability to allow the user to logon as any identity they chose: "If you don't like to hang out in a 'chat house,' you can live in a world of vampires on Elysium, or be a cartoon character on ToonMUD or be a sleek, post-pubescent otter on FurryMuck, where you can have Netsex with a fish."[11] With this fashioning of the subjectivity of the Internet user as "net"-head, or Internet user, there was a strong strain of utopian thinking emphasizing the overcoming of bodily limitations. Subjectivities and bodies online, the argument runs, are potentially very different from bodies offline. At issue here is a desire with a very long pedigree, namely the desire to transcend the body and to be released from its earthly limitations.[12] Yet such a philosophical and spiritual position has also long been contested, by those who point to the nature of bodies as far more complex. Thus we would hold that when we think about the multiple relationships between bodies and subjectivities in which technological mediation plays a critical role, it is clear that embodiment is indeed central to subjectivity.[13]

One early and influential contribution to rethinking embodiment in a net-worked computer environment is Allucquère Rosanne Stone's 1995 *The War of Desire and Technology at the Close of the Mechanical Age*.[14] Stone points to the need to reimagine the relationship between bodies and selves, and insists on the embodiment of subjectivity. She also argues that the "technosocial, the social mode of the computer nets, evokes unruly multiplicity as an integral part of social identity."[15] Stone proposes that

> The cyborg, the multiple personality, the technosocial subject, Gibson's cyberspace cowboy, all suggest a radical rewriting, in the technosocial space (which is largely constituted by textual production, much of which is the computer code by whose prosthetic mediation a significant portion of the space of technosociality exists), of the bounded individual as the standard social unit and validated social actant.[16]

Prosthesis is a key term in Stone's lexicon. In her opening chapter, Stone introduces herself:

> I have bad history: I am a person who fell in love with her own prostheses. Not once,
> but twice. Then I fell in love with somebody *else's* prosthesis.[17]

The prostheses that Stone refers to are a crystal set radio and recording console.
The other person's prosthesis to which she refers is physicist Stephen Hawking's
artificial speech device. Listening to Hawking lecturing provides a departure
point for Stone to meditate on the nature of the relationship between technology
and subjectivity:

> Hawking doesn't stop being Hawking at the edge of his visible body . . . a serious
> part of Hawking extends into the box in his lap. In mirror image, a serious part of
> that silicon and plastic assemblage in his lap extends into him as well. . . . No box,
> no discourse; in the absence of the prosthetic, Hawking's intellect becomes a tree
> falling in the forest with nobody around to hear it. On the other hand, with the box
> his voice is auditory and simultaneously electric, in a radically different way from
> that of a person *speaking* into a microphone. Where *does* he stop? Where are his
> edges? The issues his person and his communication prostheses raise are boundary
> debates, borderland/*frontera* questions.[18]

A prosthesis is a supplement to the body—an *artificial* limb, for example, with
the emphasis on artificial. For Stone, as with other theorists, the prosthesis is a
case in point of the difficulty of clearly demarcating between body and technology, human and machine, something which Donna Haraway and others have argued concerning the figure of the cyborg.[19] In Stone's case, disability provides a
touchstone, a prop, for her reflections here on the body and the difficulties of
defining where it begins and ends. Such an argument does have a point: as we
read Stone we could not help reflecting on the way in which one of us, who uses
a wheelchair, is particularly annoyed by people who lean on the chair, or put their
feet on it. It is truly a violation of personal space even if not physically part of the
body qua body.

Yet there is also something else unsettling transpiring in Stone's critical ma-
neuvers. This feeling of unease leads us to ask: what are the politics of Stone's
exemplum? Disability is invoked, to be sure. Yet, as with so much serious critical
work, disability is a category that remains curiously un(re)marked and unex-
plored.[20] We are reminded here of David T. Mitchell and Sharon L. Snyder's critique of the "extent to which a disabled citizenry is central to social theory and
postmodern philosophy."[21] They comment that the

> apparatus of disability shows up in numerous postmodern catalogs without comment
> on the conflictual relationships of disabled people to the equipment that theoretically
> affords them access to able-bodied populations, architectural structures, and cultural
> commodities.[22]

For her part, Stone does mention the "invisible ways, displaced in time and space, in which discourse of medical technology and their physical accretions already permeate him [Hawking] and us."[23] Despite this recognition of the role of medical discourse in constituting disability, she fails to identify the way in which this fundamentally shapes her own analysis and taken-for-granted views of Hawking of the disabled body.

In our view, a prosthesis is not only a signal of disability, but also an artifact of disability with all its tacit but important meanings. Hawking, and so many of us who identify as occupying that contested space which is disability, is embodied in his apparent disembodiment. In its embodiment all the problematic things attendant to his disabled body have been removed. He is asexual, is not threatening, is uniform, and has become the ultimate commodification of disability because people buy that package. Disability is pre-presented for audiences through dominant media representations; and Hawking's voice is determined through artificial speech synthesis technology in ways that reflect the power relations of disability: more than a hint of an American accent sounding curious for an Englishman. While questioning the prosthesis, Stone actually takes it for granted in a certain way, not troubling her view with any opinion of Hawking regarding the taken-for-granted notion of the prosthesis (something that is actually intimately connected with Hawking himself).[24]

We have identified how Stone relies upon yet forecloses on disability, and this might be thought to be an isolated example. However, this invocation of disability recurs in a telling context: Stone's celebrated discussion of the "cross-dressing psychiatrist" Sanford Lewin, a *locus classicus* in discussion of online identities. Stone begins with a brief history of role-playing games and MUDs. Following these preliminaries, she introduces the case of Lewin, a CompuServe user, who in the early 1980s created a persona called Julie Graham. When she first appeared online, Graham introduced herself as a New York neurophysiologist severely injured in a car accident. Stone explains that Graham claimed to have suffered "severe neurological damage to her head and spine, in particular to Broca's area, which controls speech. She was now mute and paraplegic."[25] As Stone tells the story, being online transforms Julie's life: "her personality began to flourish," "[s]he stopped thinking of suicide and began planning her life," and "as time went on, she became flamboyantly sexual."[26] Julie started a women's discussion group and policed its boundaries, unmasking pretenders, especially "men who masqueraded as women."[27] Julie related how she fell in love with a man who was not bothered by her "disability and disfigured face"[28] and how her career blossomed, with her husband's support. At this point friends became suspicious of how perfect the husband figure seemed, especially women with disabilities online. Lewin himself become worried about how to sustain the pose of Julie, and introduced himself as a close friend of Julie. Eventually the Julie Graham persona disintegrated, leaving many grieving, as well as angry with Lewin for what they felt was his deception and betrayal.

For Stone, the incident demonstrates something of the deep changes to subjectivity at stake in digital networks, "radical changes in social conventions, some of which would go unnoticed . . . until an event like a disabled woman who is revealed to be "only" a persona—not a true name at all."[29] In her following chapter elaborating the theoretical implications of this and another case study, Stone suggests that such encounters are about the "relationships between bodies and personae/selves/subjects, and the multiplicities of connections between them," and about "negotiating realities, and the conjunction of social spaces and activities bound together by webs of physical and ideological force."[30] She argues that our experience of inhabiting our bodies and the physical map we have of them is socially mediated, and so too is the location of the self that inhabits such bodies. Drawing upon this insight, Stone seeks to establish a framework that "allows us to interpret the world of high-speed communications technology as a cultural framework within which social interaction can be understood as 'normal' and can be studied in the same way as other social systems."[31]

While Stone's framework is useful, she does not use her own critical framework with regard to the taken-for-granted—disability and its social mediation in and through technology. Indeed the politics of disability in the case of the psychiatrist passing as a disabled woman is quite unremarked. The prosthesis in this text may also be a narrative one, to employ David T. Mitchell and Sharon L. Snyder's terminology, rhetorically propping up Stone's argument.[32] In any case, Stone's most direct gloss is an obviously problematic one. In the course of Stone discussing the debriefing among chat participants about Julie Graham's unmasking, she reflects on the following:

> Perhaps most telling was the rethinking, among Julie's closest friends, of their attitudes towards Julie's disability. One said, "In retrospect, we went out of our way to believe her. . . . So everybody was bending over backward to extend praise and support and caring to this disabled person. . . . in fact there was a lot of patronizing going on that we didn't recognize at the time."[33]

In interrogating this text we wish to pause at this point and remark on our response to Stone's text, in light of our own lived experience. One of us reflects, "What is the thing that I do that offends people the most? Of course, it is when I get out of my [wheel]chair and walk." We suspect that this gives offense to many because they had nicely compartmentalized the person with disability— you over *there* as the other. According to the stereotype, a person with disability is *confined* to a chair, despite the reality of most people who use wheelchairs *not* being in this situation. Everyone on the Internet adopts a persona. Nonetheless when that persona revolves around disability—even on the Internet—one is seen as faking and offensive if departing from a fixed, reified identity position (such as a person with a disability). Curiously when others take on non-disabled roles it is liberating.[34]

We have dwelt at some length on the double-movement of rhetorical reliance upon yet eclipse of disability in Stone's explorations of body and subjectivity on the Internet. While Stone's study is now just one of many accounts of these matters, we feel that there is something significant and even representative here in how studies of the Internet have engaged with disability. Take, for instance, Mark Poster's 2001 book *What's the Matter with the Internet?*[35] After making his way through such topics as subjectivity, authorship, nations, and identities, and virtual ethnicity, Poster's concluding chapter tackles the issue of "CyberDemocracy: Internet as a Public Sphere?" The final section of the chapter examines gender and virtual communities, claiming that there "is an articulation of gender on the Internet that goes beyond the reproduction of real-life hierarchies to instantiate new conditions of inscription."[36] The case Poster turns to is the same one used by Stone (although via an earlier account, upon which Stone also draws).[37] Poster provides the following gloss:

> The construction of gender in this example indicates a level of complexity not accounted for by the supposition that cultural and social forms are or are not transferable to the Internet. . . . In cyberspace, one may create and live a gendered identity that differs from one's daily life persona. . . . Nonetheless the structural conditions of communicating in Internet communities do introduce resistances to and breaks with these gender determinations, including sexual preferences. The fact of having to decide on one's gender and sexual preference itself raises the issue of individual identity in a novel and compelling manner.[38]

Poster's argument is a compelling one, yet he, like most other theorists of the Internet, does not take up the opportunity to think about embodiment and subjectivity from a disability perspective.[39]

Indeed, discourses on net bodies and disability have been rarely challenged or interrogated at a popular or theoretical level.[40] An inspection of leading anthologies and introductory textbooks on the Internet show that disability is rarely, if ever, considered. Yet the roll call of topics in these texts invariably includes community, identity, gender, race, political economy, cyberspace, governance, ideology (the titles of the first eight chapters of the 2000 text *Unspun: Key Concepts for Understanding the World Wide Web*,[41] an example chosen at random). Alternative, critical histories of the Internet are only now being written,[42] yet disability is still rarely encountered there. Likewise, the emerging discipline of Internet studies, and scholarship regarding the Internet in general, have not explored the social, cultural, and discursive construction of disability. While critical disability studies has recently emerged in a number of countries as an important body of theory, Internet studies has had very little engagement with this. Talk of cyborg bodies is obligatory—why is disability ignored?

One reason why disability is a lacuna in Internet studies is that disability at a deep level is routinely conceptualized as deficit, drawing from medical discourse. This would explain why it makes sense for such theorists to separate disability from other social categories such as gender or sexuality (and then to "forget" to discuss disability). In contrast, we would point to the need to conceptualize disability as a social space, then, think of it in terms of diversity: in this regard, to see it in analytically similar terms to gender and sexuality. The implication would be that disability is inextricably bound together with gender and sexual identity formation, and needs be recognized and analyzed.

COMPUTING DISABILITY

While the cultural construction of bodies and identities on the Internet and their relationship to disability has rarely been analyzed, disability is often mentioned in everyday discussions of web design on the Internet. We believe that this discourse on web accessibility and disability is indeed important and becoming more widespread but that it only represents a starting point; more importantly, that it needs to be critically situated in an account of how disability has been constructed in the technological world of computing and computer networks.

With the rise of personal computers, the needs of people with disabilities to be incorporated into this latest cultural technology saw a set of contests over the three main technologies involved: hardware, operating systems, and applications.[43] Issues for people with disabilities with microcomputers were well on the agenda by the early 1980s, as may be seen by a special issue of computer industry *Byte* magazine in September 1982.[44] The consumer and disability movements took an early lead, as, for instance, in the formation in Illinois in 1981 of the Committee of Personal Computers and the Handicapped (COPH-2). As one of its members describes it, COPH was an innovation in social organization, which saw people with disabilities interact as equals with others with an interest and stake in computer technology:

> Consumers, industry representatives, rehabilitation providers, and advocates are members of COPH-2, and they innovatively interact as peers. There are no referrals by physicians, no comprehensive evaluations by teams, no costly charges by institutions, no hard sells by computer representatives, and no rejections on the grounds of infeasibility as COPH-2 members readily share ideas, leads, information, and assistance. This new form of activity makes more rapid the utilization of information bearing on computer use by people with disability and tends to forestall the culture gap resulting from the computerization of society.[45]

Work on specialized assistive technology,[46] whether hardware or software, for people with disabilities continued to yield interesting results,[47] not least given the potential range of input and output devices that could be used in conjunction with computers, such as braille embossers, for instance, to provide documents readable by blind people, and software for speech synthesis.[48] Breakthroughs in accessibility of mainstream computing technology proved harder to come by, as

Mary Ellen Reihing makes plain in a 1987 article in the National Federation of the Blind (NFB)'s *Braille Monitor*:

> The Apple Macintosh is particularly hard to use because it depends heavily on graphics. Some word processors "paint" pictures of letters on the screen instead of using standard computer codes, and speech or Braille devices can't cope.[49]

Reihing spells out a crucial barrier still faced by many people with disabilities in using computers:

> Fantasy: All you have to do is plug in your computer, and it'll be the answer to your access prayers. Fact: Every speech, Braille, or large print method for getting information from computers requires the user to learn an extra skill above and beyond the skills sighted people need. Blind people must know more to get the same work done.[50]

The double-bind of computing technology led to mounting concern among people with disabilities:

> Blind computer users increasingly find that their inability to access the GUI-[graphical-user interface] based programs being used more and more in the workplace is costing jobs. Unless something is done to counteract the trend, the situation will only get worse. As if this were not bad enough, household appliances and publicly accessible information terminals are increasingly unuseable to anyone who cannot read the LCD [liquid crystal display] or CRT screen displays. Therefore, the future jobs of thousands of blind people and their ability to use household appliances and deal electronically with the rest of the world in years to come may well depend upon our capacity today to work together for the common good.[51]

The MS-DOS operating system was a text-based platform, and worked in conjunction with text-based programs such as early versions of Word or WordPerfect. Computer users who were blind or had a vision disability could use a screen reader to speak text. Microsoft's introduction of Windows, with its graphical-user interface, was hailed as a breakthrough by many, but seen as a grave threat by blind users. The seriousness of this predicament resulted in a clarion call from leaders of the blind community:

> It is extremely important that the technology experts among us settle down to work on the software and consumer-product access problems identified during our meetings and that the consumers and service providers then use our joint strength and creativity to influence mass-market computer program producers and consumer-technology manufacturers to insure that blind people have continued and increasing access to their products.[52]

This strategy had certainly been adopted by disability advocates, one of whom diplomatically remarked at the same conference, at which Greg Rosen from

Microsoft was attending, as well as other technology companies, that "Microsoft Corporation has demonstrated initiative in solving some of the problems resulting from their emphasis on the Windows computer environment."[53]

Relying on Microsoft's initiative was not sufficient, and so other strategies needed to be utilized, such as evoking legislative protections. One of these was the *Americans with Disabilities Act*, but another extremely important piece of legislation was section 508 of the 1973 *Rehabilitation Act* (as amended in 1986, 1992, then 1998). Section 508 requires that information technology procured, developed, maintained, and used by federal agencies must be accessible to people with disabilities, unless such requirement imposes an undue burden.[54] Effectively, the U.S. government and state governments could use, or be persuaded to use, their purchasing power to force companies such as Microsoft to make information technology accessible, or else miss out on lucrative government contracts. Activists in the state of Massachusetts took the lead here:

> The Massachusetts Commission for the Blind, the Massachusetts Assistive Technology Partnership, National Council on Disability [NCD], and various consumer organizations, banded together to demonstrate the incompatibility of Windows 3.1 with screen reader software to other state agencies responsible for purchasing and management of information systems. . . . The good news out of all this is that it convinced Microsoft to come to the bargaining table. After lengthy negotiations with the software giant, Microsoft has agreed to make Windows '95 more accessible across-the-board, and to work specifically on issues relating to screen reader access in general.[55]

Thus the disability movement fought pitched battles with Microsoft before they made serious efforts to make their operating system and programs accessible. As the NCD comments:

> Though mainstream developers certainly seemed in a position to pursue accessibility and compatibility, no law clearly obliged them to. Indeed, as sometimes happens in technology, some of the most highly touted advances in computer software and operating systems have actually set back the cause of computer access for people who were blind. The move from text-oriented DOS-based to graphical Windows-based computer operating systems resulted in precipitous losses in access (and, according to reports at the time, losses in jobs) for persons using speech or braille for their computer output. Largely unaided by mainstream developers, it took the AT industry several years to develop viable Windows-access strategies, and some say the ground lost has never been fully regained.[56]

Into the early 1990s Microsoft had only one person working on accessibility issues, and even as late as 1998 alienated the disability community by shipping Internet Explorer 4.0 with fewer accessibility features than version 3.0.[57] More recently, Microsoft has publicized its good corporate citizenry, such as a 2000 award from disability lifestyle *We Magazine* for leadership in hiring, accommodating, and creating accessible technologies for people with disabilities.[58] Despite the positive moves of corporations, accessibility of new software and hardware remains a threshold issue for the incorporation of people with disabilities in computing technology, and thus the information society.

WORLD-WIDE WEB AND CONTESTED ACCESSIBILITY

Accessibility for people with disabilities has figured quite prominently in the design and deployment of the World-Wide Web in the second half of the 1990s. The World-Wide Web Accessibility Initiative (WAI) was launched in April 1997, with the blessing of Tim Berners-Lee, one of those credited with inventing the web. The World-Wide Web consortium (W3C)'s three accessibility guidelines describe the common conventions that enable web accessibility: for websites (web content accessibility); for the software (authoring tools accessibility) that website designers use when they build websites (authoring tool accessibility guidelines); and for browsers (user agent accessibility). The WAI has raised the level of awareness of accessibility issues for people with disabilities among the Internet community, especially those designing and implementing web pages. In principle, information on how to make web pages accessible is easily available—through the Internet itself, of course. W3C is a *consortium* of organizations working consensually, and issuing recommendations. However, it is left to others to implement those recommendations, and many organizations do not do so. Hence accessibility for people with disabilities to the Internet remains quite precarious.

In 2000, the U.S. House of Representatives Subcommittee on the Constitution held hearings on whether it was necessary to regulate to guarantee web accessibility, such as applying the *Americans with Disabilities Act* to the Internet. Industry representatives argued against this, one of those testifying being the chair of the U.S. Internet Association, Dennis Hayes (familiar as the inventor of the Hayes asynchronous modem in 1977, the first PC modem). Hayes mentioned his own worsening eye condition, but put the view that

> the application of the ADA [Americans with Disabilities Act] to the Internet in some kind of "one-size-fits-all" mandate is not the right approach, for three reasons:
>
> 1. The Internet is an evolving media, not a physical structure. And it is a dynamic media that is changing at a rate that is not well suited to the regulatory style of the last century. If we apply regulations based on the technologies and possibilities of today, we may in fact limit the development of better access tools simply because we couldn't conceive of them when the regulation was drafted.
> 2. The variety of disabilities is too broad to address in a single piece of legislation. Attempting to define how accessibility should work for the visually-impaired will do little for the hearing-impaired, or the physically handicapped, or the cognitively challenged. Meeting the needs of some at the expense of others may be worse than no change at all.[59]

Putting an alternative perspective, Judy Brewer, director of the WAI, noted that

> in an industry with intense competition, for many companies these factors [demo-
> graphics of disability marketplace and carry-over benefits from accessible design]
> can be insufficient to lead to a critical mass of involvement in or implementation of
> Web accessibility. The presence of several regulatory processes in the background
> appears to have stimulated parties to come to the table who have not previously been
> involved in accessibility, and enabled other parties already working on accessibility
> within companies to leverage more attention and implementation commitments from
> product divisions that they work with.[60]

This contest over implementation of Internet accessibility underlines the fact
that the Internet remains inaccessible to many people with disabilities. Some of
the worst offenders in implementing basic Internet accessibility have been large
corporations, entities that surely enjoy sufficient resources to ensure that their
website administrators and designers understand and put in place accessibility
measures. Hayes and many in the Internet industry argue for ongoing dialogue as
represented by the WAI as the best way to educate providers and gain accessibility over time. Others, especially the disability movement, contest this view, and
have turned to legal remedies, such as the application of the *Americans with Disabilities Act*, to redefine accessibility.

RESISTING ACCESS

To gain a fuller sense of this contested accessibility of the Internet and World-
Wide Web, two cases are worth mentioning briefly here.

Firstly, the case of America Online (AOL) in the United States, where a number of blind people invoked the *Americans with Disabilities Act* to force AOL to
adopt accessibility measures.[61] For some years, the NFB filed a lawsuit against
AOL in November 1999, demanding that it make its online and Internet services
accessible to the blind, noting that it had nineteen million subscribers at that
time.[62] Blind citizens had been asking AOL for accessibility for some years. Following the filing of the suit, negotiations commenced between AOL and the NFB,
and the suit was suspended in July 2000 with AOL agreeing to make its software
accessible by April 2001. According to NFB sources, mixed progress was
achieved by the beginning of 2001, with accessibility for new products, such as
interactive television, being raised as matters of concern.[63] As well as improving
the accessibility of its software interfaces, AOL also appointed dedicated officers
charged with responsibility for accessibility issues—a strategy presumably aimed
at the cultivation of a company persona of sensitivity to customers with disability and thus the image of a "good corporate citizen."

These moves were part of an overall AOL accessibility policy that aimed to express the corporation's "commitment to the development of products and services

that are accessible to all users, including those with disabilities."[64] The policy included the integration of "accessibility considerations into the research and design of products and services."[65] Despite these steps, there was still widespread frustration at the beginning of 2002 with the accessibility of AOL's 7.0 software release. One of the issues was the compatibility between AOL's software and the commonly used JAWS for Windows screen reader package. Explaining the issues to a disgruntled member, Curtis Chong, the NFB's director of technology, noted in passing that

> AOL has already taken some small steps to provide useful information to customers with disabilities. The AOL Web site has an entire section devoted to issues of accessibility. . . . Ironically, the AOL Web site appears to be easier to use in some cases than the AOL client software—at least for the blind.[66]

The second case that illuminates accessibility struggles is that of the website of the 2000 Sydney Olympics, which led to the world's first successful legal challenge to an organization for discriminating against people with disabilities through an inaccessible website. As noted in chapter five, the 2000 Olympics was a titan among media events. Despite international media organizations zealously guarding their hard-fought, expensive television broadcasting rights against any unauthorized Internet broadcasting, the Internet was a crucial place for people around the world to find out latest results, breaking news, and more information on their sporting heroes, and, for those wishing to attend the Olympics, to be able to engage in transactions, such as viewing the program and purchasing tickets. With the growing popularity of the Internet as an everyday media form, the Sydney Organizing Committee for the Olympic Games (SOCOG) heavily resourced and promoted their website as the official portal and homepage for news, information, and transactions about the Olympics. However, the Sydney Olympics website was significantly inaccessible to blind users. Sydney resident Bruce Maguire was one person who wished to use the website but was unable to do so because the Olympic organizers had not ensured that the site conformed with the W3C guidelines on web accessibility.[67]

When this matter was formally brought to the attention of SOCOG, it rejected the need to make their site accessible, arguing that it was too costly to do so. Maguire made formal complaint to the Australian Human Rights and Equal Opportunity Commission in June 1999, which conducted a hearing. An initial reaction on the part of SOCOG was to suggest to Maguire that he enlist a sighted person to assist him. The commission determined in August 2000 that SOCOG had discriminated against Maguire on the basis of his disability by not providing an accessible website, something that, despite its protestations, it could have easily done:

> The provision of information by the respondent via its web site is, in the Commission's view, a service relating to the entertainment which the respondent will provide

to the world in the course of the Sydney Olympic Games. . . . The provision of an accessible web site for the complainant and other vision impaired persons constitutes a very considerable benefit. He and they could access precisely the same body of information which is available to sighted persons in relation to this event which during its currency will engage the attention of the whole nation. This considerable benefit will be available and the consequential detriment for the respondent will be modest. Indeed, had it sought to address the issue earlier it would have been easily consumed in the course of the development of the site.[68]

Despite an adverse determination, SOCOG still held out, refusing to fully comply, as the commissioner noted in his final decision on this matter:

much of the missing ALT text has been supplied,[69] although fairly important ALT text for images is either both missing or inaccurate. . . . In respect of the missing ALT text [the SOCOG representative] says that, given the level of inaccessibility, it would not have been reasonably possible for the complainant to get to the stage of identifying the missing ALT text which would affect the complainant's capacity to properly access the site.[70]

In the face of such willful obstruction, the commissioner awarded Maguire $20,000 in damages:

One cannot overstate the consequential effect upon him of his having to cope with the persistent need to counter what he saw as a negative, unhelpful and dismissive attitude on the part of an organization charged with the presentation of the most notable sporting event in the history of this country. This, in my view, was aggravated by his final inability to obtain the desired access to the web site in spite of his having established to the satisfaction of the Commission the fact that he had been unlawfully discriminated against.

DISABILITY AND THE FUTURE OF THE INTERNET

In the first part of this chapter, we argued that the social and cultural construction of disability on the Internet is a rich area of enquiry, and deserves to be taken seriously in Internet theory and scholarship. Not only does the current overlooking of disability in Internet and cultural studies need to be remedied, but the implications of critical understandings of disability need to be brought to bear on these disciplines. An engagement with disability is likely to pose serious challenges to how we understand central categories in Internet theory—something urgently needed at this time when it is being radically reconfigured, not least to comprehend the massive social changes at stake in Internet technocultures in their emergent convergent, broadband forms.

Following this, we have sought to establish that the Internet has been, and remains, a disabling technology for many people. There is a great deal of work underway on disability and the Internet, including many worthy and sophisticated endeavors that for reasons of space we have not been able to discuss here. Yet there are troubling concerns that the construction of disability on the Internet proceeds in largely unexamined and unrecognized ways, the result of which may be to circumscribe or deny the participation and aspirations of people with disabilities—as the cases of Microsoft, America Online, and the Sydney 2000 Olympics website indicate. In this light, we suspect that Shworles's concern expressed in 1983 that people with disabilities are "on the verge of experiencing a culture gap" still rings true. So too do his recommendations that

> New social forms are required in order to offset the imminent culture gap. It is recommended that consumers and consumer representatives become a part of the problem-solving process.[71]

These new social forms and broadening of the effective participation and representation of people with disabilities in the Internet is the topic of chapter seven—exploring how people with disabilities have been experimenting with and shaping Internet cultures, constructing new identities and exploring new modes of communication, subjectivity, representation, and media consumption.

NOTES

1. Gregg C. Vanderheiden, "Curbcuts and Computers: Providing Access to Computers and Information Systems for Disabled Individuals," in *Computers for the Disabled: Conference Papers*, ed. Janet E. Roehl (Menomonie: Stout Vocational Rehabilitation Institute, University of Wisconsin-Stout, 1983), 10.

2. Web Accessibility Initiative, "World Wide Web Consortium (W3C) Launches International Web Accessibility Initiative," press release, 7 April 1997, www.w3.org/Press/WAI-Launch.html.

3. Brian Kahin and James H. Keller, eds. *Coordinating the Internet* (Cambridge, Mass.: MIT Press, 1997).

4. Mark Stefik, ed., *Internet Dreams: Archetypes, Myths, and Metaphors* (Cambridge, Mass.: MIT Press, 1996).

5. Mitch Kapor, "Where Is the Digital Highway Really Heading?: The Case for a Jeffersonian Information Policy," *Wired* 1.03 (July/August 1993), www.wired.com/wired/archive/1.03/kapor.on.nii.html.

6. See John Perry Barlow, "The Economy of Ideas," *Wired* 2.03 (March 1994), www.wired.com/wired/archive/2.03/economy.ideas.html. Author and editor of *The Whole Earth Catalog*, and author of *The Media Lab: Inventing the Future at MIT* (New York: Penguin, 1988). Stewart Brand was associated with the famous Whole Earth 'Lectronic Link (WELL) bulletin board.

7. Read Eric S. Raymond, "The Cathedral and the Bazaar," *First Monday*, 3.3 (1998), www.firstmonday.org/issues/issue3_3/raymond/index.html, with Nikolai Bezroukov's "Open Source Software as a Special Type of Academic Research (Critique of Vulgar

Raymondism)," *First Monday*, 4.10 (1999), www.firstmonday.org/issues/issue4_10/ bezroukov/index.html. Also helpful is Lawrence Lessig, *Code and Other Laws of Cyberspace* (New York: Basic, 1999).

8. For critiques of dominant myths of computer and Internet culture, see Sean Cubitt, *Digital Aesthetics* (Thousand Oaks, Calif.: Sage, 1998); Rob Kling, ed., *Computerization and Controversy: Value Conflicts and Social Choices,* 2nd ed. (San Diego: Academic, 1996); Thomas Streeter, "Notes Towards a Political History of the Internet 1950–1983," *Media International Australia* 95 (2000): 131–46. See also Gerard Goggin, "Pay Per Browse?: The Web's Commercial Futures," in *Web.Studies: Rewiring Media Studies for the Digital Age*, ed. David Gauntlett (London: Arnold & Hodder, 2000), 103–12.

9. "Touch Your Customers," chapter 6 of Bill Gates, *Business @ the Speed of Thought: Using a Digital Nervous System* (New York: Warner, 1999), 91–113.

10. There is a voluminous popular and academic literature on identity and subjectivity on the Internet, including Sherry Turkle, *Life on the Screen: Identity in the Age of the Internet* (New York: Simon & Schuster, 1995); and Rob Shields, ed., *Cultures of Internet: Virtual Spaces, Real Histories, Living Bodies* (London: Sage, 1996).

11. Josh Quittner, "Johnny Manhattan Meets the Furry Muckers: Why Playing MUDs Is Becoming the Addiction of the '90s," *Wired* 2.03 (March 1994), www.wired.com/wired/archive/2.03/muds.html.

12. Margaret Wertheim, *The Pearly Gates of Cyberspace: A History of Space from Dante to the Internet* (Sydney: Doubleday, 1999).

13. Lelia Green, *Technoculture: From Alphabet to Cybersex* (Sydney: Allen & Unwin, 2002).

14. A. R. [Sandy] Stone, *The War of Desire and Technology at the Close of the Mechanical Age* (Cambridge, Mass.: MIT Press, 1995).

15. Stone, *War of Desire and Technology*, 42.

16. Stone, *War of Desire and Technology*, 43.

17. Stone, *War of Desire and Technology*, 5.

18. Stone, *War of Desire and Technology*, 5.

19. Donna Haraway, *Simians, Cyborgs, and Women: The Reinvention of Nature* (New York: Routledge, 1991).On the cyber and disability, see also Nick Moody, "Untapped Potential: The Representation of Disability/Special Ability in the Cyberpunk Workforce," *Convergence* (1997).

20. Paul Abberley, "The Spectre at the Feast: Disabled People and Social Theory," in Tom Shakespeare, *The Disability Reader: Social Science Perspectives* (London: Cassell, 1998), 79–93.

21. David T. Mitchell and Sharon L. Snyder, "Introduction: Disability Studies and the Double Bind of Representation," in *The Body and Physical Difference: Discourses of Disability*, ed. David T. Mitchell and Sharon L. Snyder (Ann Arbor: University of Michigan Press, 1997), 7.

22. Mitchell and Snyder, *The Body and Physical Difference*, 8.

23. Stone, *War of Desire and Technology*, 5.

24. On this point one of us reflects that people always want to talk about his wheelchair—far more than they want to talk about his life or relationships. When they talk about relationship they make themselves vulnerable, whereas a focus on technology can make for superficiality and a relationship at a safe remove. It is as if it is easier to fall in love with a chair than a person . . . being a person with disability one is not a "full" person any-

way. On these matters, see D. O. Braithwaite, "'Just How Much Did That Wheelchair Cost?': Management of Privacy Boundaries by Persons with Disabilities," *Western Journal of Speech Communications* 55 (1991): 254–74; and S. A. Fox and H. Giles, " 'Let the Wheelchair through': An Intergroup Approach to Interability Communication," in W. P. Robinson, ed., *Social Groups and Identity: The Developing Legacy of Henri Taffel* (Oxford: Butterworth Heinmann, 1996), 215–48.

25. Stone, *War of Desire and Technology*, 71. Here we have reproduced the terminology utilized by Stone, but would record our concern at now inappropriate terminology such as "mute" and the definition of people in accordance with disease labels, such as "paraplegic"—a critique well-made by many people with disabilities, in addition to the disability studies literature. Fulcher makes the point that this sort of nomination is part of the medical discourse of disability (Gillian Fulcher, *Disabling Policies?* [London: Falmer Press, 1989]).

26. Stone, *War of Desire and Technology*, 71–72.

27. Stone, *War of Desire and Technology*, 72.

28. Stone, *War of Desire and Technology*, 73.

29. Stone, *War of Desire and Technology*, 81.

30. Stone, *War of Desire and Technology*, 86.

31. Stone, *War of Desire and Technology*, 93.

32. D. T. Mitchell and S. L. Snyder, *Narrative Prosthesis: Disability and the Dependencies of Discourse* (Ann Arbor: University of Michigan Press, 2000).

33. Stone, *War of Desire and Technology*, 80.

34. Here we would point to the debate in the *Journal of Sexuality and Disability* on the status of people wishing to become, or pretending to be, amputees. For instance, see Richard L. Bruno, "Devotees, Pretenders and Wannabes: Two Cases of Factitious Disability Disorder," *Journal of Sexuality and Disability* 15 (1997): 243–60; John Money and Kent W. Simcoe, "Acrotomophilia, Sex and Disability: New Concepts and Case Reports," *Sexuality and Disability* 7 (1984–96): 43–50. See also Kath Duncan and Gerard Goggin, "'Something in your belly'—Fantasy, Disability and Desire in *My One-Legged Dream Lover*," *Disability Quarterly* 22.3 (Summer 2002), www.cds.hawaii.edu/DSQ/pdf/dsq_2002_summer.pdf.

35. Mark Poster, *What's the Matter with the Internet?* (Minneapolis: University of Minnesota Press, 2001).

36. Poster, *What's the Matter with the Internet?* 185.

37. L. Van Gelder, "The Strange Case of the Electronic Lover," in J. Lorber and S. Farrell, eds., *The Social Construction of Gender* (Newbury Park, Calif.: Sage, 1991).

38. Poster, *What's the Matter with the Internet?* 185.

39. In an otherwise rich and engaging essay, O'Brien also cites the Sanford Lewin case in its earlier reported form by Gelder. O'Brien uses the case to discuss sex and gender, but not does not treat disability (J. O'Brien, "Writing in the Body: Gender [Re]production in Online Interaction," in M. A. Smith and P. Kollock, eds. *Communities in Cyberspace* [London: Routledge, 1995], 88–89). In a discussion of cyborgs and bodies in cyberspace, David Bell mentions in passing another critic's discussion of disabled bodies but draws no implications for disability (David Bell, *Introduction to Cybercultures* [London: Routledge, 2001], 142).

40. A rare exception is Mike Featherstone's thoughtful discussion of age and disability in his "Post-bodies, Aging, and Virtual Reality," in David Bell and Barbara M. Kennedy,

The Cybercultures Reader (London: Routledge, 2000), 609–18. Significantly Feather-stone's essay was first published in Mike Featherstone and Andrew Wernick, ed., *Images of Aging: Cultural Representations of Later Life* (London: Routledge, 1995).

41. Thomas Swiss, ed., *Unspun: Key Concepts for Understanding the World-Wide Web* (New York: New York University Press, 2001).

42. For example, see Thomas Streeter, "Notes towards a Political History of the Internet 1950–1983," *Media International Australia* 95 (2000): 131–46.

43. For a "Brief History of Information and Technology Accessibility," see National Council on Disability, *The Accessible Future* (Washington, D.C.: NCD, 2001), chapter 2.

44. *Computers and the Disabled*, special issue of *Byte* 7, no. 9 (1982): 64–360.

45. T. Shworles, "The Person with Disability and the Benefits of the Microcomputer Revolution," in *Computers for the Disabled*, ed. Roehl, 18.

46. On assistive technology, see Barbara A. Kollodge, "Specialized Computer Applications," in *Assistive Technology: An Interdisciplinary Approach*, ed. Beverly K. Bain and Dawn Leger (New York: Churchill Livingstone, 1997).

47. For example, Julia M. Schofield, *Microcomputer-Based Aids for the Disabled* (London: Heyden & The British Computer Society, 1981).

48. A forerunner of this was the Kurzweil Reading machine invented in 1976, which converted print to speech.

49. Mary Ellen Reihing, "So You Don't Know Anything about Computers and Might Like to Nibble," *Braille Monitor* (August 1987), www.nfb.org/bm/bm87/brlm8708.htm [accessed 15 March 2002]. Despite these drawbacks, Apple Macintosh commenced their accessibility initiatives in 1985, and thus relatively early on incorporated accessibility into their standard operating system.

50. Reihing, "So You Don't Know Anything about Computers."

51. Kenneth Jernigan, "Note from the Chairman," *Proceedings of the 2nd U.S./Canada Conference on Technology for the Blind, November 4 to 6, 1993, Planned and Hosted by the National Federation of the Blind*, in *Braille Monitor* (January 1994), www.nfb.org/bm/bm94/brlm9401.htm, [accessed 15 March 2002]. At the time, Jernigan was president, North America/Caribbean Region, World Blind Union.

52. Jernigan, "Note from the Chairman."

53. T. V. Cranmer, "Emerging Research Goals in the Blindness Field," *Proceedings of the 2nd U.S./Canada Conference on Technology for the Blind*.

54. See discussion in NCD, *The Accessible Future,* chapter 2, section E.1, of the effect of the *Rehabilitation Act* and its amendments, which is dubbed the "leverage model."

55. Joseph J. Lazarro, "Light at the End of the Tunnel?" *Information Technology and Disability* 2 (1993), www.rit.edu/~easi/itd/itdv02n2/jobs.html.

56. NCD, *The Accessible Future*, chapter 2, section D.

57. "Greg Lowney: Microsoft's Director of Accessibility Is Motivated by the Millions of People His Work Will Benefit," 22 October 1998. *Microsoft Press Pass,* www.microsoft.com/presspass/features/1998/10-22lowney.asp.

58. "Microsoft Receives Award for Continued Leadership in Hiring, Accommodating and Creating Accessible Technologies for People with Disabilities," 7 February 2000. *Microsoft Press Pass*, www.microsoft.com/PressPass/features/2000/02-07we.asp.

59. Dennis C. Hayes, *Testimony before the House Subcommittee on the Constitution February 9, 2000,* Washington, D.C. www.house.gov/judiciary/hay30209.htm (1 February 2002).

60. Judy Brewer, *Statement before the U.S. House of Representatives Subcommittee on the Constitution, Wednesday, February 9, 2000,* www.w3.org/WAI/References/200002-Statement.html (1 February 2002).

61. This case is actually noted, albeit in a limited way, in one primer of Internet theory: see Andrew F. Wood and Matthew J. Smith, *Online Communication: Linking Technology, Identity, and Culture* (Mahwah, N.J.: Lawrence Erlbaum, 2001), 163.

62. Marc Maurer, "AOL Progress Report," *Braille Monitor* 42.2 (February 2001), www.nfb.org/BM/BM01/BM0102/bm010203.html [accessed 15 March 2002].

63. Maurer, "AOL Progress Report."

64. "America Online Accessibility Policy," www.corp.aol.com/access_policy.html (15 March 2002).

65. "America Online Accessibility Policy."

66. Brian Miller, "AOL Report," *Braille Monitor*, 45.2 (March 2002), www.nfb.org/bm/bm02/bm0203/bm020307.htm [accessed 15 March 2002]. For the AOL accessibility web site, see www.aol.com/accessibility/.

67. Maguire complained that SOCOG had failed to provide braille copies of the information required to place orders for Olympic Games tickets or the souvenir program, and also failed to provide an accessible website.

68. *Bruce Lindsay Maguire v. Sydney Organizing Committee for the Olympic Games,* reasons for decision, H 99/115 (Sydney: Human Rights and Equal Opportunity Commission, 24 August 2000; www.hreoc.gov.au.

69. The provision of alternative text when preparing, or marking-up, web pages (by use of the "ALT tag"), allows the provision of text to describe visual information. This ALT text information can then be interpreted by a blind user's screen reader, which uses speech synthesis to give the information. The use of ALT tags is perhaps the most basic recommended under the W3C guidelines.

70. *Bruce Lindsay Maguire v. Sydney Organizing Committee for the Olympic Games,* reasons for decision concerning relief, H 99/115a (Sydney: Human Rights and Equal Opportunity Commission, 18 November 2000; www.hreoc.gov.au).

71. T. Shworles, "Benefits of the Microcomputer Revolution," 18.

Chapter Seven

Cultures of Digital Disability

Dream with me, if you will, of a world where visually impaired people can independently have access to magazines, books, documents, data and even private mail. Imagine also a place where the most important thing is the power of your mind, a place where petty discrimination on account of your disability does not exist. In the real world, sighted people can be said to be "on-line." They can walk into any newsagent, book store or library and have access to any reading material that they desire. Visually impaired people, on the other hand, are "off-line" for the opposite reason. We cannot easily access print media without soliciting help or spending a fortune on specialized reading or magnifying equipment. . . . The *New Yorker* once carried a cartoon which showed two dogs sitting at computer terminals. One was saying to the other: "The good thing about the Internet is that no one knows you're a dog". . . . The anonymity and invisibility that the Internet provides us is a great leveller, and something much cherished by disabled people.

—Damon Rose, 1996[1]

Our discourse over cyberspace cannot be a merely passive one—even more than the nation, cyberspace must be imagined actively. . . . We study what is not because it will tell us what will be in any simple way, but because in understanding what is (and what has been) we can learn ways of imagining that discourage practices that should be hindered, as ways that help us set goals we can attain.

—David Hakkan, 1999[2]

In this chapter, we name and explore a strange phenomenon: cultures of digital disability. In previous chapters, we have developed a strong critique of disablist values within new media spaces, and indeed our technological society. Yet there are cultural spaces being transformed and created through digitization that have important implications for how disability is understood. As we will discover, some of the most exciting are those spaces created by those who live with disability themselves. Accordingly, this chapter will focus on the nature of, and possibilities for, cultural production by people with disabilities themselves in new media—including the generation of alternative representations of disability.

DISABILITY AND INTERACTIVITY

Interactivity is one of the great themes of new media. A pervasive myth is that networked digital technologies herald a shift from consumer to producer, from "couch potato" to "couch commando," as Nicholas Negroponte terms it.[3] There has been extensive debate on interactivity, and understanding what its attributes and possibilities in new media might actually be. Sally J. McMillan observes that "Interactivity is not unique to new media . . . But new media do facilitate interactivity in new environments."[4] McMillan distinguishes between user-to-user, user-to-documents, and user-to-system interactivity, contending that interactivity is a "multifaceted concept that resides in the users, the documents and the systems that facilitate interactive communication."[5] McMillan's caution regarding interactivity is an important one. Indeed the sorts of embodiment and subjectivity implied by hyperbolic claims about interactivity need to be closely scrutinized. The way interactivity is constructed discursively often naively purports to include people with disabilities, suggesting that the Internet offers us opportunities to become more active. However, the way that interactivity is framed creates new, circumscribing ways of managing people with disabilities.

Take, for instance, the well-meaning opening to an article by Susan Anne Fox on people with disabilities and computer-mediated communication:

> In 1986 it was estimated that in the United States there were 1.7 million "home-bound" people with disabilities and eight times that number who were temporarily disabled. Fifty years ago this could have meant social and personal isolation for these people who had limited physical means to interact with others, especially others with disabilities. Today assistive technologies are radically changing the lives of people with disabilities. . . . The World Wide Web . . . and computer-mediated communication . . . are greatly increasing the access of people with disabilities to information and interaction.[6]

Fox concludes that the web and computer-mediated communication "function as conduits to social interactions that were unavailable 15 years ago."[7] She notes that there is a great deal of disability-related information available via the Internet, and also that computer-mediated communication

> allows people with disabilities access to others to whom they would not normally have access in a medium that equalizes status cues. For people with disabilities,

[computer-mediated communication] may be one of the few media in which interactions are not mediated by the disability-related stigma and where a person with a disability can truly feel like a "person first."[8]

Of course, Fox has a traditional conception of interaction that she refurbishes for "computer-mediated communication." This is quite different from the revolutionary idea of interactivity favored by Negroponte and others. Yet both views share common views, we suggest, in their conception of the person—that disability, explicitly for Fox or implicitly for Negroponte, is a deficit to be overcome, redressed, or made invisible. Thus the Internet for Fox, and for Damon Rose too in another way, allows the death of disability—just as Frances Cairncross heralds the "death of distance";[9] the Internet abolishes disability, putting the disabled and temporarily able-bodied on an equal footing, courtesy of the medium that "equalizes status cues."

Common notions of disability and interactivity seem to be almost mutually exclusive. After all, dominant constructions of disability involve being the isolated "other," defined in terms of receiving and being acted upon, as opposed to imparting or contributing. Hence the agitating questions such as: "What advantages does [computer-mediated communication] provide for people with disabilities?"[10] Interactivity in a celebratory, Negropontean, sense is for someone else, the full human being, at least in the guise of possessive individualist[11] as celebrated in the pages of *Wired* magazine. The barriers for people with disabilities in achieving inclusion in utopian visions of interactivity are great, as our societies are not good at recognizing disability as part of the human condition. Despite this, we are now seeing the development of cultures that welcome and indeed embrace disability as a defining attribute for the online environment.

DISABLED ONLINE COMMUNITIES

There is a bewildering array of websites, information, newsgroups, discussion lists and groups, and chat rooms on the Internet concerned with disability, as a cursory visit to a search engine will show. Increasingly we also see that a variety of people with disabilities embrace the online world, indeed sometimes to the extent that they claim that the Internet removes their disability, as we have noted above.[12] Certainly when we reflect upon the role of the Internet in our lives as authors, academics, and activists, regardless of our disability, we can see how important it is.[13] Much of this book was written via e-mail and files exchanged over the Internet. Certainly, Christopher, as a person with mobility disability, has found his life revolutionized by the ability to work, write, and research online in the settings he requires, including home and hospital. Yet one of the questions we pondered as we logged on daily was whether the Internet removes disability, or does the online world merely create new dimensions of disability?

For many people with disabilities, the Internet offers possibilities to select, join, and shape communities of interest, if their present multiple communities are not satisfactory—or indeed if they wish to extend their realities and lives.[14] Deaf people, for instance, can search the Internet for a discussion group or chat room that piques their attention. They can log on anonymously, or with a "nic" (nickname), and post messages to the group at large. A website indexes over 175 blindness-related e-mail lists.[15] Yet upon closer examination, the online world reveals complexities and paradoxes. In searching the Internet we find that a search via common search engines, or as organized by leading providers, tends to reveal disability lists and sites defined in accordance with medical and charitable discourses.[16] There is a useful but small literature on the politics of search engines, but disability has not been addressed in such work as yet.

For example, a net search reveals a list for "Deaf and hard-of-hearing" people, and the list evidences more of single introductions than it does in-depth engagement by the participants. One person says he is "hard-of-hearing"; the next says she is "Deaf and proud of it." The cultural clash here is manifest: as discussed in chapter two, those who identify as hard-of-hearing identify as members of the hearing world, and those who see themselves as Deaf in terms of a cultural minority. Such open, indiscriminate spaces make mixing between people of different communities, cultures, and nationalities possible, as the hosts of Deaf-CHAT.com make clear: "Deaf and hearing visitors from all nations (and of all opinions) are welcome to log on and share fun chat and join in lively discussions and heated debates."[17] However, as we explored the online world we could not help reflecting that such lists can make for strange and ill-connected bed-fellows, perhaps resulting in the lack of in-depth discussion on many chat rooms, including this one. DeafCHAT.com claims to have

> attracted a sizable crowd of visitors from across the nation and around the globe. Many have become regulars, with new visitors logging on at all times. As of November 27, 2000, DeafChat has received 22,170,264 hits.[18]

Millions of hits may sound spectacular, but provides little evidence of real engagement or interest, as studies of Internet audience measure have shown. On the other hand, there is significant evidence of a thriving online world for people who identify culturally as being Deaf, where they may connect with other Deaf people. Lists abound with deep relationships and discussions built around shared meaning and understandings of the world. Interestingly such lists tend to be fostered by Deaf organizations or institutions and thus there is a significant connection between the online and offline world.

Another example is found in the online world of blind and vision impaired people, which crackles with energy, for those with adequate access (of course, that "adequate" so often depends on the notion of adaptive technology and "special needs"). However, once online we find that the technological requirements of blind and vision impaired people can assist in defining and constituting an online community. The index of blindness lists contains a category of "Index of Lists Which Are Not Blindness-Related, But Which Are Frequented by Blind and VI Members," including lists relating to computer software and languages (such as HTML web language, Java, Linux, CakeWalk music composition program, and Lynx text-only web browser) and technology (such as telephony).[19] The blind community has been constituted in accordance with medical discourse, with this being reinforced by the role of the state via legislation and welfare policy. Linked with this is the important role of charitable discourse, in particular the rise of blindness as a pressing social problem, especially following World War I, with war veterans.[20] Because of these dominant discourses and understandings of the world, and because these fit within dominant accounts of special needs and adaptive technology, the online world of a blind community is arguably more easily constituted than in other communities. Increasingly the emerging technologies help to constitute what it is to be blind. (We note, however, that the Internet is hardly a level playing field. Significantly limited options for blind people still exist because of the nature of the web, as discussed in chapter six. So much of the Internet remains inaccessible. Yet this inaccessibility is in itself constitutive and shaping. Thus chat rooms, seen as widely accessible by others, may not be favored by blind or vision impaired people.)

It is also noteworthy that a significant difference appears to exist between online blindness and other disability communities. The difference between Deaf and hard-of-hearing perspectives has already been discussed. A significant dimension of this difference lies in whether or not a person is born Deaf or becomes Deaf later in life. Likewise, in the current debates to do with developments in genetic and cloning technology, significant differences in worldview exist among people with physical disability. A difference can often be found in terms of people born with impairment or a condition, or who acquire it early in life, and people who have recently developed disability—and who still operate in accordance with disablist values.

For example, Christopher Reeve as construct and activist is much discussed by some disability activist lists. On one list, Reeve is discussed as the epitome of a person with acquired disability, prominent in media coverage as he seeks "the cure" ceaselessly.[21] Many discussants show how Reeve, while the darling of the media as a celebrated person with disability, still operates in accordance with disablist values.[22] Such online discussion helps to make clear the difference between impairment and disability. Reeve certainly has an impairment, but online discussion helps to make clear that in some lists he is not regarded as being part of the disability community—as having disability—and yet paradoxically as a male with quadriplegia surely he is the living stereotype of disability. The online community of disability becomes a key site for the discursive shaping of shared values. What is fascinating in all this is that on such a list that extends around the world there are a variety of nationalities, experiences of impairment, and hidden and obvious disability. The discussion of disablism—and the articulation of the shared and differing experience of oppression—is to be one of the constitutive parts of an online disability community. One example of many is the online bimonthly journal, *Bent: A Journal of Cripgay Voices*,[23] which received commendation from the Annenberg School of Communication's *Online Journalism Review*:

> "The twin crip/gay subject is a limited one, true, but it offers as many variations, as many ways of telling one another the truth, as there are talented and vocal gimps," writes editor Bob Guter, himself a bilateral amputee. Contributors to Bent offer highly personal essays that look unflinchingly at the problems and issues facing men who are both gay and disabled. Be warned, however: some articles are sexually explicit.[24]

The relative ease of publishing alternative material on the web and reaching disparate audiences has meant that disability cultures and subcultures can be constituted and constructed via the Internet, partaking in and contributing to the broader cultural impact of the Internet. As yet we are unaware that this cultural efflorescence has been charted and studied, as have the transformations relating to other cultural groupings.

These instances of the formation of communities of interest on the Internet—in the diverse and growing interactions of people with disabilities on e-mail discussion lists, web-based chat rooms, Internet messaging, websites, online magazines and journals, and other technologies—add to our understanding of the possibilities for disability cultures, and the way in which these are sociotemporal spaces. The notion of disability culture suggests that people with disabilities potentially have a shared "culture." Of course, culture is a notoriously slippery term, but remains an important one.[25] Disability studies scholars and those in the disability movement have been actively developing and debating ideas about how people with disabilities have a shared, if contested, notion of culture. Examples of disability culture are the disability arts movement, filmmaking by people with disabilities, and expressive writing, music, and art by people with disabilities. Official state arts funding and policy bodies typically now recognize "disability" as a legitimate, if firmly marginalized, quadrant of contemporary, more-or-less multicultural arts policy—an example of diversity in action, if not exception. Theorists of disability culture have sought to register some of the dimensions of disability culture.[26]

If we accept the notion of disability culture, contested as it is, we may argue that use of new media and communications technologies is actually constituting new cultural spaces for people with disabilities. As this phenomenon unfolds, there is as yet little critical discussion of the politics of digitization of disability. A starting point for such analysis in our view is the recognition, as we have argued before, that disability is constructed even in affirmative exchanges and rituals, in habitus (to use Pierre Bourdieu's term)[27] of everyday life. Both authors routinely participate in international lists about disability—and in so doing we help to create new dimensions of disability. Our point here is that a critical understanding of disability as culture means that we must move beyond disability as something done to us, to seeing that all of us, disabled or temporarily ablebodied, have a role in constituting disability, and that online disability is a vital and increasing dimension to this. The dominant construct is that we work to remove disability or barriers for people with disabilities. If what we suggest is correct, we will always have disability while society wishes to—and we actually create disability—including in discursive ways via the Internet.

"MAINSTREAM" NET SPACES

It is worth contrasting here the specialist or niche disability virtual spaces, inhabited by people with disabilities and those with diverse interests in disability, with more "mainstream" spaces. We deliberately take the terms "mainstream" and "mainstreaming" from the disability area. During the past decade in particular, mainstreaming was a central if problematic aim with regard to accommodation, education, and other life options for people with disabilities. It is still regarded as important, but when we visit the high-traffic, much visited, areas of the Internet, such as popular and "brand name" webs, "portals," and established media sites, we could not help concluding that there is a long way to go before people with disabilities are incorporated into the mainstream of online activity. At present, disability in its diversity is not often visible in such spaces, and thus such mainstream spaces are hardly disability friendly.

To elaborate this critique, we would like to go "walkabout" on the Internet, a trope we take from writing on Internet culture.[28] As David Bell suggests:

> Cyberspace is, I think, something to be understood as it is lived—while maps and stats give us one kind of insight into it, they are inadequate to the task of capturing the thoughts and feelings that come from, to take a mundane example, sending and receiving email. At one level, thinking of cyberspace as culture emphasizes this point: it is lived culture, made from people, machines and stories in everyday life. That's why I often turn to stories of my own and others' experiences with cyberspace.[29]

Accordingly, we asked a blind colleague, John, if we could visit several Internet sites with him. In visiting the Internet he used the screen-reading program JAWS for Windows (mentioned in chapter six). First, we visited a major telecommunications company site. The company in question has a well established consultation process with disability organizations, has had to respond to legal action on the grounds of discrimination against it by vision impaired advocates, and certainly has reason to seek to make its website disability friendly. As we trawl through the website and its links we discover the way in which disablist values shape it. Certainly the web page has a text only option that works, but the very number of links—over 150—provides a substantial challenge. The very number of choices constitutes a real navigation challenge, posing obstacles rather than merely being an impressive range of options. John tells how his advocacy organization had talked to the corporate affairs section of this corporation about the high number of web links and how difficult it was to navigate the site. In the name of choice some people with disabilities are presented with increasing challenges, so their actual choice diminishes. Unfortunately the result of the dialogue between the corporation and John's organization was that the amount of links on the site actually increased.

As we traveled with John, we noted that increasingly mainstream sites present a text only option for vision impaired people. This effectively means that there are *two* websites, with most web design resulting in the dominance of the non-disabled norm. Yet many people with vision impairment will not necessarily just want a text only option. There is a danger that the text only option will become a form of managing some people with disabilities. Accordingly we see the online environment incorporating non-disabled values and the notion of "special needs" being incorporated uncritically into the online world values that dominate the mainstream environment.

Another example of the apartheid of "special needs" was revealed with links from the telecommunications corporation website to other web pages to do with health, lifestyle, and travel. A visit to a linked health website was especially revealing. The discussion of disability prevention and dominant accounts of health and disease evident there presented dominant discourses long critiqued by the disability community. As we discover links to lifestyle and health products we also encounter images that speak volumes about what health, vitality, and normality are. Just as feminist accounts of advertising and health have critiqued dominant images, accounts that have largely been disregarded in the corporate world, so too can we reflect critically upon the disablist images widespread in the online world. Disabling representations are complicated by the fact that one of us, our blind colleague John, cannot even see them. With respect to some of the images encountered, Christopher ruefully reflects upon his own body and his struggle with fat since being very young, especially in light of medication he takes that causes excessive weight gain. The online world encountered in these links speaks volumes to those of us with disability about our bodies and our lives.

With John we then visited some travel sites directly linked to the corporate entity that in rhetoric supports diversity and antidiscrimination against people with disabilities. Christopher wants to make some plans to travel to a regional area, and very real issues exist as to how viable this will be for him as a person who uses wheelchair assistance and an oxygen cylinder. The rhetoric of, and images accompanying, the travel company website suggest that travel is seamless, one stop, and customer focused. Yet customer focus somehow left out people with disabilities. The information we require is not there and a response to an online inquiry says that "we will need to get back to you about your special needs request." A message later that day states that "you will need to contact the airline directly about your special needs and provide medical certification." Christopher's request is about his daily life experience and needs, he travels every week, and yet his travel requirements are treated as "special needs" by an online system that parallels and incorporates all of the disablist values found in the offline world. Rather than removing disability, the online world has incorporated another dimension.

Visions of e-commerce, in which those delivering products and services use the Internet, have proliferated, and now constitute a dominant aspect of the online medium. Despite the possibilities for reconceiving disability in the online environment, our travels in cyberspace with John reveal that many large companies are simply engaging in digital disability "shovel ware"—taking their existing disablist services and shifting them online. E-commerce has a long way to go before accessible, nondiscriminatory services are the norm, as the Australian Human Rights and Equal Opportunity Commission (HREOC) noted in 2001: "physical barriers, affordability and equipment access barriers, and attitudinal and awareness barriers are preventing some Australians with a disability and some older Australians from having equally effective access to e-commerce and other services using new technologies."[30]

Of course, many would argue that commerce is not the place to find pioneering work on removal of discrimination, espousal of equality, and recognition of diversity. Such critics are likely to suggest that a more auspicious space is civil society, a concept that has gained great popularity for its democracy potential.[31] Yet civil society too routinely overlooks disability, as national celebrations reveal. One interesting exception to this situation may be found in a case study in which an advocacy organization sought to use the online environment to create a discussion of disability across diverse sectors of society.

THE FASHIONING OF DISABILITY CULTURE: CIVILLY ONLINE

As we have shown, the online world can be disabling in a variety of ways. Yet people with disabilities and those interested in disability have created online communities and cultures that have significant positive dimensions, fostering supportive online environments. A particularly apposite case study is a 2001 online forum, "Action 2001: Turning Rhetoric into Reality," hosted by an Australian disability advocacy organization, Queensland Advocacy Inc.[32] This forum featured an online discussion list, active from May to August 2001, which complemented a face-to-face forum for four days in July 2001. Discussion, decisions, and action during the online forum focused on broad issues of community living, justice for all, and health and well-being. The online forum involved people with disabilities, their families and service providers, policymakers, service practitioners, governments, politicians, and the broader community drawn from the city of Brisbane, Queensland, as well as participants from national and international level with leaders in the disability arena, the social and economic policy arena, human rights arena, and the private sector.

The online forum was designed to provide energetic discussion, challenges, and opportunities for many people who otherwise would not have the chance to be involved in this event. Topical papers were presented on the Internet for discussion, and discussion was moderated. The online process had a number of aims: to generate information from people unable to attend the face-to-face discussion; to build interest in the activities following the forum; to help the participants to develop realistic expectations about the activity as a whole, and about the forum; and to build communication networks, for distributing and receiving information. The electronic forum was organized around topics which included bioethics, community living, education, employment, funding and support issues, and justice. The forum was very active, with 227 subscribers generating 724 e-mails, including a substantial international participation from fifteen countries, and heavy traffic on the QAI forum website.

We consider the Queensland Advocacy online forum to be a good example of how people with disabilities can participate in and help to constitute a civil society, including the online component of a civil society. The forum deliberately sought to eschew biomedical and charitable models of disability, even though there is no doubt some of the approaches of the diverse participants were informed by these. It is significant that a starting point was ensuring that people could participate equitably, and that issues of people not being able to participate readily using information technology were recognized. Organizers sought to include people who did not have direct Internet access, did not own a computer. If a participant needed someone else to relay the contents of the discussion list to them and to reply accordingly, this was possible, and several participants chose to do this.[33]

The online forum had particular rules of participation based upon the experience of people with disabilities in a variety of forums. The rules were about facilitating respectful relationships and understanding how deeply people who had spent their whole lives being marginalized and precluded from discussing their own lives could be hurt by e-mail comments. It was impressive to observe how comments that were ad hominem and struck a jarring note were dealt with. People with disabilities are just as capable of being hurtful toward each other as nondisabled people. Indeed many posts made by people were extremely personal, telling stories of abuse, sexuality, relationships, grief, and all other dimensions of life. People who had never met each other encountered each other in a space in which they obviously felt safe and affirmed as part of a supportive community.

Mediation was done by the coordinator of Queensland Advocacy, Kevin Cox, who lives with disability himself. This also meant that when breaches of protocol necessary to foster the mores of civil society occurred, rather than having a nondisabled person mediating it was someone who lives with disability who could shape this. The online forum culminated in a face-to-face forum of people with disabilities, focusing on their careers and families. People who wished to participate via the online world received a daily summary and transcript of sessions and were able to post comments for incorporation into the next day's face-to-face proceedings. Here the organizers sought to provide a variety of ways of people participating in a community that spanned the online and offline worlds.

We suspect that one of the main reasons that this online forum worked well for participants was because it was convened by Queensland Advocacy, as an organization where people with disabilities constitute the majority of the board. In effect, people with disabilities were able to establish their own discussion group, chat context, and cultural values, as opposed to much of the mainstream Internet, where one has to conform to norms and values—despite the wide range of possibilities in the Internet for alternative cultural practices and approaches. Indeed, we should not underestimate the importance of such an online event for the people concerned. It is also a symbol of a comprehensive, equitable conception of civil society online. For some people it was their first opportunity to talk about their experience of disability and to explore a vision of disability as part of a civil society, something difficult to do in an indifferent if not hostile public sphere. The online space provided a zone where anxiety could be nuanced and reduced as topics of daily importance were discussed. The way in which these topics were discussed stand in stark contrast with the mainstream websites discussed above. People were able to talk of how dominant notions of health oppressed them, to explore the paradox of being forced to rely upon health and disability services but in also being effectively disabled via such services.

Yet, even in such a seemingly benign and enabling environment we need to recall that disability is constructed; in online, as well as offline (RL or "real life") communities we create and replicate ideas of disability. Thus we contend that it is not that people lost their disability or even impairment in participating online. Rather in online interaction and exchange, those of us participating learned to understand the social nature of disability—while still clearly being online as embodied people with disabilities. The limits of the construction of disability can also still be observed. For example, there is no doubt that a variety of people, including people with intellectual disabilities, were effectively barred from equitable participation. People with intellectual disability are not well served by computers and computer network technology, precisely because of the tacit values built in the computers, screens, programs, and interfaces. Yet issues facing people with intellectual disabilities are rarely considered in relation to new media technologies. Instead, new media designers and providers tacitly share the dominant conception that it is the impaired intellect—even the retarded nature—of the individual that is the problem. This view of intellectual disability stands to reason in a world that reifies intellectual achievement. Rather than the experience of intellectual disability being too difficult (or irrelevant) to be considered in the design and implementation of new media technology, we suggest that, like other dimensions of disability, it is crucial to rethink the problem from the perspective of people with disabilities. For instance, if we care to put ourselves in the shoes of a person with intellectual disability, is it our problem? Or is it that of an unaccepting society and design that sees that person's realities as being too difficult, and thus incorporates disabling values? Here we cannot but help reflect that if all people with intellectual disabilities were multimillionaires, it is more likely that market-driven solutions would be incorporated into mainstream information technology design. Likewise, many people fitting within other constructs of disability may not communicate so well via text online, where face-to-face contact is preferred. Of course, this does raise the promise of future broadband potential, which would be important for a variety of disability groupings.

Among the many electronic forums that spring up and fade away, what then is the significance of the Queensland Advocacy Forum? Certainly it is another affirmative example of a creative electronic forum among the extraordinary diverse disability community, and thereby a contribution toward the evolving ensembles of disability cultures. It teaches us about the discursive shaping of disability within a broadly supportive virtual disability community. We also submit that the Queensland Advocacy Forum serves as an exemplar of things that are possible, showing us how aspects of an online civil society might operate. In the online exchange it was apparent that there is no agreed upon notion within the disability community as to what should constitute appropriate dialogue. Some people started with narratives of their life stories—compelling to the point that we were moved to tears. Those stories helped the forum to focus on how these were not just private troubles but public issues. Conflict seemed to center on the contested nature of ways in which one should analyze the issues facing people with disabilities, with language being the crucial issue. For some, academic analysis was seen as disempowering—they *knew* what disability was and indeed the problems. Others sought to use the tools of the academy to identify issues: in particular, to introduce topics that the disability community in Australia has largely been ill-equipped to deal with. Among people who are the subject and recipients of services, it is customary to talk about de-institutionalization or accommodation options, but topics such as technology policy and bioethics were felt by some to be alienating. The way in which these conflicts were managed was crucial to fostering a notion of community. In particular, people shared intimate details of their lives, making themselves vulnerable, and leading to a significant feeling of community.

THE ONLINE UNIVERSE

We have thus far reflected critically in this book on the way in which disability is created in new media spaces, based upon dominant accounts of disability. This is also encountered in exploring so-called mainstream online worlds. Yet we have also sought in this chapter to identify ways in which people who inhabit the online environment as members of the disability community have utilized specialized spaces in positive community building ways. There is certainly an ill-explored and insufficiently resourced possibility for emerging new media spaces for people with disabilities to provide more than disabling practices on the margins of digitization. In designing mainstream and specialized online spaces we need to ask: Whom do I wish to include in my moral community and whom do I wish to exclude?

This requires a move beyond the rhetoric of "inclusion" or "universal design,"[34] notwithstanding the importance of these strategies (as discussed in chapter eight). A starting point is the life experience and participation of those who are usually deemed "too difficult" to imagine as users of digital technology, especially newer technologies. This would involve putting the margins at the center. There is still great potential for fostering affirmative, creative, diverse, and capacious cultures of digital disability. The political question is whether we as a society will do so, or instead merely allow the online world to continue to be dominated and informed by the dominant approaches and discourses of disability that continue to create the need for positive but ultimately segregated specialized disability communities online.

NOTES

1. Damon Rose, "The Internet: Made for Blind People," *The New Beacon*, Royal National Institute of the Blind (U.K.), July 1996.

2. David Hakken, *Cyborgs@Cyberspace?: An Ethnographer Looks to the Future* (New York: Routledge, 1999), 228.

3. Nicholas Negroponte, *Being Digital* (New York: Knopf, 1995).

4. Sally J. McMillan, "Exploring Models of Interactivity from Multiple Research Traditions: Users, Documents, and Systems," in Leah Lievrouw and Sonia Livingstone, eds., *Handbook of New Media* (London: Sage, 2002), 163.

5. McMillan, "Exploring Models of Interactivity," 175.

6. Susan Anne Fox, "The Uses and Abuses of Computer-Mediated Communication for People with Disabilities," in *Handbook of Communication and People with Disabilities,* ed. Dawn O. Braithwaite and Teresa L. Thompson (Mahwah, N.J.: Lawrence Erlbaum Associates, 2000), 319.

7. Fox, "Use and Abuses of Computer-Mediated Communication," 333.

8. Fox, "Use and Abuses of Computer-Mediated Communication," 333.

9. Frances Cairncross, *The Death of Distance: How the Communications Revolution Will Change Our Lives* (London: Orion Business Books, 1998).

10. Fox, "Use and Abuses of Computer-Mediated Communication," 333.

11. Crawford Brough Macpherson, *The Political Theory of Possessive Individualism: Hobbes to Locke,* corrected ed. (Oxford: Clarendon Press, 1962).

12. "You can lose your disability on the Internet," suggests Jacob Baldwin, something that he implies comes from successfully mastering the medium: "Where do we find it all? On the Internet, if we know what we're looking for. If we don't, the gates of Internet Hades

will open and swallow us into Cyberspace, disability and all." See Baldwin's *The ADC Network Consumer's Guide to the Internet; or How I Lost My Disability on the Internet*; www.adcnetwork.net.au/lost_disability.htm [accessed 15 March 2002].

13. For an early account, see J. A. Nelson, "The Internet, the Virtual Community and Those with Disabilities," *Disability Studies Quarterly* 15 (1995): 15–20.

14. We note here the ongoing debate in relation to cyberculture as elsewhere on the dense, conflicted, and problematic category of community. See David Bell, *Introduction to Cybercultures* (London: Routledge, 2001), 92–112, or David Gauntlett, "Web.Studies: A User Guide," in David Gauntlett, ed., *Web.Studies* (London: Arnold and Hodder, 2000). Elsewhere Gauntlett has punctured the balloon of tired scholarship on virtual communities: "Publishers are still churning out books called Virtual Something and Cyber Something Else. They might as well be called 'Wow! Virtual communities!' and 'Holy cow! In cyberspace, no-one knows who you are!' Even the journals are still publishing those articles which people were pulling out of the drawer in 1996. Has no-one changed the record?" ("Internet Studies: What Went Wrong?" *Times Higher Education Supplement*, 22 September 2000; www.newmediastudies.com/webbook2.htm [accessed 24 March 2002]).

15. *BLIST: Comprehensive Index of Blindness-Related Emailing Lists*, www.hicom.net/~oedipus/blist.html [accessed 15 March 2002].

16. Vincent Miller, "Search Engines, Portals, and Global Capitalism," in *Web.Studies*, 113–21.

17. "About DeafCHAT.com," www.deafchat.com/learnmore.html [accessed 15 March 2002].

18. "About DeafCHAT.com."

19. BLIST: Comprehensive Index of Blindness-Related Emailing Lists.

20. Gabriel Farrell, *The Story of Blindness* (Cambridge, Mass.: Harvard University Press, 1956); Frances A. Koestler, *The Unseen Minority: A Social History of Blindness in America* (New York: David McKay, 1976); Floyd Maston, *Walking Alone and Marching Together: A History of the Organized Blind Movement in the US, 1940–1990* (Baltimore, Md.: National Federation of the Blind, 1990); June Rose, *Changing Focus: The Development of Blind Welfare in Britain* (London: Hutchinson, 1970).

21. See for example Reeve's advocacy with regard to stem cell research in stark contrast with such groups as the World Institute on Disability and the American Association of People with Disabilities, which have called for a moratorium on so-called "therapeutic cloning." See "Statement of Christopher Reeve, Chairman of the Christopher Reeve Paralysis Foundation," www.paralysis.org/news/releases.cfm?storyID=372 [accessed 20 March 2002].

22. For a sense of this debate, see the following exchange: Christopher Newell, "Christopher Reeve, Utilitarianism and Human Rights," *Access* (June/July 2002): 4–5; Christopher Reeve, "Christopher Reeve Responds to Dr. Newell," *Access* (June/July 2002): 6–7.

23. Bent: A Journal of Cripgay Voices, www.bentvoices.org/ [accessed 25 March 2002].

24. "Spike Report," *Online Journalism Review*, 13 April 2001, ojr.usc.edu/ [accessed 25 March 2002].

25. Raymond Williams, "Culture," *Keywords: A Vocabulary of Culture and Society* (New York: Oxford University Press, 1976); Tony Bennett, *Culture: A Reformer's Science* (Sydney: Allen & Unwin, 1998).

26. Susan Crutchfield and Marcy Epstein, ed., *Points of Contact: Disability, Art, and Culture* (Ann Arbor: University of Michigan Press, 2000).

27. Pierre Bourdieu, *Outline of a Theory of Practice*, trans. Richard Nice (Cambridge: Cambridge University Press, 1977).

28. "Sitting here, at my computer, pondering how to start this book, how to introduce my own 'walkabout' in cyberspace, I find myself struggling," David Bell, *Introduction to Cybercultures* (London: Routledge, 2001). Hakken's theory of a more engaged, experiential, reflexive ethnography of cyberspace leads him to confess: "My personal walkabout in cyberspace has given me glimpses of a truly different world, and I wish to share them," Hakken, *Cyborgs@Cyberspace?* 227. Christine Hine examines the role of travel in the "construction of a ethnographic authority" with respect to online worlds in her *Virtual Ethnography* (London: Sage, 2000), 44ff.

29. Bell, *Introduction to Cybercultures*, 2. See also his longer discussion of storytelling and cultures, 6–64.

30. HREOC, *Accessibility of Electronic Commerce and New Service and Information Technologies for Older Australians and People with a Disability* (Sydney: HREOC, 2001), www.hreoc.gov.au/disability_rights/inquiries/ecom/ecomrep.htm [accessed 24 March 2002].

31. See Sandra Braman and Annabelle Sreberny-Hohammadi, eds., *Globalization, Communication and Transnational Civil Society* (Cresskill, N.J.: Hampton Press, 1996).

32. See Queensland Advocacy website, www.qai.org.au.

33. There is some evidence suggesting that people with multiple and speech disabilities are not as well served by the Internet as even many other people with disabilities (Owens, J. et al., *Telecommunication Needs of People with Communication/Speech Difficulties* [Geelong, Australia: Deakin University, 1988]).

34. On universal design, see the work of the Trace Research and Development Centre, and explanation given at trace.wisc.edu/world/gen_ud.html ([accessed 28 March 2002].

Part Four

The Politics of Disabling Digitization

Chapter Eight

Rewiring Disability

We started this book in a sterile so-called "accessible" hotel room overlooking the Brisbane River. As we conclude this book in the same location, we would suggest that, in the spirit of our reexamination of that room as being indicative of power relations and dominant understandings of disability, so too have we sought to provide a book in which we rethink how we in society create disability, especially in relation to existing and emerging media technologies.

The hotel had proudly given us its "accessible" room. But what do we mean by "access"? Predominantly this room was designed for people who use small wheelchairs, who do not need hoists, and who do not have any other form of impairment, except of course the red and yellow emergency lights prominently displayed so as to ensure that those who cannot hear know when to evacuate the room. (We cannot help wryly reflecting on how useful the wheelchair accessible features will be for your "average" Deaf person.) In the name of inclusion, seeking to do the right thing, perhaps in part because of government regulations, the hotel has created further apartheid. Those with "special needs" are directed to this room. If you are Deaf—and do not see yourself as being disabled—welcome to the social technology that requires you to fit into dominant notions of disability and access. Furthermore, this room is hardly accessible for a whole range of people with impairments. For example, neither hotel owners, architects, and designers, nor the disability rights movement, has paid much regard to the needs of people with chemical sensitivities. Where is the access to be found in a carpet and chipboard furniture that outgasses? How accessible is this room really for a blind person (apart from the nice flashing light to tell them when they need to evacuate the building)?

In this book we have sought to show how society, consciously and unconsciously, has built in disability into digital technologies. Time and time again in the field of new media and communications technologies, our needs as people with disabilities are not met by a preexisting product or service. Then, just like

147

our accessible room, we are offered a special solution—and usually the stigma that accompanies being so very special, so other. Paradoxically, these new media technologies have become central to and formative of disability communities. For example, the text telephone typewriter has become a cultural artifact of the Deaf community, something that short-messaging via mobile phones is now in the process of becoming. For hard-of-hearing people the cochlear implant is an icon of hope and salvation, and inducts one into a cultural club. Similarly braille as a form of technology—and more recently the screen reader program JAWS for Windows—has been enormously important for and constitutive of the blind community, where endless debates otherwise occur around whether to use canes, dogs, or the latest sonic device. Regardless of whether we inhabit the techno-science worlds of disability, inevitably we find everyday media and communications technologies that not only enable or limit our activities but that frame our notions of choice and viable options.

We have argued for the need to critically analyze the ways in which disability is constructed in these central technologies of contemporary society, namely new digital media and communications technologies. We have sought to map the different discourses, institutions, politics, cultures, and histories that go together to produce "digital disability." One of the most surprising findings of our study is the persistent, willed, subterranean, enduring neglect of disability, and the reluctance of government, media and communications businesses, regulatory organizations, academics, and other important groups to seriously and critically engage with disability or with people with disabilities. With alarming regularity, wealthy corporations and governments have adopted new media policies that explicitly militate against the interests of people with disabilities; have again and again excluded people with disabilities from positions of power, authority, and decision making; have remained disinterested in new knowledge about disability and communications; have explicitly and implicitly discriminated against people on the basis of disability; have judged people with disabilities as costing more money than they are worth as customers; have relegated people with disabilities to the digital margins by seeing them as a "special" case, not part of the mainstream; have clung tightly to disabling value systems, such as those that ensure that disability products and services are the responsibility of junior staff, rather than senior managers or officials. In short, at the center of the new economy, of the information superhighway, of electronic commerce, of the dot.coms (and tech wreck), has been the eclipse of disability—the creation of digital disability.

On the face of it, one would expect that a great deal has changed over the last hundred years, as society has moved from the basic telephone and telegraph, through the telex and data communications, to the ubiquitous "always-on," ever-present, networked personal, wireless, and broadband devices of the twenty-first century. In the very origins of telephony, we see disability constructed: Bell inventing a device with deaf people in mind, yet the uses of this technology for most of the next hundred years excludes significant numbers of people with disabilities.

In the directions that telecommunications and new media are taking today, we see disability still being constructed—and this phenomenon still is not understood, appreciated, or acted upon. Digital disability for the majority remains framed by stubborn, deeply rooted, taken-for-granted notions. We critique such dominant cultural understandings of the world in this book, and highlight their limitations.

There have been significant initiatives taken by many organizations and individuals to look differently at disability: long-term pan-European initiatives on telecommunications and accessibility; participatory standards-setting activity such as the World-Wide Web Accessibility Initiative; partnerships among technologists, telecommunications and new media organizations, people with disabilities, and disability organizations, to develop new media and communications technologies that better meet the needs and expectations of people with disabilities. We note important work of the sort undertaken by the U.S.A. Trace Center or Gallaudet Institute, British Royal Institute of the Blind, or the European committees COST219 and COST 219bis; video telephony trials involving the Swedish Federation of the Deaf, technology companies, and Swedish carrier Telia, as partners; experiments in consumer consultation and research in Australia. We have sought to provide a critical assessment of such initiatives, and also to indicate the ways in which these too create, manage, and ultimately construct digital disability.

INCLUSION OR UNIVERSAL DESIGN

If we are to heed dominant accounts of disability and the incorporation of people with disabilities into all aspects of society, surely we must aim for inclusion. Certainly, inclusion has been one of the catchwords of the 1980s and 1990s. Yet in so striving or even achieving inclusion, we help to perpetuate the underlying problem, one that we have sought to identify in this book. Call it "inclusion," or "assimilation," dare we say "normalization,"[1] if we are not careful, then we privilege dominant disablist notions and structures, rather than challenging these. People with disabilities are expected to cut their cloth to fit the temporarily ablebodied world, and its new media technologies. Paradoxically, in its desire for the same, inclusion always requires the "other" to stay in its niche as it is pressed into the mold of the normal, rather than engaging with the real alterity and difference in an "us" relationship.

One way in which the problem of inclusion has been dealt with is in the emerging notion of universal design. Universal design is one of the solutions to accessibility and disability urged upon policymakers and technology shapers by the disability community and others. As an idea it has simplicity on its side, and so is easy for new media providers to grasp, in theory at least. There is no doubt that such an approach offers a great deal in reorienting thinking and design to factor in a variety of functional needs. Yet, a challenge for universal design is found in the very diversity of situations and human circumstances. How do we design a mobile phone handset that will meet all needs? We may need a small handset but the very smallness of the keys will preclude the use by many people with disabilities. Admittedly, provision for a variety of peripherals or "add-ons," such as an extended or modified keyboard, to be fitted, may take care of this particular issue. However, part of the problem in all of these technologies is that so often the change recommended comes down to designing for particular abstracted disability needs, rather than ensuring an engagement in the process of design and implementation with people with disabilities with all the messy realities they bring with them.

Underlying this abstracted notion, we suspect, is the question of whose vision of design is reflected in universal design. Certainly, universal design is worthy of aiming for, but whose account of universal design will win the day? Design of new technologies must take account of the different desires and visions of different groups in its process. Design itself needs to become genuinely participatory, allowing people with diverse and contradictory perspectives to bring these to bear upon the shaping of technology in all its facets, as well as the situations in which technology is used. We are more likely to come close to achieving universal design when we routinely have people with disabilities participating in not just all aspects of research and development but in all aspects of life. In reality, the challenge for new media and communications technology is to enable, sustain, and institutionalize the very relationships that will help to bring about those identified with disability as being the "us," part of the normal, and the natural. Accordingly, we would suggest that universal design joins a long list of discourses that could prove to be little more than window dressing unless the dominant discourses, understandings of the world, and structures—in short, disablism—are also addressed.

INSTITUTIONS OF DISABILITY

There are a variety of institutions, sites of power, in which occurs the framing of technology as salvation and inherently good. The state plays a crucial role in terms of funding, regulation, and shrouding disabling new media technologies with legitimacy, as the government leaders enjoy yet another media moment of triumph in helping those poor disabled folk. Regulatory institutions, established and bound by state legislation, yet very often playing an independent and extremely important role in shaping policy on technology, have also proved crucial to the construction of disability, and indeed its management.

In an epoch in which the state is being reshaped, the market takes on additional significance as a disabling institution. The market is now seen in dominant accounts to be the ultimate efficient, frictionless enabler of the goods of society. As such, its social relations of disability are all too rarely appreciated or put under the microscope. Yet given that the competition model has now been adopted by most countries, and underpins convergent media, information, and communications technologies, it is the policy making of corporations that grows in importance. The power of transnational corporations has become more keenly sensed, and registered in debates over governance and demands for transparency. John Ralston Saul has proposed that

> It is therefore a matter of inserting a citizen into the system in whatever way we can. Then letting the mechanisms of criticisms combined with high levels of involvement take effect.[2]

Despite such a desideratum, the populace is very rarely allowed to participate in the significant decisions of the boardroom, the office, or the shop front. Since its enunciation by then British Prime Minister Margaret Thatcher, and adoption by many governments since, shareholder democracy through privatization has not seen individual citizens sharing in the effective control and power of large corporations (even in the country that Napoleon once dubbed a "nation of shopkeepers"). Decisions made by transnational media and communications corporations directly affect people's everyday lives, yet citizens, even as titular shareholders, have little or no say in these.

To understand contemporary shaping of disability in new media, we need to map and engage with the shaping of technology by corporations, governments, and technologies. We also need to recognize and chart the ways that new institutions are purveying power. Thus in chapter three, for instance, we have pointed to the importance that "self-regulation" has assumed in telecommunications, becoming a twilight zone straddling the divide between traditional notions of the state and market. Here new analytics of power and disability are needed, drawing on and going beyond the work of theorists such as Foucault, to describe and critique the way that the state morphs into the market. We point here to the emergence of new organizational forms, to be observed in the example of the "third sector" of not-for-profit and nongovernmental organizations, even social movements, such as the disability movement itself, assuming new roles in response to changing notions of the state providing welfare assistance for citizens, and newly deeply implicated responsibilities for managing and constructing disability.

INTERVENTIONS WITH DISABILITY

A new disability-oriented vision of telecommunications requires a comprehensive set of strategies for each of the institutions that play a role in constructing the social, economic, political, and cultural dimensions of universal service.

Firstly, as the paramount democratic institution in telecommunications, governments may lay claim, in most cases, to being representative of citizens. As they represent people with disabilities and others who believe accessibility and a full engagement with disability is important, the state needs to take an active and responsive leadership role in embodying in policy and legislation accessibility and disability requirements. With the changes of nations and nation-states under the impress of globalization, supranational forums, such as the Organization for Economic Cooperation and Development, Asia-Pacific Cooperation, World Trade Organization, the World Bank, International Telecommunications Union, and international standards-setting bodies, accumulating power and influence daily, should also take similar steps.

Secondly, corporations have both an obligation and an opportunity to demonstrate their support for a new vision of disability. By understanding disability in all its dimensions, companies will enhance their understanding of the diverse needs and expectations of their customers. In this respect, accessibility and disability have much in common with marketing and product design where an understanding of consumer needs is critical for success. Shareholders, boards, management, and staff all need to incorporate accessibility, and a full understanding of disability, into their business plans, policies, strategies, and operations. New technologies can thereby incorporate the needs and aspirations of people with disabilities at the earliest stage, avoiding expensive and avoidable retrofitting of systems. The end result will definitely be better corporate image, but is also likely to be better corporate profitability.

Thirdly, government regulators have a key role to play in working with corporations and the community to ensure that telecommunications systems are accessible. Although regulators are often given the task of working through details of policy implementation, they are also policymakers in their own right—though in many countries, this fact is obscured or downplayed for political reasons. Regulators need to insert people with disabilities back into the circuits of policy and regulatory decision making, and also must ensure that people with disabilities are on staff in positions of power and authority in order that a critical capacity on disability be incorporated as an organizational strength.

Fourthly, reformation of the civil society and its institutions is pivotal for any vision of equality for people with disabilities in new media. Whereas dominant accounts of the civil society tend to avoid engagement with the realities of disability; whereas disability and people with disabilities are routinely excluded or "forgotten" in discussions of how society should work, how political arrangements are structured, who is a suitable leader, and other key questions of civil society; we pose this question: will the civil society of the future have a disabled face? Rather, we propose that civil society is a crucial space in which disability needs to be embraced, and that the institutions of civil society must be accorded greater recognition by commerce and the state. This is absolutely critical for democratic and diverse imaginings of disability in new media. The disability movement, community organizations, social welfare groups, consumer and public interest groups, older peoples' organizations, residents' associations, tenants' groups, and a myriad of other voluntary, not-for-profit, and nongovernmental organizations have a stake in telecommunications and new media policy, yet are forced to the margins of government and corporate decision making. Commitment to embracing disability requires innovative policy making processes that are open, transparent, and accountable. Citizens and their organizations should be involved at every level of decision making, and this means that participatory public inquiries into new technologies are essential. The representative nongovernmental organizations with an interest in telecommunications—the likes of Consumers' Telecommunications Network and Communications Law Centre in Australia, Consumers Federation of America in the United States, and the Consumers Association in the United Kingdom, as well as disability and other nongovernmental organizations—need to be adequately funded on an arms-length independent basis so that articulation of policy can be based on real needs of citizens, not just the perceptions and interests of business, government, or technology elites.

Finally, researchers and scholars of new media and communications technologies also need to grapple with questions of disability and accessibility. Some theorists do attempt to incorporate accessibility and equity into their concepts of new media, but the majority take a narrower view and continue to overlook disability, to conceptually straiten rather than engender new conceptions of new media.

WHITHER DIGITAL DISABILITY?

Will the promises accompanying new media be realized? In different accents and voices, we are ceaselessly promised that technology will deliver us from disability. Yet we would suggest not only that technology will never deliver society from the reality of disability, but that disability continues to be constructed through such technology. We can never supersede or overcome or do away with disability. As a sociopolitical space, disability will continue to exist, and technology will remain an important site in which it is constructed. New communications and media technologies will also offer some putative solutions—but these may well be solutions to social problems masked by the beneficent face of technology.

In the end, we face some disconcerting questions that are not easily answered. Is our focus to be on rewiring disability, with those responsible for new communications and media technologies, their design, implementation, purposes, and uses, continuing to locate the problem within deviant individuals or even groupings? We face serious challenges here: after all we blame Deaf people as a class for not hearing, and dominant media representations ceaselessly reiterate the stigmatizing message that chided people with disabilities for their bad genes that could be fixed by biotechnology and the genetic revolution. Or are we to see the disability we build into new media as requiring a sustained engagement as a matter that concerns diverse publics, and that is the crux of delivering a civil society for all?

It is not so much the latest add-on, the fastest computer, or even the more expansive application of universal design that will confer the greatest benefit for people with disabilities. Rather, we need to recognize that in whatever we do we have the opportunity to disable or enable. We recommend that it is time for society to decide that it wishes to reconnect with people with disabilities in the digital futures that will be our emerging society. This is not so much a technological question, as a political one. As we interrogate our technologies, and see them as reflecting the values and lived social policy, we propose that society dare to ask: whom do I count as a member of my moral community, and whom do I exclude in the everyday taken-for-granted technology and its uses? Whom do we disable in the scramble to the networked digital society? Or, more hopefully, how can we bring about a future in which disability in its digital incarnations may unfold in new, unexpected, and fairer ways to the genuine benefit, and with the assured, ubiquitous participation and imaginings of people with disabilities? These are ultimately political questions as every day, individually and collectively, we engage with a pressing reality: disabling new media.

NOTES

1. Normalization is an important concept in the history of disability, first conceptualized by Wolf Wolfensberger, who later proposed in its place the notion of "Social Role Valorization." See Wolf Wolfensberger, "Social Role Valorization Is Too Conservative. No, It Is Too Radical," *Disability & Society* 10 (1995): 365–68.

2. John Ralston Saul, *The Unconscious Civilization* (Melbourne: Penguin Australia, 1997), 172.

Bibliography

Abberley, Paul. "The Spectre at the Feast: Disabled People and Social Theory." In *The Disability Reader: Social Science Perspectives,* ed. Tom Shakespeare. London: Routledge, 1998, 79–93

———. *Handicapped by Numbers.* Occasional Papers in Sociology No 9. Bristol: Bristol Polytechnic, 1990.

———. "The Concept of Oppression and the Development of a Social Theory of Disability." *Disability, Handicap & Society* 2 (1987): 5–20.

Ad hoc Committee on Ear Surgery, the Greater Los Angeles Council on Deafness, *Position Paper: Cochlear Implant Surgery.* Greater Los Angeles Council on Deafness, 1985.

Adamson, Linda, et al. *Planning for an Information Society: Population Group Discussion Papers and Policy Issue Discussion Papers.* Melbourne: Telecom Australia, 1994.

Advisory Committee on Telecommunications for Disabled and Elderly People, Office of Telecommunications (OFTEL). *Communicating with Customers Who Are Disabled—A Guide for Telecoms Companies.* London: OFTEL, 2001. www.oftel.gov.uk/publications/consumer/gpm0901.htm [accessed 14 February 2002].

Agre, Phil, and Marc Rotenberg, eds. *Technology and Privacy: The New Landscape.* Cambridge, Mass.: MIT Press, 1997.

Albrecht, G. L., and L. M. Verbrugge. "The Global Emergence of Disability." In *The Handbook of Social Studies in Health and Medicine,* ed. G. L. Albrecht, R. Fitzpatrick, and S. C. Scrimshaw. London: Sage, 2000.

Allen, Bob, ed. *Complete but Not Finished: The Final Report of COST 219.* Brussels: COST 219, CEC, 1997. www.stakes.fi/cost219/COSA120.html [accessed 15 March 1997].

Althusser, Louis. *Lenin and Philosophy, and Other Essays.* Trans. Ben Brewster. London: New Left Books, 1971.

Altman, Barbara M. "Disability Definitions, Models, Classification Schemes, and Applications." In *Handbook of Disability Studies,* ed. Gary L. Albrecht, Katherine D. Seelman, and Michael Bury. Thousand Oaks, Calif.: Sage, 2001, 11–68.

Anderson, Benedict. *Imagined Communities.* London: Verso, 1983.

Asch, Adrienne, and Michelle Fine. "Introduction: Beyond Pedestals." In *Women with Disabilities: Essays in Psychology, Culture, and Politics*, ed. Adrienne Asch and Michelle Fine. Philadelphia: Temple University Press, 1988, 1–37.

Astbrink, Gunela. *Participation by People with Disabilities in Telecommunications Standards-Setting Processes in Europe.* Consumer discussion paper prepared for Consumers' Telecommunications Network *International Standards Project* User Workshop, Global Standards Collaboration Forum (GSC7), Sydney, September 2001. www.ctn.org.au/internationalstandards.htm [accessed 15 March 2002].

Aufderheide, Patricia. Communications Policy and the Public Interest: The Telecommunications Act of 1996. New York: Guildford, 1999.

Australian Association of the Deaf (AAD). *Review into the Captioning Requirements of the* Broadcasting Services Act 1992*: Options Paper: Submission.* Sydney: AAD, 1999. www.dcita.gov.au [accessed 15 November 2000].

Australian Caption Centre (ACC). *Review into the Captioning Requirements of the* Broadcasting Services Act 1992*: Options Paper: Submission.* Sydney: ACC, 1999. www.dcita.gov.au [accessed 15 November 2000].

Babe, R. E. *Communication and the Transformation of Economics: Essays in Information, Public Policy, and Political Economy.* Boulder, Colo.: Westview, 1995.

Baldwin, Jacob. *The ADC Network Consumer's Guide to the Internet; or How I Lost My Disability on the Internet.* www.adcnetwork.net.au/lost_disability.htm [accessed 15 March 2002].

Barlow, John. "The Economy of Ideas." *Wired* 2.03 (March 1994). www.wired.com/wired/archive/2.03/economy.ideas.html.

Barnartt, Sharon N., and Richard K. Scotch. *Disability Protests: Contentious Politics, 1970–1999.* Washington, D.C.: Gallaudet Press, 2001.

Barnes, Colin. "The Social Model of Disability: A Sociological Phenomenon Ignored by Sociologists?" In *The Disability Reader: Social Science Perspectives,* ed. Tom Shakespeare. London: Cassell, 1998, 65–78.

———. "Institutional Discrimination against Disabled People and the Campaign for Anti-Discrimination Legislation." In *Critical Social Policy: A Reader. Social Policy and Social Relations,* ed. David Taylor. London: Sage, 1996, 95–112.

———. *Disabled People in Britain and Discrimination: A Case for Anti-Discrimination.* London: Hurst & Co., 1991.

———, Geoff Mercer, and Tom Shakespeare. *Exploring Disability: A Sociological Introduction.* Cambridge: Polity Press, 1999.

Barr, Trevor. *New Media.com.au.* Sydney: Allen & Unwin, 2000.

Barton, Len, and Mike Oliver, eds. *Disability Studies: Past, Present and Future.* Leeds: The Disability Press, 1997.

Battye, Louis. "The Chatterley Syndrome." In *Stigma: The Experience of Disability,* ed. Paul Hunt. London: Geoffrey Chapman, 1966.

Baudrillard, Jean. *"L'esprit du terrorisme." Harper's Magazine* 304, no.1821 (February 2002): 13–18.

———. *The Gulf War Did Not Take Place.* Trans. Paul Patton. Sydney: Power Publications, 1995.

Baym, Nancy K. *Tune In, Log On: Soaps, Fandom, and Online Community.* Thousand Oaks, Calif.: Sage, 2000.

Baynton, Douglas C. *Forbidden Signs: American Culture and the Campaign against Sign Language.* Chicago: University of Chicago Press, 1996.

Becher, Tony. *Academic Tribes and Territories: Intellectual Enquiry and the Cultures of Disciplines*. Milton Keynes, U.K.: Open University Press, 1989.

Becker, Howard S. *Art Worlds*. Berkeley: University of California Press, 1992.

Bell, Daniel. *The Coming of Post-Industry Society: A Venture in Social Forecasting*. New York: Basic, 1973.

Bell, David. *Introduction to Cybercultures*. London: Routledge, 2001.

Bennett, Tony. *Culture: A Reformer's Science*. Sydney: Allen & Unwin, 1998.

Bezroukov, Nikolai. "Open Source Software as a Special Type of Academic Research (Critique of Vulgar Raymondism)." *First Monday* 4.10 (1999). www.firstmonday.org/issues/issue4_10/bezroukov/index.htm.

Bijker, W. E., T. P. Hughes, and T. Pinch. *The Social Construction of Technological Systems*. Cambridge, Mass.: MIT Press, 1987.

Borsay, A. "Personal Trouble or Public Issue? Toward a Model of Policy for People with Physical and Mental Disabilities." *Disability, Handicap and Society* 1 (1986): 179–95.

Bourdieu, Pierre. *Distinction: A Social Critique of the Judgment of Taste*. Trans. Richard Nice. Cambridge, Mass.: Harvard University Press, 1984.

———. *Outline of a Theory of Practice*. Trans. Richard Nice. Cambridge: Cambridge University Press, 1977.

———, and Jean-Claude Passeron, *Reproduction in Education, Society and Culture*. Trans. Richard Nice. 2nd ed. London: Sage, 1990.

Bourk, Michael J. *Universal Service?: Telecommunications Policy in Australia and People with Disabilities*. Ed. Tom Worthington. Canberra: Tomw Communications Pty Ltd, 2000. www.tomw.net.au/uso.

Bowe, F. G. "Access to the Information Age: Fundamental Decisions in Telecommunications Policy." *Policy Studies Journal* 21(1993): 765–74.

Boyle, Deirdre. *Subject to Change: Guerrilla Television Revisited*. New York: Oxford University Press, 1997.

Braithwaite, D. O. " 'Just How Much Did That Wheelchair Cost?': Management of Privacy Boundaries by Persons with Disabilities." *Western Journal of Speech Communications* 55 (1991): 254–74.

Braithwaite, Dawn O., and Teresa L. Thompson. "Introduction: A History of Communication and Disability Research: The Way We Were." In *Handbook of Communication and People with Disabilities: Research and Applications,* ed. D. O. Braithwaite and T. L. Thompson. Mahwah, N.J.: Lawrence Erlbaum Associates, 2000, 1–14.

Braithwaite, John, and Peter Drahos. *Global Business Regulation*. Cambridge: Cambridge University Press, 2000.

Braman, Sandra, and Annabelle Sreberny-Hohammadi, eds. *Globalization, Communication and Transnational Civil Society*. Cresskill, N.J.: Hampton Press, 1996.

Brewer, Judy. *Statement before the U.S. House of Representatives Subcommittee on the Constitution,* Wednesday, February 9, 2000, Washington, D.C. www.w3.org/WAI/References/200002-Statement.html [accessed 1 February 2002].

Brisenden, S. "Independent Living and the Medical Model of Disability." *Disability, Handicap & Society* 1 (1986): 174.

Broadband Services Expert Group. *Networking Australia's Future: Final Report*. Canberra: Australian Government Publishing Service, 1994.

———. *Networking Australia's Future: Interim Report*. Canberra: Australian Government Publishing Services, 1994.

Brock, G. W., and G. L. Rosston, eds. *The Internet and Telecommunications Policy: Selected Papers from the 1995 Telecommunications Policy Research Conference.* Mahwah, N.J.: Lawrence Erlbaum, 1996.

Brock, Gerald W. Telecommunication Policy for the Information Age: From Monopoly to Competition. Cambridge, Mass.: Harvard University Press, 1994.

Brotman, Stuart N. *Extending Telecommunications Service to Americans with Disabilities: A Report on Telecommunications Services Mandated under the* Americans with Disabilities Act *of 1990.* Washington: Annenberg Washington Program, Northwestern University, 1991.

Brueggeman, Brenda Jo. *Lend Me Your Eyes: Rhetorical Constructions of Deafness.* Washington, D.C.: Gallaudet University Press, 1999.

———. "On (Almost) Passing." *College English* 59 (1997): 647–60.

———. "The Coming Out of Deaf Culture and American Sign Language: An Exploration into the Visual Rhetoric and Literacy." *Rhetoric Review* 13 (1995):409–20.

———, and James A. Fredal. "Studying Disability Rhetorically." In *Disability Discourse,* ed. Mairian Corker and Sally French. Buckingham, U.K.: Open University Press, 1999, 129–35.

Bruno, Richard L. "Devotees, Pretenders and Wannabes: Two Cases of Factitious Disability Disorder." *Journal of Sexuality and Disability* 15 (1997): 243–60.

Bureau of Transport and Communications Economics. *Communication Futures Project: Final Report.* Canberra: Australian Government Publishing Service, 1995.

———. *The Cost of Telecom's Community Service Obligations.* Canberra: Australian Government Publishing Service, 1989.

Burwood, E., and R. Le Strange. *Interference to Hearing Aids by the New Digital Mobile Telephone Systems, Global Systems for Mobile (GSM) Communications Standard.* Sydney: National Acoustic Laboratories, 1993.

Butler, Judith. *The Psychic Life of Power: Theories in Subjection.* Stanford, Calif.: Stanford University Press, 1997.

Cairncross, Frances. *The Death of Distance: How the Communications Revolution Will Change Our Lives.* London: Orion Business Books, 1998.

Campbell, Helen. "Choosing Telecommunications?: Consumers in a Liberalised, Privatised Telecommunications Sector." *Media International Australia* 96 (2000): 59–68.

Castells, Manuel. *The Information Age.* 3 vols. Oxford: Blackwell, 1996–98.

Chambers, D. W., and D. Turnbull. "Science Worlds: An Integrated Approach to Social Studies of Science Teaching." *Social Studies of Science* 19 (1989): 155–79.

Clark, G. M. et al., eds. *Cochlear Prostheses.* Edinburgh: Churchill Livingstone, 1990.

Clark, G. M., P. J. Blamey, A. M. Brown, P. A. Gusby, R. C. Dowell, B. K. H. Franz, B. C. Pyman, R. K. Shepherd, Y. C. Tong, R. L. Webb, M. S. Hirshorn, J. Kuzma, D. J. Mecklenburg, D. K. Money, J. F. Patrick, and J. M. Seligman. "The University of Melbourne-Nucleus Multi-Electrode Cochlear Implant." *Advances in Otorhinolaryngology* 38 (1987): 1–190.

Clogston, John. *Disability Coverage in Sixteen Newspapers.* Louisville, Ky.: Avocado Press, 1990.

Collins, Richard, and Cristina Murroni. *New Media, New Policies: Media and Communications Strategies for the Future.* Cambridge: Polity Press, 1996.

Comor, E. A., ed. *The Global Political Economy of Communication: Hegemony, Telecommunication, and the Information Economy.* London: St. Martin's, 1994.

Computers and the Disabled. Special issue of *Byte Magazine* 7, no. 9 (1982): 64–360.

Consumers' Telecommunications Network (CTN). *Voices in the Market: Consumer Consultation and Advocacy in an Era of Competition.* Sydney: CTN, 1995.

Cooper, Margaret. "The Australian Disability Movement Lives." *Disability & Society* 14 (1999): 217–26.

Corker, Mairian. "Disability Discourse in a Postmodern World." In *The Disability Reader: Social Science Perspectives*, ed. Tom Shakespeare. London: Cassell, 1998, 221–33.

———, and Sally French, eds. *Disability Discourse.* Buckingham, U.K.: Open University Press, 1999.

Cornes, P. "Impairment, Disability, Handicap and New Technology." In *Social Work, Disabled People and Disabling Environments,* ed. Mike Oliver. London: Jessica Kingsley, 1991.

COST 219bis. "COST 219bis." www.stakes.fi/cost219/COSA120.html [accessed 1 December 2001].

Coulon, Alain. *Ethnomethodology.* Trans. Jacqueline Coulon and Jack Katz. London: Sage, 1995.

Cranmer, T. V. "Emerging Research Goals in the Blindness Field." Proceedings of the 2nd U.S./Canada Conference on Technology for the Blind, November 4 to 6, 1993, Planned and Hosted by the National Federation of the Blind, in *Braille Monitor* (January 1994). www.nfb.org/bm/bm94/brlm9401.htm [accessed 15 March 2002].

Crouch, R.A. "Letting The Deaf Be Deaf: Reconsidering the Use of Cochlear Implants In Prelingually Deaf Children." *Hastings Center Report* 27 (1997): 14–21.

Crutchfield, Susan, and Marcy Epstein, eds. *Points of Contact: Disability, Art, and Culture.* Ann Arbor: University of Michigan Press, 2000.

Cubitt, Sean. *Digital Aesthetics.* Thousand Oaks, Calif.: Sage, 1998.

Cumberbatch, Guy, and Ralph Negrine. *Images of Disability on Television.* London: Routledge, 1992.

Davis, D. S. "Cochlear Implants and the Claims of Culture? A Response to Lane and Grodin." *Kennedy Institute of Ethics Journal* 7 (1997): 253–58.

Davis, Lennard J. *The Disability Studies Reader.* London: Routledge, 1997.

———. "Introduction." In *The Disability Studies Reader*, ed. Lennard J. Davis. New York: Routledge, 1997, 9–28.

Day, Lawrence H. "Telecommunications Policy: Teamwork." *Telecommunications Policy* 1 (1976).

De Moragas Spà, M., N. K. Rivenburgh, and J. F. Larson. *Television in the Olympics.* London: John Libbey, 1995.

De Solla Price, D. J. "Notes towards a Philosophy of the Science/Technology Interaction." In *The Nature of Scientific Knowledge: Are Models of Scientific Change Relevant?* ed. R. Laudan. Dordrecht: D. Reidel, 1984, 105–14.

Dean, Mitchell. Governmentality: Power and Rule in Modern Society. London: Sage, 1999.

Deleuze, Gilles, and Félix Guattari. *A Thousand Plateaux: Capitalism and Schizophrenia.* Trans. Brian Massumi. Minneapolis: University of Minnesota Press, 1987.

Dennis, Dion. "The World Trade Centre and the Rise of the Security State." Event-scene 9. *Ctheory: Theory, Technology and Culture* 24.3 (2001). www.ctheory.com.

Department of Commerce. *A Framework for Global Electronic Commerce.* Washington, D.C.: Department of Commerce, 1997. www.iitf.nist.gov/eleccomm/ecomm.htm [accessed 15 February 2002].

Department of Communications, Information Technology and the Arts (DCITA). *Review into the Captioning Requirements of the* Broadcasting Services Act 1992*: Options Paper*. Canberra: DCITA, 1999. www.dcita.gov.au [accessed 15 November 2000].

Department of Trade and Industry. *Creating the Superhighways of the Future: The Potential of Broadband Communications*. London: HMSO, 1994. www.archive. official-documents.co.uk/document/dti/dticmd/ [accessed 15 February 2002].

Dickson, David. Alternative Technology and the Politics of Technical Change. Glasgow: Fontana/Collins, 1974.

Drake, R. F. "The Exclusion of Disabled People from Positions of Power in British Voluntary Organisations." *Disability and Society* 9 (1994): 461–80.

Dreachslin, Janice L. *Diversity Leadership*. Chicago: Health Administration Press, 1996.

Driedger, Diane. *The Last Civil Rights Movement: Disabled Peoples' International*. London: Hurst & Co; New York: St. Martin's, 1989.

Duncan, Kath, and Gerard Goggin. " 'Something in your belly'— Fantasy, Disability and Desire in *My One-Legged Dream Lover*." *Disability Quarterly* 22.3 (Summer 2002). www.cds.hawaii.edu/DSQ/pdf/dsq_2002_summer.pdf.

Dutton, W. H., J. G. Blumer, and K. L. Kraemer. *Wired Cities: Shaping the Future of Communications*. Boston: G.K. Hall & Co, 1987.

Dutton, William, et al. *The Information Superhighway: Britain's Response: A Forum Discussion*. Policy Research Paper 29. Programme on Information and Communications Technologies, Economic and Social Research Council: London 1994.

Elix, Jane, and Jane Lambert. *Final Report: "Have Your Say" National Seminar Series on Future Communications Technologies: Issues and Opportunities*. Sydney: Community Solutions, 1994.

Ellul, Jacques. *The Technological Society*. New York: Vintage, 1964.

Farrell, Gabriel. *The Story of Blindness*. Cambridge, Mass.: Harvard University Press, 1956.

Federal Communications Commission (FCC). *Implementation of Video Description of Video Programming: Report and Order,* MM Docket No. 99-339 (Washington: FCC, 2000); www.fcc.gov [accessed 2 December 2000].

——. *Report & Order in the Matter of Federal-State Joint Board on Universal Service.* 97-157 (CC Docket No. 96-45). Washington, D.C.: FCC, 1997.

——. *Building Bridges to the Information Superhighway: Annual Report of the Disabilities Issues Task Force.* Washington, D.C.: FCC, 1996.

——. *Notice of Inquiry, in re Closed Captioning and Video Description of Video Programming.* MM Docket No. 95-176, FCC 95-484. www.fcc.gov [accessed 2 December 2000].

Featherstone, Mike. "Post-bodies, Aging, and Virtual Reality." In *The Cybercultures Reader,* ed. David Bell and Barbara M. Kennedy. London: Routledge, 2000, 609– 18.

——, and Andrew Wernick, ed. *Images of Ageing: Cultural Representations of Later Life*. London: Routledge, 1995.

Feyerabend, Paul. Against Method: An Outline of an Anarchistic Theory of Knowledge. London: New Left Books, 1975.

Finkelstein, Vic. "Emancipating Disability Studies." In *The Disability Reader: Social Science Perspectives,* ed. Tom Shakespeare. London: Cassell, 1998, 28–49.

——. "To Deny or Not to Deny Disability." In *Handicap in a Social World,* ed. A. Brechin, P. Liddiard, and J. Swain. Kent: Hodder and Stoughton, 1981, 34–36.

Fiske, John. *Television Culture.* London: Routledge, 1987.

Fleischer, Doris Zames, and Frieda Zames. *The Disability Rights Movement: From Charity to Confrontation.* Philadelphia: Temple University Press, 2001.

Flew, Terry. *New Media Technologies: An Introduction.* Oxford: Oxford University Press, 2002.

———, and Christina Spurgeon. "Television after Broadcasting." In *The Australian Television Book,* ed. Graeme Turner and Stuart Cunningham. Sydney: Allen & Unwin, 2000, 69–85.

Forrester, Chris. *The Business of Digital Television.* Oxford: Focal Press, 2000.

Foucault, Michel. "Governmentality." In *Power,* ed. James D. Faubion and trans. Robert Hurley et al. *The Essential Works 1954–1984.* Vol. 3. London: Allen Lane The Penguin Press, 2000.

———. History of Sexuality: An Introduction. London: Allen Lane, 1979.

Fox, S. A., and H. Giles. "'Let The Wheelchair through': An Intergroup Approach to Interability Communication." In *Social Groups and Identity: The Developing Legacy of Henri Taffel,* ed. W. P. Robinson. Oxford: Butterworth Heinmann, 1996, 215–48.

Fox, Susan Anne. "The Uses and Abuses of Computer-Mediated Communication for People with Disabilities." In *Handbook of Communication and People with Disabilities,* ed. D. O. Braithwaite and T. L. Thompson. Mahwah, N.J.: Lawrence Erlbaum, 2000, 319–36.

Frow, John, and Meaghan Morris. "Cultural Studies." In *Handbook of Qualitative Research,* 2nd ed., ed. Norman K. Denzin and Yvonna S. Lincoln. Thousand Oaks, Calif.: Sage, 315–46.

Fulcher, Gillian. *Disabling Policies?* London: Falmer Press, 1989.

Gantz, B. J. "Issues of Candidate Selection for a Cochlear Implant." *Otolaryngologic Clinics of North America* 22 (1989): 239–47.

Gartner, A., and T. Joe, ed. *Images of the Disabled: Disabling Images.* New York: Praeger, 1987.

Gatens, Moira. *Imaginary Bodies: Ethics, Power, and Corporeality.* New York: Routledge, 1995.

Gates, Bill. *Business @ the Speed of Thought: Using a Digital Nervous System.* New York: Warner, 1999.

———, with Nathan Myhrvold and Peter Rinearson. *The Road Ahead.* New York: Viking, 1995.

Gauntlett, David. "Internet Studies: What Went Wrong?" *Times Higher Education Supplement,* 22 September 2000.

———. "Web.Studies: A User's Guide." In *Web.Studies,* ed. David Gauntlett. London: Arnold and Hodder, 2000.

Germon, Penny. "Activists and Academics: Part of the Same or a World Apart?" In *The Disability Reader: Social Science Perspectives,* ed. Tom Shakespeare. London: Cassell, 1998, 245–55.

Gibson, B. "Cochlear Implants—Some Questions Answered." *SHHH News* (February 1988).

Gibson, W. "Opposition from Deaf Groups to the Cochlear Implant." *Medical Journal of Australia* 155 (1991): 212–14.

Gibson, William. *Neuromancer.* New York: Ace, 1984.

Gilder, George. *Life after Television.* New York: Norton, 1992.

Gill, John, and Tony Shipley. *The Impact of Telecommunications Deregulation on People with Disabilities: A Review for COST 219bis by the UK Group.* London: Royal National Institute of the Blind, 1997. www.stakes.fi/cost219/DISASTER.HTM [accessed 15 March 2002].

Given, Jock. *Turning Off the Television.* Sydney: University of New South Press, 2002.

Gluckman, A., and B. Reed. "The Gay Marketing Moment." *Dollars and Sense* (1993).

Goggin, Gerard. "Pay Per Browse?: The Web's Commercial Futures." In *Web.Studies: Rewiring Media Studies for the Digital Age,* ed. David Gauntlett. London: Arnold & Hodder, 2000, 103–22.

——. "Universal Service: Voice Telephony and Beyond." In *All Connected: Universal Service in Telecommunications,* ed. Bruce Langtry. Melbourne: Melbourne University Press, 1998.

——, and Claire Milne. "Literature Review: Residential Consumers and Australian Telecommunications 1991–94." In *For Whom the Phone Rings: Residential Consumers and Telecommunications Competition,* ed. Trish Benson. Sydney: Consumers' Telecommunications Network, 1995, 27–95.

Goggin, Gerard, and Christopher Newell. "Crippling Competition: Critical Reflections on Disability and Australian Telecommunications Policy." *Media International Australia* 96 (2000): 83–94.

——. "Crippling Paralympics?: Media, Disability and Olympism." *Media International Australia* 97 (2000): 71–84.

——. "Reflections from the Roadside: Residential Consumers and Information Super-highways." *Media Information Australia* 74 (1994): 34–41.

Gold, N., and G. Auslander. "Newspaper Coverage of People with Disabilities in Canada and Israel: An International Comparison." *Disability and Society* 14 (1999): 709–31.

Gonsoulin, T. P. "Cochlear Implant/Deaf World Dispute: Different Bottom Elephants." *Otolaryngology Head and Neck Surgery* 125, no. 5 (Nov. 2001): 552–56.

Goodman, James, and Patricia Ranald, eds. Stopping the Juggernaut: Public Interest Versus the Multilateral Agreement on Investment. Sydney: Pluto Press, 2000.

Goodwin, P. "British Media Policy Takes to the Superhighway," *Media, Culture & Society* 17 (1995): 677–89.

Gordon, Colin. "Governmental Rationality: An Introduction." In *The Foucault Effect: Studies in Governmentality with Two Lectures by and an Interview with Michel Foucault,* ed. Graham Burchell, Colin Gordon, and Peter Miller. Chicago: University of Chicago Press, 1991.

Gore, Al. *Opening Speech.* International Telecommunications Union, First World Telecommunications Development Conference. Buenos Aires, Argentina, 21 March 1994. www.iitf.nist.gov/documents/speeches/032194_gore_giispeech.html [accessed 24 March 2002].

Green, Lelia. *Technoculture: From Alphabet to Cybersex.* Sydney: Allen & Unwin, 2002.

Groce, N. L. *Everyone Here Spoke Sign Language.* Cambridge, Mass.: Harvard University Press, 1988.

Hakken, David. Cyborgs@Cyberspace?: An Ethnographer Looks to the Future. New York: Routledge, 1999.

Haller, B. "If They Limp, They Lead: News Representations and the Hierarchy of Disability Images." In *Handbook of Communication and People with Disabilities: Research and Application,* ed. D. O. Braithwaite and T. L. Thompson. Mahwah, N.J.: Lawrence Erlbaum, 2000, 273–88.

Haller, Beth. "Rethinking Models of Media Representations of Disability." *Disability Studies Quarterly* 15 (1995): 26–30.

Hansen, K.A. "Bibliographies and Scholarly Communication." *Journal of Communication* 44 (1994).

Haraway, Donna. *Simians, Cyborgs, and Women: The Reinvention of Nature.* New York: Routledge, 1991.

Hartley, John. *Uses of Television.* New York: Routledge, 2000.

———. *The Politics of Pictures: The Creation of the Public in the Age of Popular Media.* London: Routledge, 1992.

———, and Alan McKee. *The Indigenous Public Sphere: The Reporting and Reception of Aboriginal Issues in the Australian Media.* Oxford: Oxford University Press, 2000.

Hayes, Dennis C. *Testimony before the House Subcommittee on the Constitution February 9, 2000.* www.house.gov/judiciary/hay30209.htm [accessed 1 February 2002].

Hellström, Gunnar. "Standardization of Text Telephony." www.omnitor.se/english/standards [accessed 15 March 2002].

Henry Vlug and Canadian Human Rights Commission and Canadian Broadcasting Corporation, Reasons for Decision, Canadian Human Rights Tribunal, T557/1500, 15 November 2000.

Hervey, David. *The Creatures That Time Forgot: Photography and Disability Imagery.* New York: Routledge, 1992.

High-Level Group on the Information Society. *Europe and the Global Information Society: Recommendations to the European Council (Bangemann Report).* Brussels: European Commission, 1994. www.medicif.org/Dig_library/ECdocs/reports/Bangemann.htm.

Hill, Stephen. *The Tragedy of Technology.* London: Pluto Press, 1988.

Hills, Jill. *The Democracy Gap: The Politics of Information and Communications Technologies in the United States and Europe.* Westport, Conn.: Greenwood, 1991.

Hillyer, Barbara. *Feminism and Disability.* Norman: University of Oklahoma Press, 1993.

Hine, Christine. *Virtual Ethnography.* London: Sage, 2000.

Holzer, Brigitte, Arthur Vreede, and Gabriele Weigt, ed. *Disability in Different Cultures: Reflections on Local Concepts.* Bielefeld, Germany: Transcript Verl, 1999.

Hoynes, William. *Public Television for Sale: Media, the Market and the Public Sphere.* Boulder, Colo.: Westview, 1994.

Human Rights and Equal Opportunity Commission (HREOC). *Accessibility of Electronic Commerce and New Service and Information Technologies for Older Australians and People with a Disability* (Sydney: HREOC, 2001). www.hreoc.gov.au/disability_rights/inquiries/ecom/ecomrep.htm [accessed 24 March 2002].

———. *Bruce Lindsay Maguire v. Sydney Organizing Committee for the Olympic Games,* Reasons for Decision Concerning Relief, H 99/115a. Sydney: Human Rights and Equal Opportunity Commission, 18 November 2000. www.hreoc.gov.au [accessed 15 March 2002].

———. *Bruce Lindsay Maguire v. Sydney Organizing Committee for the Olympic Games,* reasons for decision, H 99/115. Sydney: Human Rights and Equal Opportunity Commission, 24 August 2000. www.hreoc.gov.au (15 March 2002).

———. *Inquiry on Mobile Phone Access for Hearing Aid Users.* Sydney: HREOC, 2000. www.hreoc.gov.au/disability_rights/communications/communications.html [accessed 11 November 2001].

Hurst, Rachel. "International Classification of Functioning, Disability and Health." *Disability Tribune* (September 2001): 10–11.

———. "To Revise or Not to Revise?" *Disability & Society* 15, no. 7 (2000): 1083–87.

Imrie, Rob. *Disability and the City: International Perspectives.* London: Paul Chapman Publishing, 1996.

Information Infrastructure Taskforce. *The National Information Infrastructure: Agenda for Action.* Washington, D.C.: Department of Commerce, 1993. www.ibiblio.org/nii/toc.html [accessed 15 February 2002].

Innes, Harold. *The Bias of Communication.* Toronto: University of Toronto Press, 1951.

Jenkins, Henry. *Textual Poachers: Television Fans and Participatory Culture.* London: Routledge, 1992.

Jernigan, Kenneth. "Note from the Chairman." Proceedings of the 2nd U.S./Canada Conference on Technology for the Blind, November 4 to 6, 1993, Planned and Hosted by the National Federation of the Blind, in *Braille Monitor* (January 1994), www.nfb.org/bm/bm94/brlm9401.htm [accessed 15 March 2002].

Jussawalla, M., ed. *Telecommunications: A Bridge to the 21st Century.* Amsterdam: Elsevier, 1995.

Kahin, Brian, and Keller, James H., eds. *Coordinating the Internet.* Cambridge, Mass.: MIT Press, 1997.

Kahin, Brian, and Wilson, Ernest J., III, eds. *National Information Infrastructure Initiatives: Vision and Policy Design.* Cambridge, Mass.: MIT Press, 1997.

Kamenetz, Herman L. "A Brief History of the Wheelchair." *Journal of the History of Medicine and Allied Sciences* 24 (1969): 205–10.

———. *The Wheelchair Book: Mobility for the Disabled.* Springfield, IL.: Charles C. Thomas, 1969.

Kapor, Mitch. "Where Is the Digital Highway Really Heading?: The Case for a Jeffersonian Information Policy." *Wired* 1.03 (July/August 1993). www.wired.com/wired/archive/1.03/kapor.on.nii.html.

Kennard, William. *Note of Proposed Rulemaking on Video Description.* 18 November 1999, Federal Communications Commission (FCC) (Washington: FCC); www.fcc.gov [accessed 2 December 2000].

Kittay, Eva, and Anita Silvers, and Susan Wendell, ed. "Feminism and Disability, Part 1." Special issue of *Hypatia: A Journal of Feminist Philosophy* 16.4 (2001).

Kling, Rob, ed. *Computerization and Controversy: Value Conflicts and Social Choices.* 2nd ed. San Diego: Academic, 1996.

Klobas, Lauri E. *Disability Drama in Television and Film.* Jefferson, N.C.: McFarland & Company, 1988.

Knorr-Cetina, K. *The Manufacture of Knowledge: An Essay on the Constructivist and Contextual Nature of Science.* Oxford: Pergamon, 1981.

Koestler, Frances A. *The Unseen Minority: A Social History of Blindness in America.* New York: David McKay, 1976.

Kollodge, Barbara A. "Specialized Computer Applications." In *Assistive Technology: An Interdisciplinary Approach,* ed. Beverly K. Bain and Dawn Leger. New York: Churchill Livingstone, 1997.

Kuhn, Thomas S. *The Structure of Scientific Revolutions.* 2nd ed. Chicago: University of Chicago Press, 1970.

Lamberton, Don, ed. *Beyond Competition: The Future of Telecommunications.* Amsterdam: Elsevier, 1995.

———, ed. *The New Research Frontiers of Communications Policy.* Amsterdam, Elsevier, 1999.

Lane, H., and B. Bahan. "Ethics of Cochlear Implantation in Young Children." *Otolaryngology Head and Neck Surgery* 121 (1999): 672–75.

——. "Ethics of Cochlear Implantation in Young Children: A Review and Reply from a Deaf-World Perspective." *Otolaryngology Head and Neck Surgery* 119.4 (1998): 297–313.

Lane, H., and M. Grodin. "Ethical Issues in Cochlear Implant Surgery: An Exploration into Disease, Disability, and the Best Interests of the Child." *Kennedy Institute of Ethics Journal* 7 (1997): 231–51.

Lane, Harlan. *The Mask of Benevolence.* New York: Vintage, 1993.

Latour, Bruno. *Science in Action.* Milton Keynes, U.K.: Open University Press, 1987.

——, and Steve Woolgar. *Laboratory Life: The Construction of Scientific Facts.* Princeton, N.J.: Princeton University Press, 1986.

Law, John, and John Hassard, eds. *Actor Network Theory and After.* Boston, Mass.: Blackwell, 1999.

Lax, Stephen, ed. *Access Denied: Exclusion in the Information Age.* Basingstoke, U.K.: Macmillan, 2000.

Lazarro, Joseph J. "Light at the End of the Tunnel?" *Information Technology and Disability* 2 (1993). www.rit.edu/~easi/itd/itdv02n2/jobs.html.

Lazarus, Wendy, and Francisco Mora. *Online Content for Low-Income and Underserved Americans: The Digital Divide's New Frontier.* Santa Monica, Calif.: The Children's Partnership, 2000. www.childrenspartnership.org/ [accessed 20 June 2000].

Lea, A. R. *Cochlear Implants.* Australian Institute of Health Care Technology Series No. 6. Canberra: Australian Government Publishing Service, 1991.

Lehoux, P., and S. Blume. "Technology Assessment and the Sociopolitics of Health Technologies." *Journal of Health Politics, Policy & Law* 25 (2000): 1083–120.

Lessig, Lawrence. *Code and Other Laws of Cyberspace.* New York: Basic, 1999.

Lievrouw, Leah, and Sonia Livingstone, eds. *The Handbook of New Media.* London: Sage, 2002.

Linder, Laura R. *Public Access Television: America's Electronic Soapbox.* Westport, Conn.: Praeger, 1999.

Lindström, Jan-Ingvar, ed., *Universal Services Issues.* Brussels: COST219b, CEC, 1998.

Linton, Simi. "Disability Studies/Not Disability Studies." *Disability and Society* 13 (1998): 525–40.

Longmore, Paul K., and Lauri Umansky, eds. *The New Disability History: American Perspectives.* New York: New York University Press, 2001.

Macdonald, S., and J. Nightingale, eds. *Information and Organization: A Tribute to the Work of Don Lamberton.* Amsterdam: North-Holland, 1999.

Macintyre, Alasdair. "The Need for a Standard of Care." In *Americans with Disabilities: Exploring Implications of the Law for Individuals and Institutions,* ed. Leslie Pickering Francis and Anita Silvers. New York: Routledge, 2000.

MacKenzie, Donald, and Judy Wajcman, eds. *The Social Shaping of Technology.* 1st ed. Milton Keynes, U.K.: Open University Press, 1985.

——. *The Social Shaping Of Technology.* 2nd ed. Buckingham: Open University Press, 1999.

Macpherson, Crawford Bough. *The Political Theory of Possessive Individualism: Hobbes to Locke.* Corrected ed. Oxford: Clarendon Press, 1962.

Malhotra, Y., A. Al-Shehri, and Jeff J. Jones. "National Information Infrastructure: Myths, Metaphors and Realities" (1995). www.brint.com/papers/nii/ [accessed 1 February 2002].

Mansell, Robin. *The New Telecommunications: A Political Economy of Network Evolution.* London: Sage, 1993.

Marcuse, Herbert. *One Dimensional Man.* London: Abacus, 1972.

Marvin, Carolyn. *When Old Technologies Were New: Thinking about Electric Communication in the Late Nineteen Century.* Oxford: Oxford University Press, 1990.

Maston, Floyd. *Walking Alone and Marching Together: A History of the Organized Blind Movement in the US, 1940–1990.* Baltimore, Md.: National Federation of the Blind, 1990.

Maurer, Marc. "From the President's Mail Basket: Reflections on Descriptive Videos." *Braille Monitor.* 41.5 (May 2001). www.nfb.org/BM/BM01/BM0105/bm010506.htm [accessed 15 March 2002].

———. "AOL Progress Report." *Braille Monitor* 42.2 (February 2001), www.nfb.org/BM/BM01/BM0102/bm010203.htm [accessed 15 March 2002].

———. "From the President's Mail Basket." "Recent NFB Resolutions Concerning Descriptive Video." *Braille Monitor* 41.5 (2001).

McChesney, Robert. *Rich Media, Poor Democracy: Communications Politics in Dubious Times.* Urbana-Champaign: University of Illinois Press, 1999.

McMillan, Sally J. "Exploring Models of Interactivity from Multiple Research Traditions: Users, Documents, and Systems." In *The Handbook of New Media,* ed. Leah Lievrouw and Sonia Livingstone. London: Sage, 2002, 162–82.

Meekhosha, Helen. "The Politics of Recognition or the Politics of Presence: The Challenge of Disability." In *Speaking for the People: Representation in Australian Politics,* ed. Marian Sawer and Gianni Zappalà. Melbourne: Melbourne University Press, 2001, 225–45, 298–321.

Meekhosha, Helen, and Leann Dowse. "Distorting Images, Invisible Images: Gender, Disability and the Media." *Media International Australia* 84 (1997) 91–101.

Melody, William H., ed. *Telecom Reform: Principles, Policies and Regulatory Practices.* Copenhagen: Lyngby University Press, 1997.

Metts, R. L. *Disability Issues, Trends and Recommendations for the World Bank.* Washington, D.C.: World Bank, 2000.

Microsoft. "Microsoft Receives Award for Continued Leadership in Hiring, Accommodating and Creating Accessible Technologies for People with Disabilities," 7 February 2000. *Microsoft Press Pass.* www.microsoft.com/PressPass/features/2000/02-07we.asp.

———. "Greg Lowney: Microsoft's Director of Accessibility Is Motivated by the Millions of People His Work Will Benefit." 22 October 1998. *Microsoft Press Pass.* www.microsoft.com/presspass/features/1998/10-22lowney.asp.

Miller, Toby. *Technologies of Truth: Cultural Citizenship and the Popular Media.* Minneapolis: University of Minnesota Press, 1998.

Miller, Vincent. "Search Engines, Portals, and Global Capitalism." In *Web.Studies,* ed. David Gauntlett. London: Arnold and Hodder, 2000, 113–21.

Mitchell, David T., and Sharon L. Snyder, eds. "Representation and Its Discontents: The Uneasy Home of Disability in Literature and Film." In *Handbook of Disability Studies,* ed. Gary L. Albrecht, Katherine D. Seelman, and Michael Bury. Thousand Oaks, Calif.: 2001, 195–218.

———. *Narrative Prosthesis: Disability and the Dependencies of Discourse.* Ann Arbor: University of Michigan Press, 2000.

———. *The Body and Physical Difference: Discourses of Disability.* Ann Arbor: University of Michigan Press, 1997.

———. "Introduction: Disability Studies and the Double Bind of Representation." In *The Body and Physical Difference: Discourses of Disability*, ed. David T. Mitchell and Sharon L. Synder. Ann Arbor: University of Michigan Press, 1997, 1–31.

———. *Vital Signs: Crip Culture Talks Back*. Video; 48 min., Marquette, Mich.: Brace Yourselves Productions, 1996.

Mohay, Heather. "Deafness in Children." *Medical Journal of Australia* 154 (March 18, 1991): 372–74.

Money, John, and Kent W. Simcoe. "Acrotomophilia, Sex and Disability: New Concepts and Case Reports." *Sexuality and Disability* 7 (1984–96): 43–50.

Moody, Nick. "Untapped Potential: The Representation of Disability/Special Ability in the Cyberpunk Workforce." *Convergence* (1997).

Morris, Jenny. *Encounters with Strangers: Feminism and Disability*. London: Women's Press, 1999.

———. "Personal and Political: A Feminist Perspective on Researching Physical Disability." In *Debates and Issues in Feminist Research and Pedagogy: A Reader*, ed. J. Holland and M. Blair with S. Sheldon. Philadelphia: Clevedon; Adelaide: Multilingual Matters, and Milton Keynes, U.K.: Open University, 1995, 262–72.

Mosco, Vincent. "Teaching Telecommunications Policy, Critically." *Canadian Journal of Communications* 11 (1985): 51–62.

Moyal, Ann. "The Gendered Use of the Telephone: An Australian Case Study." *Media, Culture and Society* 14 (1992): 51–72.

———. "The Feminine Culture of the Telephone: People, Patterns and Policy." *Prometheus* 7.1 (1989): 5-31.

———. *Clear across Australia: A History of Telecommunications*. Melbourne: Thomas Nelson, 1984.

Mulgan, Geoff. *Communication and Control: Networks and the New Economies of Communication*. Cambridge: Polity Press, 1991.

Mumford, Lewis. *Technics and Civilization*. London: Routledge & Kegan Paul, 1934.

Munster, Anna. "Net Affects: Responding to Shock on Internet Time." In *Politics of a Digital Present: An Inventory of Australian Net Culture, Criticism and Theory*, ed. H. Brown et al. Melbourne: Fibreculture, 2001, 9–18.

Murdock, Graham, and Peter Golding. "Information Poverty and Political Inequality: Citizenship in the Age of Privatised Communications." *Journal of Communications* 39 (1989).

———. "Unequal Communications Access and Exclusion in the New Communications Marketplace." In *New Communications Technologies and the Public Interest: Comparative Perspectives on Policy and Research*, ed. Marjorie Ferguson. London: Sage, 1986, 71–83.

Naficy, Hamif. *The Making of Exile Cultures: Iranian Television in Los Angeles*. Minneapolis: University of Minnesota Press, 1993.

National Council on Disability (NCD). *The Accessible Future*. Washington, D.C.: NCD, 2001. www.ncd.gov/newsroom/publications/accessiblefuture.html [accessed 24 March 2002].

———. *Access to the Information Superhighway and Emerging Information Technologies by People with Disabilities*. Washington, D.C.: NCD, 1996. www.ncd.gov/newsroom/publications/superhwy.html [accessed 15 February 2002].

National Telecommunications and Information Administration (NTIA). *Falling through the Net: Defining the Digital Divide*. Washington, D.C.: 1999. www.ntia.doc.gov/ntiahome/fttn99/contents.html [accessed 20 June 2000].

————. *The Global Information Infrastructure: Agenda for Cooperation.* Washington: National Telecommunications and Information Administration, 1994. www.ntia.doc.gov/reports/giiagend.html [accessed 15 February 2002].

Naussbaum, Felicity, and Helene Deutsch, eds. *DEFECT!: Engendering the Modern Body.* Ann Arbor: University of Michigan Press, 2000.

Needham, K. "Who Needs Tickets When the Web Serves Up Front Row Seats?" "Olympics Historic Edition." *Sydney Morning Herald,* 16–17th September 2000, 11.

Negroponte, Nicholas. *Being Digital.* New York: Knopf, 1995.

Nelson, J. A. "The Internet, the Virtual Community and Those with Disabilities." *Disability Studies Quarterly* 15 (1995): 15–20.

Newcomb, Horace, ed. *Television: The Critical View.* 6th ed. New York: Oxford University Press, 2000.

Newell, Christopher. "Bioethics and Disability." Special issue of *Interaction* 13, no. 3 and 4 (2000).

————. "Christopher Reeve, Utilitarianism and Human Rights." *Access* (June/July 2002): 4–5.

————. "Debates Regarding Governance: A Disability Perspective." *Disability and Society* 13 (1998): 295–96.

————. "Disabling Consultation? A Report Card from the Disability Sector." *Communications Update* 145 (1998): 13–14.

————. "A Critical Evaluation of the [National Health & Medical Research Council] 'The Ethics of Limiting Life-Sustaining Treatment' and Related Perspectives on the Bioethics of Disability." *Australian Disability Review* 4 (1991): 46–57.

————, and Judy Walker. "'Openness' in Distance and Higher Education as the Social Control of People with Disabilities: An Australian Policy Analysis." In *Research in Distance Education 2,* ed. T. Evans and P. Juler. Geelong, Victoria, Australia: Institute of Distance Education, Deakin University, 1992, 68–80.

Noam, Eli M., ed. *Telecommunications in Africa.* New York: Oxford University Press, 1999.

Noam, Eli M., S. Komatsuzaki, and D. A. Conn, eds. *Telecommunications in the Pacific Basin: An Evolutionary Approach.* Oxford University Press, Oxford, 1994.

Noble, D. F. *America by Design.* Oxford: Oxford University Press, 1977.

Norden, Martin F. *The Cinema of Isolation: A History of Physical Disability in the Movies.* New Brunswick, N.J.: Rutgers University Press, 1994.

Northfield, Dianne. *The Information Policy Maze: Global Challenges—National Responses.* Melbourne: RMIT, 1999.

Nunes, R. "Ethical Dimensions of Pediatric Cochlear Implantation." *Theoretical Medicine & Bioethics* 22.4 (2001): 337–49.

O'Brien, J. "Writing in the Body: Gender [Re]production in Online Interaction." In *Communities in Cyberspace,* ed. M. A. Smith and P. Kollock. London: Routledge, 1995.

Offe. Claus. *The Contradictions of the Welfare State.* Ed. John Keane. London: Hutchinson, 1989.

Office of Telecommunications (OFTEL). *Telecommunications Services for People with Disabilities: Consultative Document.* London: OFTEL, 1998. www.oftel.gov.uk [accessed 15 March 2002].

————. *Telecommunications Services for People with Disabilities: Statement.* London: OFTEL, 1998. www.oftel.gov.uk [accessed 5 September 1999].

———. *Universal Telecommunications Services.* London: OFTEL, 1997. www.oftel. gov.uk [accessed 5 September 1999].

Oliver, Mike. *Understanding Disability: From Theory to Practice.* London: Macmillan Press, 1996.

———. "Social Policy and Disability: Some Theoretical Issues." *Disability, Handicap and Society* 1 (1986): 5–17.

———, and Colin Barnes. "All We Are Saying Is Give Disabled Researchers a Chance." *Disability and Society* 12 (1997): 811–13.

Ong, Walter J. *Orality and Literacy: The Technologizing of the Word.* London: Methuen, 1982.

O'Regan, Tom, and Stuart Cunningham. "Marginalised Audiences." In *The Australian Television Book,* ed. Graeme Turner and Stuart Cunningham. Sydney: Allen & Unwin, 2001, 201–12.

Organization for Economic Cooperation and Development (OECD). *Information Infrastructure Policies in OECD Countries.* Paris: OECD: 1996. www.oecd.org/dsti/iccp/iip.html [accessed 15 February 2002].

Owen, Bruce W. *The Internet Challenge to Television.* Cambridge, Mass.: Harvard University Press, 1999.

Owens, J., et al. *Telecommunications Needs of People with Communication/Speech Difficulties.* Geelong, Australia: Deakin University, 1998.

Padden, Carol, and Humphries, Tom. *Deaf in America: Voices from a Culture.* Cambridge, Mass.: Harvard University Press, 1988.

Peach, T. *Confronting Nature: The Sociology of Solar-Neutrino Detection.* Dordrecht: Ridell, 1986.

Pointon, Ann, with Chris Davies, ed. *Framed: Interrogating Disability in the Media.* London: British Film Institute, 1997.

Pool, Ithiel de Sola, ed. *The Social Impact of the Telephone.* Cambridge, Mass.: MIT Press, 1977.

Popper, Karl R. *The Logic of Scientific Discovery.* London: Hutchinson, 1959.

Poster, Mark. *What's the Matter with the Internet?* Minneapolis: University of Minnesota Press, 2001.

Power, D .J., and M. B. Hyde. "The Cochlear Implant and the Deaf Community." *The Medical Journal of Australia* 157 (1992): 421–22.

Productivity Commission. *Broadcasting Inquiry: Final Report.* Melbourne: Productivity Commission, 2000.

Quiggin, John. *Great Expectations: Microeconomic Reform in Australia.* Sydney: Allen & Unwin, 1996.

Quittner, Josh. "Johnny Manhattan Meets the Furry Muckers: Why Playing MUDs Is Becoming the Addiction of the '90s." *Wired* 2.03 (March 1994). www.wired.com/wired/archive/2.03/muds.html.

Raymond, Eric S. "The Cathedral and the Bazaar," *First Monday* 3.3 (1998). www. firstmonday.org/issues/issue3_3/raymond/index.html.

Reeve, Christopher. "Christopher Reeve responds to Dr. Newell." *Access* (June/July 2002): 6–7.

Reihing, Mary Ellen. "So You Don't Know Anything about Computers and Might Like To Nibble." *Braille Monitor* (August 1987). www.nfb.org/bm/bm87/brlm8708.htm [accessed 15 March 2002].

Reinecke, Ian, and Julianne Schultz. *The Phone Book: The Future of Australia's Commu-nications on the Line.* Melbourne: Penguin, 1983.

Rice, R. E., C. L. Borgman, and B. Reeves. "Citation Networks of Communication Jour-nals, 1977–1985: Cliques and Positions, Citations Made and Citations Received." *Hu-man Communications Research* 15 (1988): 256–83.

Richards, E. *Vitamin C and Cancer: Medicine or Politics?* London: Macmillan, 1991.

Roe, Patrick, ed. *Bridging the Gap? Access to Telecommunications for All People.* Brus-sels: Commission of the European Communities, 2001. www.tiresias.org/phoneabil-ity/bridging_the_gap/ [accessed 15 March 2002].

———. *Guidelines-Booklet on Mobile Phones: A COST 219bis Guidebook.* Brussels: COST 219bis, Commission of the European Communities, 1999.

———. *Telecommunications for All.* Brussels: COST 219bis, CEC, 1995.

Rose, Damon. "The Internet: Made for Blind People." *The New Beacon* (July 1996).

Rose, June. *Changing Focus: The Development of Blind Welfare in Britain.* London: Hutchinson, 1970.

Rose, Nikolas. *Powers of Freedom: Reframing Political Thought.* Cambridge: Cambridge University Press, 1999.

Rosenthal, Sally. "Adrift on the Information Highway: Confessions of a Wannabe Com-puter Nerd." *Electric Edge: Web Edition of the Ragged Edge* (Sept/Oct. 1997). www.ragged-edge-mag.com/sep97/net.htm [accessed 1 February 2002].

Roulstone, A. *Enabling Technology: Disabled People, Work and New Technology.* Buck-ingham, U.K.: Open University Press, 1998.

Rouse, J. R. *Knowledge and Power.* Ithaca, N.Y.: Cornell University Press, 1987.

Rowe, David. *Sport, Culture and the Media.* Buckingham, U.K.: Open University Press, 1999.

Rowland, W. H. "The Traditions of Communication Research and Their Implications for Telecommunications Study." *Journal of Communication* 43 (1993): 207–17.

———. "American Telecommunications Policy Research: Its Contradictory Origins and Influences." *Media Culture and Society* 8 (1986): 159–82.

Royal National Institute of the Blind (RNIB). *May I Use the Phone?: A Seminar Held by the COST219 UK Group on Wednesday 9th July 1997, Summary of Proceedings.* Lon-don: RNIB, 1997. www.stakes.fi/cost219/DDASUM.HTM [accessed 15 March 2002].

Rushton, Dave, ed. *Citizen Television: A Local Dimension to Public Service Broadcasting.* London: John Libbey, 1993.

Sapey, Bob. "Disablement in the Informational Age." *Disability and Society* 15 (2000): 619–36.

Saul, John Ralston. *The Unconscious Civilization.* Melbourne: Penguin Australia, 1997.

Sawhney, Harmeet. "Dynamics of Infrastructure Development: The Role of Metaphors, Political Will and Sunk Investment." *Media, Culture & Society* 23 (2001): 33–53.

———. "Information Superhighway: Metaphors as Midwives." *Media, Culture & Society* 18 (1996): 291–314.

Schiller, Dan. *Digital Capitalism: Networking the Global Market System.* Cambridge, Mass.: MIT Press, 1999.

Schofield, Julia M. *Microcomputer-Based Aids for the Disabled.* London: Heyden and The British Computer Society, 1981.

Schon, Donald A., Bisch Sanyal, and William J. Mitchell, ed. *High Technology and Low-Income Communities: Prospects for the Positive Use of Advanced Information Technol-ogy.* Cambridge, Mass.: MIT Press, 1998.

Schroeder, Frederic K. "Research and the Organized Blind Movement." *Braille Monitor* 44.8 (August/September 2001). www.nfb.org/BM/BM01/BM0108/BM010807.HTM [accessed 15 March 2002].

Seelman, Katherine D. "Science and Technology Policy: Is Disability a Missing Factor?" In *Handbook of Disability Studies,* ed. Gary L. Albrecht, Katherine D. Seelman, and Michael Bury. Thousand Oaks, Calif.: Sage, 2001, 663–92.

Shakespeare, Tom, "Cultural Representations of Disabled People: Dustbins for Disavowal." *Disability & Society* 9 (1994): 283–99.

——, ed. *The Disability Reader: Social Science Perspectives.* London: Cassell, 1998.

——, and Nick Watson. "Making the Difference: Disability, Politics, and Recognition." In *Handbook of Disability Studies,* ed. Gary L. Albrecht, Katherine D. Seelman, and Michael Bury. Thousand Oaks, Calif.: Sage, 2001, 546–64.

Shapiro, M. J. "Disability and the Politics of Constitutive Rules." In *Cross-National Rehabilitation Policies,* ed. G. L. Albrecht. Beverley Hills, Calif.: Sage, 1981, 84–96.

Shields, Rob, ed. *Cultures of Internet: Virtual Spaces, Real Histories, Living Bodies.* London: Sage, 1996.

Shipley, Tony. *Interference and Electro-Magnetic Compatibility.* London: Royal National Institute of the Blind, 2000. www.tiresias.org/reports/emc.htm [accessed 15 March 2002].

——, and John Gill. *Call Barred?: Inclusive Design of Wireless Systems.* London: Royal National Institute of the Blind, 2000. www.tiresias.org/phoneability/wireless.htm.

Shultz, Kara. "Deaf Activists in the Rhetorical Transformation of the Construct of Disability." In *Handbook of Communication and People with Disabilities,* ed. D. O. Braithwaite and T. L. Thompson. Mahwah, N.J.: Lawrence Erlbaum, 2000, 257–70.

Shworles, T. "The Person with Disability and the Benefits of the Microcomputer Revolution." In *Computers for the Disabled: Conference Papers,* ed. Janet E. Roehl. Menomonie: Stout Vocational Rehabilitation Institute, University of Wisconsin-Stout, 1983.

Silverstone, R., E. Hirsch, E., and D. Morley. "Listening to a Long Conversation: an Ethnographic Approach to the Study of Information and Communication Technologies in the Home." *Cultural Studies* 5 (1991): 204–27.

Simpson, John. *When a Word Is Worth a Thousand Pictures: Improved Television Access for Blind Viewers in the Digital Era.* Melbourne: Blind Citizens Australia, 1999.

Skovman, Michael, and Kim Christian Schroder, eds. *Media Cultures: Reappraising Transnational Media.* London: Routledge, 1992.

Slot, Owen. "More Paralympic Cheats Than Originally Feared." *The (Melbourne) Age.* February 2001.

Sofoulis, Zoe. "Of Spanners and Cyborgs: De-homogenising Feminist Thinking on Technology." In *Transitions: New Australian Feminisms*, ed. Barbara Caine and Rosemary Pringle. Sydney: Allen & Unwin, 1995, 147–163.

Speck, B. W. *Publication Peer Review: An Annotated Bibliography.* Westport, Conn.: Greenwood, 1993.

Stefik, Mark, ed. *Internet Dreams: Archetypes, Myths, and Metaphors.* Cambridge, Mass.: MIT Press, 1996.

Stevenson, Nick. *Understanding Media Cultures: Social Theory and Mass Communication.* London: Sage, 1995.

Stone, A. R. [Sandy]. *The War of Desire and Technology at the Close of the Mechanical Age.* Cambridge, Mass.: MIT Press, 1995.

Streeter, Thomas. "Notes towards a Political History of the Internet 1950–1983." *Media International Australia* 95 (2000): 131–46.

Summers, I. R., ed. *Tactile Aids for the Hearing Impaired.* London: Whurr Publishers, 1992.

Swiss, Thomas, ed. *Unspun: Key Concepts for Understanding the World-Wide Web.* New York: New York University Press, 2001.

Synder, Sharon, Brenda Brueggeman, and R. G. Thompson, eds. *Enabling the Humanities: A Disability Studies Sourcebook.* New York: Modern Language Association, 2001.

Stiker, Henri-Jacques. *A History of Disability*, trans. William Sayers. Ann Arbor: University of Michigan Press, 1999,

Tellez, F. A. "Ethics of Cochlear Implantation in Young Children." *Otolaryngology—Head and Neck Surgery* 121 (1999).

Thomas, Carol. *Female Forms: Experiencing and Understanding Disability.* Milton Keynes, U.K.: Open University Press, 1999.

Thomas, Julian. "It's Later Than You Think: The Productivity Commission's Broadcasting Inquiry and Beyond." *Media International Australia* 95 (2000): 9–18.

Thomson, Rosemary Garland. *Freakery: Cultural Spectacles of the Extraordinary Body.* New York: New York University Press, 1996.

Thornton, P. "Communications Technology—Empowerment or Disempowerment." *Disability, Handicap & Society* 8 (1993): 339–49.

Thussu, Dayan Kishan, ed. *Electronic Empires: Global Media and Local Resistance.* London: Arnold, 1998.

Titchkosky, T. "Disability Studies: The Old and the New." *Canadian Journal of Sociology* 25 (2000): 197–234.

Toffler, Alvin. *Future Shock.* New York: Bantam, 1974.

Tracey, Michael. *The Decline and Fall of Public Service Broadcasting.* Oxford: Oxford University Press, 1998.

Tremain, Shelley, ed. *Foucault and the Government of Disability.* Forthcoming, 2003.

——, ed. Pushing the Limits: Disabled Dykes Produce Culture. Toronto: Women's Press, 1996.

Turkle, Sherry. *Life on the Screen: Identity in the Age of the Internet.* New York: Simon & Schuster, 1995.

Turnbull, David. *Technoscience Worlds.* Geelong, Australia: Deakin University Press, 1991.

Turner, Bryan S. *The Body and Society.* Oxford: Basil Blackwell, 1984.

Uniacke, Michael. "Of Miracles, Praise—of Anger—the Bionic Ear." *In Future* 6 (1987): 11–14.

U.S. Architectural and Transportation Barriers Compliance Board [Access Board]. *Market Monitoring Report on Accessible Telecommunications.* Access Board: Washington, D.C., 1998. www.access-board.gov/telecomm/marketrep/index.htm [accessed 25 March 2002].

Van Berlo, Ad, ed. *Design Guidelines on Smart Homes: A COST 219bis Guidebook.* Brussels: COST, Commission of the European Communities, 1999. www.stakes.fi/cost219/smarthousing.htm [accessed 15 March 2002].

Van der Wilt, G. J., R. Reuzel, and H. D. Banta. "The Ethics of Assessing Health Technologies." *Theoretical Medicine & Bioethics* 21 (2000): 103–15.

Van Gelder, L. "The Strange Case of the Electronic Lover." In *The Social Construction of Gender,* ed. J. Lorber and S. Farrell. Newbury Park, Calif.: Sage, 1991.

Vanderheiden, G. C. "Curbcuts and Computers: Providing Access to Computers and Information Systems for Disabled Individuals." In *Computers for the Disabled: Conference Papers,* ed. Janet E. Roehl. Menomonie: Stout Vocational Rehabilitation Institute, University of Wisconsin-Stout, 1983.

Veatch, R. M. ed. *Cross Cultural Perspective in Medical Ethics: Readings.* Boston: Jones and Bartlett Publishers, 1989.

Vermeij, Geerat J. "Research and the Blind." *Braille Monitor* 45.2 (March 2002). www.nfb.org/bm/bm02/bm0203/bm020305.htm [accessed 15 March 2002].

Victorian Council of Deaf People (VCOD). *Cochlear Implant Forum Report.* Melbourne: VCOD, 1988.

Von Tetzchner, S., ed. *Issues in Telecommunication and Disability.* Brussels: COST 219, DGXIII, Commission of the European Communities [CEC], 1991.

Wacjman, Judy. *Feminism Confronts Technology.* Blackwell: Polity; Sydney: Allen & Unwin, 1991.

Wallis, R. ed. On the Margins of Science: The Social Construction of Rejected Knowledge. Keele, Staffordshire, U.K.: University of Keele, 1979.

Wareing, David, and Christopher Newell. "Responsible Choice: The Choice between No Choice." *Disability & Society* 17, vol. 4 (June 2002).

Wark, McKenzie. *Virtual Geography: Living with Global Media Events.* Bloomington: Indiana University Press, 1994.

———. "What Does Capital Want?" *Media Information Australia* 94 (1994).

Wendell, Susan. *The Rejected Body: Feminist Philosophical Reflections on Disability.* London: Routledge, 1996.

Wertheim, Margaret. *The Pearly Gates of Cyberspace: A History of Space from Dante to the Internet.* Sydney: Doubleday, 1999.

White, Peter B. *Community Service Obligations and the Future of Telecommunications in Australia: Final Report.* Melbourne: Commission for the Future, 1989.

Wieten, Jan, Graham Murdock, and Peter Dahlgren, eds. *Television across Europe.* London: Sage, 2000.

Williams, Raymond. *Keywords: A Vocabulary of Culture and Society.* New York: Oxford University Press, 1976.

Wilson, Ian R., and Gerard Goggin. *Reforming Universal Service: The Future of Consumer Access and Equity in Australian Telecommunications.* Sydney: Consumers' Telecommunications Network, 1993.

Wilson, Kevin G. *Deregulating Telecommunications: U.S. and Canadian Telecommunications, 1840–1997.* Lanham, Md.: Rowman & Littlefield, 2000.

WIN TV. *Review into the Captioning Requirements of the* Broadcasting Services Act 1992*: Options Paper: Submission.* Wollongong, Australia: WIN, 1999. www.dcita.gov.au [accessed 15 November 2000].

Wise, J. Macgregor. *Exploring Technology and Social Space.* London: Sage, 1997.

Wolfensberger, Wolf. "Social Role Valorization Is Too Conservative. No, It Is Too Radical." *Disability & Society* 10 (1995): 365–68.

Wood, Andrew F., and Matthew J. Smith. *Online Communication: Linking Technology, Identity, and Culture.* Mahwah, N.J.: Lawrence Erlbaum, 2001.

World Institute on Disability (WID). *Report Card on Telecommunications Accessibility.* WID: Oakland, Calif., 1998.

———. *Telecommunications and Persons with Disabilities: Building the Framework.* Oakland, Calif.: WID, 1993.

Index

Abberley, Paul, 21, 24
ABC. *See* Australian Broadcasting
  Corporation
ableism, 42–43
accessibility: and AOL, 120–21; building
  design and, 147; personal computers
  and, 116–19, 130–31; of Sydney
  Olympics web site, 121–22;
  telecommunications and, 43–46;
  television and, 96; universal service
  and, 46–48; World-Wide Web and,
  119–20
"Action 2001: Turning Rhetoric into
  Reality", 137–40
ADA. *See Americans with Disabilities Act*
advertisements, people with disabilities in,
  93–94, 103
Advisory Committee on
  Telecommunications for Disabled and
  Elderly People (DIEL) (United
  Kingdom), 46
Age & Disability Unit (British Telecom),
  45
aging, 125n33
Albrecht, G. L., 22
All Media Sports (AMS), 91
ALT text, 122, 127n62
Amending Voice Telephony Directive
  (AVTD), 47
America Online (AOL), 120–21, 123

American Association of People with
  Disabilities, 142n21
Americans with Disabilities Act (ADA),
  43, 96, 118, 119, 120
AMS. *See* All Media Sports
Annenberg School of Communication, 134
AOL, 120–21, 123
Apple Macintosh computers, 117
Asch, Adrienne, 19
ASCII (American Standard Code for
  Information Interchange) standard,
  67–68
Asia-Pacific Cooperation, 152
assistive technologies. *See* accessibility
AT&T, 73
Australia: access issues in, 44–45; and
  information superhighway, 66;
  television policies in, 99–102
Australian Action Centre (ACC), 100
Australian Association of the Deaf, 100
Australian Broadcasting Commission, 100
Australian Broadcasting Corporation
  (ABC), 91–92
Australian Communication Industry
  Forum, 54, 101
Australian Communications Authority, 54,
  101
Australian Council on Social Service, 74
Australian Human Rights and Equal
  Opportunity Commission, 121–22, 137

Australian Labor Party, 101
Australian Telecommunications Act
  (1997), 40
AVTD. *See* Amending Voice Telephony
  Directive

Bangemann Report (1994), 65
Barnes, Carl, 14
Baudot, 67–68
Baudrillard, Jean, 90
Bell, Alexander Graham, 42, 148
Bell, David, 135
Bent: A Journal of Cripgay Voices, 134
Berners-Lee, Tim, 109, 119
Bijker, W. E., 12
blind people: and AOL, 120–21; and
  Internet use, 135–37; and online
  communities, 132–33; and personal
  computers, 116–18; and Sydney
  Olympics web site, 121–22
body: control of, and personal
  responsiblity, 24; cyborg, 30, 112;
  Internet and, 111–16
Bourdieu, Pierre, 134
Boyd, Raelene, 93
braille, 148
Braille Monitor, 117
Brand, Stewart, 110
Brewer, Judy, 120
British Telecom (BT), 45, 73
Broadband Services Expert Group (BSEG)
  (Australia), 66, 69–70, 75, 77
Broadcasting Services Act (1992)
  (Australia), 99, 100
BSEG. *See* Broadband Services Expert
  Group (Australia)
BT. *See* British Telecom
BTCE. *See* Bureau of Transport and
  Communications Economics
  (Australia)
Bureau of Transport and Communications
  Economics (BTCE) (Australia), 71
Byte, 116

Cairncross, Frances, 63, 131
Canadian Broadcasting Corporation, 101
Canadian Human Rights Tribunal, 101

Capitol, 104
captioning, of television, 96–97, 99–101
Castells, Manuel, 68–69, 80
CDMA. *See* Code Division Multiple
  Access
Centre for Deafness Studies and Research
  (Griffith University), 29
Channel 7 (Australia), 91–92
charity discourse, 24, 133
chatrooms: blind people and, 133; Deaf
  people and, 132; and online identities,
  111, 113–14
children, and cochlear implants, 26–27
Children's Cochlear Implant Centre (New
  South Wales), 28
Chong, Curtis, 121
citizenship, 53–54; cultural, 102–4; and
  decision-making, 151; do-it-yourself,
  102–4
civil society, 152–53; Internet and, 138–40
Clinton, Bill, 44, 64, 68
closed captioning, 96–97, 99–101
cochlear implants: cost effectiveness of,
  27; description of, 25; ethics of, 25–27;
  parent-child issues concerning, 26–28;
  perspectives on, 6, 8, 11–12, 25; risks
  of, 26; social aspects of, 11, 148;
  standards for, 8
Code Division Multiple Access (CDMA),
  48, 50
Committee of Personal Computers and the
  Handicapped (COPH-2), 116
Common Ground (Australia), 75
Communications Act (United States,
  1996), 40
Communications Futures Project
  (Australia), 66, 71
Communications Law Centre (Australia),
  153
communities, online (disabilities),
  131–35
Consumer/Disability Telecommunications
  Advisory Committee (FCC), 44
consumer discourse, 24
consumer research, 71, 74–77
consumers: active role of, 53–54; interests
  of, 73–74; policy-making and, 77–78

Consumers Association (United
  Kingdom), 153
Consumers Federation of America (United
  States), 153
Consumers' Telecommunications Network
  (CTN) (Australia), xv, 75, 153
convergence, 63–80; description of, xiv, 5
COPH-2. *See* Committee of Personal
  Computers and the Handicapped
Corker, Mairian, 24
corporate discourse, 30, 42–43
corporate-government relations, 72
corporations, 152. *See also* market factors
COST 219, 54–56, 149
Cox, Kevin, 138
CTN. *See* Consumers'
  Telecommunications Network
  (Australia)
culture: construction of disability, 133–35,
  139–40; and digital disability, 129–41;
  role of, 12–14
Cunningham, Stuart, 104
Cuthbert, Betty, 93
cyborgs, 30, 112

Davis, Lennard J., 39
Day, Lawrence H., 84n50
De Solla Price, Derek, 7
Deaf culture: characteristics of, 26; and
  cochlear implants, 6, 8, 11–12, 25–27;
  and online communities, 132
DeafCHAT.com, 132
deafness: parent-child issues in, 26–28;
  postlingual, 25–26
decision making, politics of, 69–70
Deleuze, Gilles, 49
Department of Communications,
  Information Technology, and the Arts
  (Australia), 101
Descriptive Video Service, 97
digital communications technologies:
  versus analog, 4–5; emergence of, xiv;
  in everyday life, 3–4. *See also* new
  media technologies
digital disability, cultures of, 129–41
digital divide, 68
digital television, 96–102

disability: as category, 20–21; congenital
  versus recently developed, 133; versus
  impairment, 21; social model theory of,
  20–22; as social phenomenon, 19–32;
  study of, 19–25 (*see also* disability
  studies)
Disability Discrimination Act (Australia,
  1992), 44, 52
Disability Discrimination Act (United
  Kingdom, 1995), 45, 46, 47
disability movement, 24, 43; FCC and, 44;
  legal action by, 120
Disability Rights Commission (United
  Kingdom), 46
Disability Rights Office (FCC), 44
disability studies, 20–25
Disabled Peoples' International
  (Australia), xv, 24, 45
disablist values, 133, 135–37
discourse approach, 22–25. *See also*
  charity approach; consumer approach;
  corporate approach; medical approach
diversity, as management issue, 30–31
dominant versus marginalized groups,
  76–77
DOS operating system, 117, 118
Dreachslin, Janice, 30

electronic commerce, 64, 137. *See also*
  information superhighway
electronic forum, 137–40
ethics, cochlear implants and, 25–27
ethnographic research, 78
European Commission, 65
European Economic Community, 47

FCC. *See* Federal Communications
  Commission
Federal Communications Commission
  (FCC), 44, 96–97, 98, 102
Federation of Australian Commercial
  Television Stations Code of Practice,
  99
Federation of the Deaf (Sweden), 149
feminism, 21–22; and disability, 22
Feyerabend, Paul, 7
Fine, Michelle, 19

Index

Finkelstein, Vic, 20
forum, online, 137–40
Foucault, Michel, 24, 41, 52, 53, 151
Fox, Susan Anne, 130–31
Fulcher, Gillian, 22–24, 125n25

Gallaudet Institute (United States), 149
Gatens, Moira, 21
Gates, Bill, 4, 110
Gibson, B., 26
Gibson, W., 28
Gibson, William, 4
Gilder, George, 89
Gill, John, 51
global context: for disability, 22; for
    telecommunications, 40–41
Global Information Infrastructure, 64
global positioning system, 49
Global System for Mobiles (GSM), 48
Global Television, 91
Gore, Al, 39, 64
government-corporate relations, 72
Graham, Julie (persona of Sanford Lewin),
    113–14
graphical-user interface (GUI), 117–18,
    120–21
Great Britain, and information
    superhighway, 66
Groce, N. L., 27
GSM. *See* Global System for Mobiles
Guattari, Félix, 49
GUI, 117–18, 120–21
Guter, Bob, 134

Hahn beer, 93
Hakkan, David, 129
hands-free kits, 50
Haraway, Donna, 112
Harper, Phil, 100
Hartley, John, 102–3
Hawking, Stephen, 112, 113
Hayes, Dennis, 119, 120
Hearing Aid Compatibility Act (United
    States, 1988), 43
hearing aids: legislation for, 43; mobile
    phones and, 49–50

Hill, Stephen, 12
Hirsch, E., 78
HREOC. *See* Human Rights and Equal
    Opportunity Commission (Australia)
Human Rights and Equal Opportunity
    Commission (HREOC) (Australia), 45,
    50, 52, 53, 101
humor, about disability, 93–95
Hyde, M. B., 29

identity, on Internet, 111, 113–14
impairment, versus disability, 21
inclusion, 149–50
information superhighway, 63–69;
    advantages of, 65; control of, 67–68;
    disadvantages of, 65; U.S. policy on,
    64–65
intellectual disability: and new media
    technologies, 139–40; and
    Paralympics, 104
interactivity, 130–31
International Paralympic Committee, 104
International Telecommunications Union,
    64, 152
Internet, 109–23; civil society and,
    138–40; development of, 109–10;
    disability versus mainstream aspects
    of, 135–37; embodiment and disability
    on, 111–16; forums on, 137–40; myths
    concerning, 110; Olympics on, 95,
    121–22, 123; Paralympics on, 95;
    social aspects of, 11; and wireless
    access protocol, 51. *See also* World-
    Wide Web
Internet Explorer, 118

JAWS for Windows, 121, 135, 148
Jefferson, Thomas, 110

Kamenetz, Herman, 9
Kennard, William E., 44, 98
knowledge(s): construction of, 77–80;
    dominant versus marginalized, 76–77;
    social nature of, 6–7
Kuhn, Thomas, 6
Kurzweil Reading machine, 125n41

Labor Party (Australia), 101
laboratories, scientific, 7
language, inappropriate, 125n25
Latour, Bruno, 7
legislation, 43–46, 118, 119–20, 150, 151–52
Lewin, Sanford, 113
Liberal and National party coalition (Australia), 101

Macintosh computers, 117
Macintyre, Alasdair, 104
MacKenzie, Donald, 8
Maguire, Bruce, 121–22
MAI. *See* Multilateral Agreement on Investment
managing disability. *See* corporate discourse
marginalized groups, 74, 76–77
market factors, 41, 42, 47, 73, 150–51
market research. *See* consumer research
Martha's Vineyard, 27
Marxism, 21
Massachusetts Assistive Technology Partnership, 118
Massachusetts Commission for the Blind, 118
Matrix, The, 4
Maurer, Marc, 98
McDonald's, 94
McLuhan, Marshall, 14
McMillan, Sally J., 130
media, culture and, 13–14
medical discourse, 23, 27–30, 125n25, 133
Medical Journal of Australia, The, 28–29
Melbourne Cochlear Implant project, 26
Mercer, Geoff, 14
Microsoft, 110, 117–19, 123
Mitchell, David, 24, 112, 114
mobile phones, 48–51; hands-free kits, 50; and hearing aids, 49–50; history of, 48–49; second generation, 50; and short-messaging, 49, 148; social aspects of, 11; third generation, 51
modems, 119
Mohay, Heather, 28

Morley, D., 78
Morley, E., 78
Mosco, Vincent, 13
Moyal, Ann, 78
Multilateral Agreement on Investment (MAI), 72

Narrative Television Network (NTN), 97
National Broadcasting Company (NBC), 95
National Center for Accessible Media (NCAM), 98
National Council on Disability (NCD) (United States), 35n64, 63, 65, 118
National Federation of the Blind (NFB), 98, 120, 121
National Information Infrastructure (United States), 64
NBC. *See* National Broadcasting Company
NCAM. *See* National Center for Accessible Media
NCD. *See* National Council on Disability
Negroponte, Nicholas, 3, 130, 131
neoclassical economics, 72
networks (communications), 5
new media technologies: characterization of, 4–5; and disability communities, 148; intellectual disability and, 139–40. *See also* digital communications technologies
New Yorker, 129
NFB. *See* National Federation of the Blind
Noble, David F., 3
nongovernmental organizations, 151, 152–53
Norden, Martin F., 94
not-for-profit organizations, 151

objectivity, scientific, 7
OECD. *See* Organization for Economic Cooperation and Development
Offe, Claus, 72, 73
Office of Population, Censuses and Surveys (OPCS) (United Kingdom), 21

Office of Telecommunications (OFTEL)
    (United Kingdom), 45–46, 47–48
OFTEL. *See* Office of Telecommunications
    (United Kingdom)
Oliver, Mike, 20–21, 22
Olympics, 91–93; disability and, 93–95;
    web site for Sydney, 121–22, 123
online communities (disabilities), 131–35
online forum, 137–40
OPCS. *See* Office of Population, Censuses
    and Surveys
O'Regan, Tom, 104
Organization for Economic Cooperation
    and Development (OECD), 63–64, 152

Paralympics, 91–93; intellectual disability
    in, 104; on Internet, 95
participation, of persons with disabilities,
    54, 55–56, 71, 139, 150, 152, 153
Pasteur, Louis, 7
PBS. *See* Public Broadcasting Service
personal computers, accessibility of,
    116–19, 130–31
Pinch, T., 12
politics, role in technology of, 9–10
Popper, Karl, 6
Poster, Mark, 115
postlingual deafness, and cochlear
    implants, 25–26
postmodernism, 112
Power, D. J., 29
prostheses, 112, 113
Public Broadcasting Service (PBS), 96

Queensland Advocacy Inc., 137–40

Reeve, Christopher, 133, 142n21
regulation, 40–41, 52, 54. *See also*
    legislation
Rehabilitation Act (1973), 118
Reihing, Mary Ellen, 116–17
representation (ethical), of persons with
    disabilities. *See* participation, of
    persons with disabilities
research, 71; consumer, 71, 74–77; context
    of, 78–80; ethnographic, 78; by people
    with disabilities, 79; standards of, 79

Ribagorda, Carlos, 104
Ritchie, Donna, 92
Roosevelt, Franklin D., 57
Rose, Damon, 129, 131
Rose, Nikolas, 53–54, 57
Rosen, Greg, 117–18
Royal Institute of the Blind (Great
    Britain), 149

Sapey, Bob, 80
Saul, John Ralston, 151
science: objectivity in, 7; society and,
    5–12; and technology, 8
Scott, DPI v Telstra, 45, 52
screen displays, 117–18, 120–21
search engines, and definitions of
    disability, 132
Seven Network, 99
Shakespeare, Tom, 14, 24
Shapiro, M. J., 24
Shipley, Tony, 51
Short Messaging Services (SMS), 49, 148
Shworles, T., 123
sign language: Deaf culture and, 26; on
    Martha's Vineyard, 27
Silverstone, R., 78
Simpson, John, 89
smart houses, 5
Smokey and the Bandit, 48
SMS. *See* Short Messaging Services
Snyder, Sharon, 24, 112, 114
SOCOG. *See* Sydney Organizing
    Committee for the Olympic Games
special needs, 42–43, 136–37
standards: for cochlear implants, 8; for
    research, 79; social aspect of, 8; for
    wheelchairs, 8
Star Wars, 98
statistics, 21
stem cell research, 142n21
Stiker, Henri-Jacques, 19
Stone, Allucquère Rosanne, 111–12,
    113–15, 125n25
subjectivity, on Internet, 111, 113–14
Sydney Olympics, 91–95, 121–22, 123
Sydney Organizing Committee for the
    Olympic Games (SOCOG), 121–22

TCCC. *See* Telstra, Consumer Consultative Council
technology: as autonomous, 9–10; character of, 8; and science, 8; society and, 5–12
Technology-Related Assistance Act (United States, 1988), 43
technoscience worlds, 5–12
Telecom Australia. *See* Telstra
telecommunications, 39–58; access to, 43–46; global context for, 40–41; mobile phones, 11, 48–51; and nation building, 42; perspectives on, 13; regulation of, 40–41, 52, 54
Telecommunications Act (Australia, 1991), 44
Telecommunications Act (Australia, 1997), 45, 52
Telecommunications Act (Canada, 1993), 40
Telecommunications Act (United Kingdom), 47–48
Telecommunications Act (United States, 1996), 43–44, 97
Telecommunications for the Disabled Act (United States, 1982), 43
Telecommunications Policy, 84n50
telephone, invention of, 42, 148
teletypewriters. *See* text telephone equipment
television, 89–104; captioning of, 96–97, 99–101; and citizenship, 103–4; Olympics on, 91–93; Paralympics on, 91–93; transformations in, 90; video description on, 97–98
Television Decoder Circuitry Act (1990) (United States), 96
Telia, 149
Telstra, 44, 45, 52, 73, 74–76; Consumer Consultative Council (TCCC), 74, 75; Regional Consumer Councils, 75
terminology, inappropriate, 125n25
text telephone equipment, 148; access to, 44–45
Thatcher, Margaret, 21, 151
therapeutic cloning, 142n21
3G. *See* mobile phones: third generation

Times, London, 104
Toffler, Alvin, 3
Toohey's beer, 93–94, 102–3
Trace Center (United States), 149
TTYs. *See* text telephone equipment
Turnbull, David, 5–6, 7, 8

UMTS. *See* Universal Mobile Telecommunications System
United Kingdom, access issues in, 45–46
United States: access issues in, 43–44; and information superhighway, 64–65; television policies in, 99–102
universal design, 149–50
Universal Mobile Telecommunications System (UMTS), 51
universal service, 42, 43–45; accessibility and, 46–48; information superhighway and, 64–65
University of Queensland, 28
U.S. Internet Association, 119

values, disablist, 133, 135–37
Vanderheiden, Gregg C., 109
Verbrugge, L. M., 22
video description, 97–98; rules for, 98
vision-impaired people. *See* blind people

W3C. *See* World-Wide Web consortium
Wacjman, Judy, 3, 8
WAI. *See* World-Wide Web Accessibility Initiative
WAP. *See* wireless access protocol
We Magazine, 118
We Media Inc., 95
We Sports, 95
welfare, 23
Westpac, 94
WGBH, 97, 98
wheelchairs: effectiveness of, 8; in imaginary society, 20; meaning of, 8; and personal interaction, 124n24; perspectives on, 9; social aspects of, 10–11; standards for, 8; as symbol of disability, 6; writings on, 9
WID. *See* World Institute on Disabilitiy

WIN TV, 100
Windows operating system, 117–18;
    JAWS for Windows, 121, 135, 148
Winner, Langdon, 6
Wired, 131
wireless access protocol (WAP), 50–51
women, with disability, versus men, 22
Word software, 117
WordPerfect software, 117
World Bank, 152

World Health Organization, 21
World Institute on Disabilitiy (WID), 43,
    142n21
World Trade Organization, 40, 152
World-Wide Web, 109–10; and
    accessibility, 119–20, 130
World-Wide Web Accessibility Initiative
    (WAI), 119, 120, 149
World-Wide Web consortium (W3C), 119,
    121

About the Authors

Gerard Goggin is a postdoctoral research fellow at the Centre for Critical and Cultural Studies, University of Queensland, Australia. Goggin has published widely on telecommunications and new media. From 1993 to 1997, he was policy advisor for Consumers' Telecommunications Network, Australia. After that, he taught media studies at Southern Cross University, Lismore, Australia. Goggin holds a Ph.D. from the University of Sydney; his doctoral research focused on Mary Wollstonecraft, William Godwin, and Percy Bysshe Shelley.

Goggin's current research projects include a cultural history of the Internet in Australia, and an investigation of the cultural implications of broadband media technologies.

Christopher Newell is senior lecturer in the School of Medicine of the University of Tasmania, Australia, teaching at undergraduate and graduate levels in the areas of bioethics and disability studies. He is a person who lives with disability; this life experience influences his active research interests in a variety of areas including new media, telecommunications, bioethics, and biotechnology. He is a member of a variety of boards including the Council of the Australian Telecommunications Industry Ombudsman and the Australian Medical Council.

Newell is active with a variety of community and disability organizations and has received several awards for his work including recognition from the Australian Human Rights and Equal Opportunity Commission. In 2001 he was presented the "Australian Achiever" award in the Australia Day Awards by the Prime Minister. In 2001 he was appointed as a Member of the Order of Australia.